Defining Modernism

Studies in Literary Criticism and Theory

Hans H. Rudnick
General Editor

Vol. 8

PETER LANG
New York • Washington, D.C./Baltimore • Boston
Bern • Frankfurt am Main • Berlin • Vienna • Paris

Andrea Gogröf-Voorhees

Defining Modernism

Baudelaire and Nietzsche on Romanticism, Modernity, Decadence, and Wagner

PETER LANG
New York • Washington, D.C./Baltimore • Boston
Bern • Frankfurt am Main • Berlin • Vienna • Paris

Library of Congress Cataloging-in-Publication Data

Gogröf-Voorhees, Andrea.
Defining modernism: Baudelaire and Nietzsche on romanticism, modernity,
decadence, and Wagner / Andrea Gogröf-Voorhees.
p. cm. — (Studies in literary criticism and theory; v. 8)
Includes bibliographical references and index.
1. Modernism (Literature). 2. Romanticism. 3. Decadence (Literary
movement). 4. Baudelaire, Charles, 1821–1867—Criticism and interpretation.
5. Nietzsche, Friedrich Wilhelm, 1844–1900. 6. Wagner,
Richard, 1813–1883. I. Title. II. Series.
PN56.M54G64 809'.9112—dc21 97-52193
ISBN 0-8204-3793-X
ISSN 1073-2004

Die Deutsche Bibliothek-CIP-Einheitsaufnahme

Gogröf-Voorhees, Andrea:
Defining modernism: Baudelaire and Nietzsche on romanticism,
modernity, decadence, and Wagner / Andrea Gogröf-Voorhees.
–New York; Washington, D.C./Baltimore; Boston; Bern;
Frankfurt am Main; Berlin; Vienna; Paris: Lang.
(Studies in literary criticism and theory; Vol. 8)
ISBN 0-8204-3793-X

Cover design by James F. Brisson

The paper in this book meets the guidelines for permanence and durability
of the Committee on Production Guidelines for Book Longevity
of the Council of Library Resources.

© 1999 Peter Lang Publishing, Inc., New York

Printed in the United States of America

For my parents:

Gisela and Helmut

Acknowledgements

The author wishes to express sincere appreciation to Professor Ernst Behler for his kind encouragement and assistance in the preparation of this manuscript. In addition, many thanks to the members of my committee: to Professor Richard T. Gray and Professor Marian Sugano, whose constructive criticism and readiness to dialogue was helpful during the many phases of this undertaking.

Thank you to my husband Rich Voorhees, whose unlimited patience, emotional support and intellectual energy were invaluable for the completion of this project.

I would like to express many thanks to my friends Valerie Conlon and Jura Avizienis for their invaluable help during the production phase of the book.

Table of Contents

Introduction

Nietzsche's interest in French culture is well known. Throughout his work, there is a constant if not increasing preoccupation with French philosophy, history, and above all, literature and art.[1] The connection between Nietzsche and Baudelaire, however, does not seem obvious at first glance. In fact, Nietzsche mentions Baudelaire only twice in his published works. In the *Twilight of the Idols* (1888), addressing the question of taste, he sees the French literary critic Sainte-Beuve as a "preliminary form of Baudelaire."[2] In *Ecce Homo* (1888) Baudelaire appears in the company of the "high-flying" and "rousing" artists of late French romanticism, such as Delacroix and Berlioz, and stands out as the first "intelligent adherent" of Wagner.[3] With the publication of Nietzsche's voluminous collection of posthumous fragments in the late 1960s through the mid-1970s by Giorgio Colli and Mazzino Montinari, new material became available containing proof of his thorough reading of Baudelaire. This reading took place between the winter of 1887 and the spring of 1888 at a time when Nietzsche was at the height of his reevaluation of romantic pessimism and decadence as they appeared most radically in France. Indeed, seventy-one nearly consecutive entries can be counted—fragments from Baudelaire's posthumously published intimate journals, *"Mon coeur mis à nu"* and *"Fusées."* Most of these fragments are copied directly in French. Some are interspersed with a German translation and a few times, Nietzsche adds a personal remark. That Nietzsche was also acquainted with Baudelaire's poetry has been known ever since access was allowed to the Nietzsche archives located in Weimar.

Many cultural and literary critics, most of them French, have perceived an affinity between Nietzsche and Baudelaire even before this new material became available to scholarly research.[4] Charles Andler assumes that Baudelaire, as a type of decadent Catholic, may have been Nietzsche's best choice for learning about decadence (Andler VI,261). Georges Blin offers occasional comparisons between Baudelaire and Nietzsche in regard to the theme of the double, the question of religion, and their resistance to the ideology of progress (Blin 38, 57, 151). And Marcel Raymond writes in the introduction of his book *From Baudelaire to Surrealism* that "Baudelaire, Mallarmé, Rimbaud . . . dreamt of 'transcending man'. (At the same time Nietzsche was wearing himself down to madness in the same endeavor)" (Raymond 31). Other philosophical and theoretical texts have

also dealt with Nietzsche and Baudelaire as critical and innovative thinkers who, although deeply rooted in their own century, have anticipated and
profoundly influenced modern issues concerning literary history and criticism, philosophy, and the arts. The richness and complexity of their cultural and ideological critiques have attracted the attention of such writers
as Walter Benjamin,[5] Albert Camus,[6] George Bataille,[7] and Paul de Man.[8]
In some of their texts parallels are specifically drawn between Baudelaire's
and Nietzsche's sensitivities toward the modernity of their own century,
specifically on the topic of "high capitalism," and "modern heroism" for
Benjamin, dandyism and nihilism for Camus, the question of laughter for
Bataille, and literary modernity for de Man. These parallels are stimulating
because the authors, while suggesting sometimes in the briefest fashion
particular points of connection, also highlight common concerns regarding
the development of literary modernity and cultural criticism.

    The more recent investigations on Nietzsche and Baudelaire tend
to focus more on Nietzsche's reception of Baudelaire.[9] They are indebted
to Karl Pestalozzi's ground-breaking article which provoked a chain of
reactions and reflections on the topic by French, German, and American
scholars.[10] Pestalozzi sees Nietzsche and Baudelaire as belonging together.
He places them among the founders of a modern consciousness, whose
foremost concern is to comprehend the human being outside of its imma-
nent condition. As such "they are to be seen as representatives of a post-
Christian era who know themselves to be formed by that from which they
turn away" (Pestalozzi 158). In other words, Nietzsche and Baudelaire both
attempt a literary and poetic reformulation of existential conditions in a
world without God as the guiding principle. As the title shows, Pestalozzi
proceeds in his article from Nietzsche's "horizon of expectation," i.e., his
intellectual outlook at the time he was reading Baudelaire. Basing his discussion on the concrete traces the poet and critic leaves in Nietzsche's
published works, journals, and correspondence, Pestalozzi's article represents a most valuable source of information and a stunning example of
philological prowess.

    Given the enormous amount of information, Pestalozzi resorts to
dividing his article into two main periods of reception. The first phase,
which Pestalozzi characterizes as "positive," extends from 1883 to 1885,
when Nietzsche encountered Baudelaire in Paul Bourget's essay on the
poet in his *Essais de psychologie contemporaine* and read the *Flowers of
Evil* with an introductory essay on Baudelaire by Théophile Gautier. Ac-

cording to Pestalozzi, Nietzsche, preoccupied at the time with the future of Europe and the role of the arts there, saw Baudelaire figuring among the great innovators who prepared the way for a new synthesis and who transcended their own nationality. In the second phase, around 1888, according to Pestalozzi, Baudelaire appears as a problematical figure, exemplifying the weaknesses inherent in decadence. In both phases Baudelaire stands in close relation to Wagner, a fact that, as Pestalozzi emphasizes, contributes to Nietzsche's ambivalence toward Baudelaire. Critics, however, have disparaged Pestalozzi's method for its somewhat reductive approach.[11]

It is precisely the continuity of Nietzsche's interest in Baudelaire that is striking, according to Jacques Le Rider. Dividing Nietzsche's interest into phases only creates a false distinction. Furthermore, Nietzsche's continuing interest goes hand in hand with his deepening understanding of Baudelaire. From beginning to end, a certain ambivalence, however, is never dispelled. Baudelaire is simultaneously one of the best among the "good Europeans," an "alter ego of Nietzsche,"—and a Parisian replica of Wagner: decadent, morbid, a comedian. Le Rider is right in stressing that this ambivalence is analogous to Nietzsche's feelings toward Wagner, and even of Nietzsche toward himself: "A love-hate relationship toward Wagner, toward Baudelaire, toward oneself . . . few contemporaries occupy in Nietzsche's pantheon such an eminent place" (Le Rider 99). Although Le Rider takes ambivalence into account, he also makes a distinction between two phases. Nietzsche's first encounter with Baudelaire in 1883–85 was colored by Bourget's and Gautier's interpretation, leading him to see Baudelaire as the "French master of décadence." The second encounter in 1887–88, placed in the context of the posthumous works, reveals Baudelaire as an "alter ego" to Nietzsche (Le Rider 92).

This distinction is problematical, however, because Nietzsche's famous passage in Aphorism 256 of *Beyond Good and Evil* (1885) already formulates the main characteristics of decadent aesthetics in a tone of unmistakable affirmation. By placing Wagner in the context of late French romanticism—for Nietzsche the hearth of decadence—he expresses enthusiasm for the interplay between the various spheres of art (painting, poetry, and music) and pays tribute to extraordinary artists such as Wagner, Delacroix, and Balzac, "those fanatics of expression", those "discoverers of the realm of the sublime, the ugly, and gruesome," those "virtuosos through and through" who have "uncanny access to everything that seduces, allures, compels, overthrows," those "born enemies of logic and straight lines, lusting after the foreign, the exotic, the tremendous, the crooked, the self-contradictory."[12] Although Baudelaire is not specifically mentioned, it does not seem unreasonable to count him—and to some extent Nietzsche himself—among this group.

That Nietzsche's critique of decadence later intensifies and sharpens is not to be seen as a disavowal of his earlier formulation in 1885 but rather a deepening of an interest in the psychological grounds of the phenomenon of decadence. This means that Nietzsche's understanding of Baudelaire and decadence becomes more complex but also remains sympathetic throughout.

In response to Pestalozzi, Stéphane Michaud suggests that, despite their own modernity, Baudelaire and Nietzsche both remain "untimely" and "displaced" individuals who could not be affiliated with any particular school of thought (Michaud 137). He sees the relationship between Nietzsche and Baudelaire as a dialogue between "two creators united by the same cult of art," who both subscribe to what Baudelaire had stated in his *Salon* of 1859, namely that "artistic matters are to be treated only between aristocrats."[13] According to Michaud, in spite of their differences, both share a concern in their cultural and ideological critique of modern times. Nietzsche and Baudelaire endeavored to shatter the mirror in which their epoch complacently viewed itself by denouncing bourgeois society, its morals, its materialism, and its idealism expressed by its trust in progress.

Nietzsche's constant discontent with the state of European culture and the role of art is expressed as early as *The Birth of Tragedy* (1872). Apart from being a tribute to the Wagnerian *Gesamtkunstwerk*, the text can be considered a response to Nietzsche's observation: "There has never been another period in the history of art in which so-called culture and true art have been so estranged and opposed as we may observe them to be at present." *(Es gibt keine andere Kunstperiode, in der sich die sogenannte Bildung und die eigentliche Kunst so befremdet und abgeneigt gegenübergestanden hätten, als wir das in der Gegenwart mit Augen sehen).*[14]

It is against the intrusion of extra-artistic elements—the century's scientific spirit and moralistic tendencies—into art that Nietzsche always speaks, and it is from this perspective that Nietzsche joins Baudelaire, who never tired of expressing very similar views on the arts. For example, in his *Salon* of 1859, Baudelaire writes:

True, mediocrity has always dominated the scene in every age, that is beyond dispute; but what is also true as it is distressing is that the reign of mediocrity is stronger than ever, to the point of triumphant obtrusiveness. . . . Our exclusive taste for the true . . . oppresses and smothers the taste for the beautiful. Where only the beautiful should be looked for . . . our people look only for the true. They are not artistic, naturally artistic; philosophers perhaps, or moralists, engineers, lovers of instructive anecdotes, anything you like, but never spontaneously artistic. They feel, or rather judge, successively, analytically. Other more favored peoples feel things quickly, at once, synthetically.

(Que dans tous les temps, la médiocrité ait dominé, cela est indubitable; mais qu'elle règne plus que jamais, qu'elle devienne absolument triomphante et encombrante, c'est ce qui est aussi vrai qu'affligeant. . . . Le goût exclusif du Vrai . . . opprime ici et étouffe le goût du Beau. Où il ne faudrait voir que le Beau notre public ne cherche que le vrai. Il n'est pas artiste, naturellement artiste; philosophe peut-être, moraliste, ingénieur, amateur d'anecdotes instructives, tout ce qu'on voudra, mais jamais spontanément artiste. Il sent ou plutôt il juge successivement, analytiquement. D'autres peuples, plus favorisés, sentent tout de suite, tout à la fois, synthétiquement).[15]

For Michaud, the affinities between Nietzsche and Baudelaire lie beyond what he terms "obvious antagonisms": Nietzsche's celebration of the Dionysian and the culture of ancient Greece, and Baudelaire's obsession with evil and original sin, concepts which Nietzsche dismisses as inventions of priests and lies created by the weak. Indeed, their affinities can be found in their respective recognition and critique of the idea of *l'art pour l'art*. Both Nietzsche and Baudelaire exhibit a very similar ambiguity toward the idea. Nietzsche recognizes *l'art pour l'art* as a struggle against the moralizing tendency in art: *"L'art pour l'art* means: the devil take morality."[16] He continues to say, however, that even if one excludes morality from art, it does not follow that art is purposeless.

On the contrary, Nietzsche thinks that the artist's basic instinct is not so much directed toward art than toward "the meaning of art, which is life." Since all art "praises," "selects," and "highlights," it stands in the service of life. Nietzsche comes to the following conclusion, summed up in this one sentence: "Art is the great stimulus to life: how could it be thought purposeless, aimless, *l'art pour l'art?"* And to this thought he adds yet another one which is essentially Baudelairian, namely that art is all the more valuable because it brings to light and transforms into beauty the often repressed and consciously ignored side of life, all that is "ugly, hard, and questionable." Although Baudelaire, as a friend of Théophile Gautier—the author of the official manifesto of *l'art pour l'art*[17]—is often thought of as a supporter of the idea, he participated in this "trend" only briefly. He shared the conviction that art is not in the service of morality, that it is is not a means to a useful end. "Is art useful? Yes. Why? Because it is art. Is there such a thing as a pernicious form of art? Yes! The form that distorts the underlying conditions of life."[18] From this proposition, the connection between art and life seems as crucial to Baudelaire as to Nietzsche. The credo of *l'art pour l'art* since it excluded historical, social, and existential dimensions of life while concentrating exclusively on form, soon became too narrow a framework for Baudelaire. As Marcel Ruff points out, Baudelaire broke with the "childish dream world of the School of Art for Art's sake," which, "by doing away with ethics and emotions, necessarily became sterile. It placed itself in violent opposition to man's genius."[19]

Other affinities connect the two authors in what Michaud calls "the new and problematic zones of modernity," with Richard Wagner as its cornerstone. Indeed, in the summer of 1885 Nietzsche wrote in his notebook one of his first impressions of Baudelaire:

> The poets who flourish at this time in France do so under the influence of Heinrich Heine and Baudelaire . . . As for the pessimistic Baudelaire, he belongs among the almost unbelievable amphibians who are as German as they are Parisian; his poetry has something of that which one characterizes in Germany as 'soul' or 'infinite melody' and sometimes 'hangover.' Apart from that, Baudelaire is a man of a perhaps corrupt, but also very distinct, sharp, and self-assured taste: with this he tyrannizes over the indecisive ones of today. If during his time he was the first supporter of Delacroix, perhaps today he would be the first 'Wagnerian' in Paris. There is a lot of Wagner in Baudelaire.
> *(Was von Dichtern jetzt in Frankreich blüht, steht unter Heinrich Heines und Baudelaires Einfluß . . . Was den pessimistischen Baudelaire betrifft, so gehört er zu jenen unglaublichen Amphibien, welche ebensosehr deutsch als pariserisch sind; seine Dichtung hat etwas von dem, was man in Deutschland Gemüth oder 'unendliche Melodie' und mitunter auch 'Katzenjammer' nennt. Im Übrigen war Baudelaire der Mensch eines vielleicht verdorbenen, aber sehr bestimmten und scharfen, seine selbst gewissen Gechmacks: damit tyrannisiert er die Ungewissen von Heute. Wenn er seiner Zeit der erste Fürsprecher Delacroix war: vielleicht, dass er heute der erste 'Wagnerianer' von Paris sein würde. Es ist viel Wagner in Baudelaire).*[20]

Although Michaud, like Pestalozzi and Le Rider, states that the relationship Nietzsche-Baudelaire has to be situated "in the heart of its very ambivalence," his main concern is to show how Nietzsche discovered Baudelaire as a double of himself. In fact, at the time he wrote the note of

1885 Nietzsche was not certain that Baudelaire actually was a great admirer of Richard Wagner. It is only in 1888, while spending the fall and winter in Nice, reading the posthumous works of Baudelaire published in 1887, that he found his supposition confirmed. In a letter to Peter Gast on February 26, 1888, he wrote:

> Today I was pleased to be confirmed in an extremely hazardous question: namely 'Who until now was best prepared for Wagner? Who was most naturally Wagnerian, despite and even without Wagner?' I told myself a long time ago: it was this demi-fool Baudelaire, the poet of *Les Fleurs du mal*. I regret not having discovered this kindred spirit of Wagner while he was alive. . . .
> As I leaf through a recently published collection of the posthumous works of this genius, so respected and even loved by the French, . . . suddenly an unedited letter from Wagner jumps out at me, regarding an essay by Baudelaire. . .
> *(Ich hatte heute das Vergnügen, mit einer Antwort recht zu bekommen, wo schon die Frage außerordentlich hazardirt scheinen konnte: nämlich—'wer war bisher am besten vorbereitet für Wagner? wer war am Naturgemäßesten und Innerlichsten Wagnerisch trotz und ohne Wagner?'—Darauf hatte ich mir schon seit lange gesagt: das war jener bizarre Dreiviertels-Narr Baudelaire, der Dichter der Fleurs du mal. Ich hatte es bedauert, daß dieser grundverwandte Geist W(agner)n nicht bei Lebzeiten entdeckt habe. . . .*
> *Ich blättere in einer jüngst erschienenen Sammlung von Oeuvres posthumes dieses in Frankreich auf's Tiefste geschätzten und selbst geliebten Genies . . . springt mir ein uneditierter Brief Wagners in die Augen, bezüglich auf eine Abhandlung Baudelaire's. . .).*[21]

In this letter to Gast, Nietzsche takes the time to copy the entire letter Wagner wrote in 1861 to Baudelaire to express his gratitude for the poet's supportive essay *"Tannhäuser à Paris."* Nietzsche's discovery of this letter makes it indeed possible to speak of Nietzsche's identification with Baudelaire, for Nietzsche continues: "If I am not mistaken, Wagner wrote a letter expressing this kind of gratitude and even enthusiasm only one other time: after receiving *The Birth of Tragedy." (Einen Brief dieser Art Dankbarkeit und selbst Enthusiasmus hat, wenn mich nicht alles trügt, Wagner nur noch einmal geschrieben: nach dem Empfang der* Geburt der Tragödie) *(SB* VIII 264).

As Le Rider points out, Nietzsche, who in all probability did not read Baudelaire's essay, would have recognized in it themes central to *The Birth of Tragedy*: a quasi-Schopenhauerian analysis of the liberating power of music and the idea of *Gesamtkunstwerk* (total work of art) which Baudelaire translates into his own language, speaking of a system of correspondences and the relation between music and space (Le Rider 93).

Nietzsche's later characterization of the phenomenon of the intermingling of various art spheres as a symptom of decadence is also present in Baudelaire who, in his essay *"L'Art philosophique,"* wonders if it is not a sign of the fatality of decadence that each art encroaches on the neighboring art in such a way that the power of suggestiveness of each separate art is lost in favor of an encyclopedic frenzy (*PL2* 598). Philipp Rippel, whose article investigates particular themes in Nietzsche's critique of decadence, such as decadent Wagnerism, the idea of progress, the dandy and the overman, also sees a connection between Nietzsche's *The Birth of Tragedy* and Baudelaire's essay on Wagner: "Baudelaire and the young Nietzsche, both independently from each other, have described, in their apologetic writings on Wagner, the subversive quality inherent in the myths of decadence as a doubling of metaphysical angst and metaphysical delight."[22]

In his article on Nietzsche, Baudelaire, and Wagner, Robert Kopp follows the lines of Pestalozzi and Michaud with the difference, however, that he stresses more forcefully that Baudelaire illuminated Nietzsche's analysis of decadence, stating that Baudelaire unquestionably provided Nietzsche with the only example of a "lucid decadent."[23] From this point of view, Baudelaire seems to surpass Wagner, whose superiority Nietzsche paradoxically sees in *The Case of Wagner* in that he had "the naïveté of décadence," i.e., a lack of distance. It is precisely Baudelaire's critical distance from the ideological tendencies of his century and most importantly from himself, his decisive role in the development of decadence as an aesthetic phenomenon reflecting modern sensitivity in its extremes, which connects him with Nietzsche.

From this point of view, Baudelaire's *Intimate Journals* prove to be of great value to Nietzsche's own assessment of the times and a striking example of self-critical awareness. The passages Nietzsche copies all contain a sharp criticism of modern civilization and the French character. For Nietzsche, who viewed France as the "seat of the most spiritual and sophisticated culture in Europe," Baudelaire's remarks must have seemed an extraordinary exercise in analysis and self-criticism.

Baudelaire seemed to be the one Nietzsche was looking for when he asked in *On the Genealogy of Morals*: "What prudent man would write a single honest word about himself today?" Of course, the question of "honesty" in regard to both authors' autobiographical statements has to be approached with caution. Nietzsche himself warns against the dangers of accepting a writer's "honest" self-description as truth. At the beginning of

Ecce Homo, which is considered his most autobiographical work, Nietzsche concedes how difficult he finds such self-portraiture: "I have a duty against which my habits, even more the pride of my instincts, revolt at bottom—namely to say: Hear me! For I am such and such a person. Above all, do not mistake me for someone else" (*. . . gibt es eine Pflicht, gegen die im Grunde meine Gewohnheit, noch mehr der Stolz meiner Instinkte revoltiert, nämlich zu sagen: Hört mich! denn ich bin der und der. Verwechselt mich vor Allem nicht!*).[24]

Some of the most important themes in Baudelaire selected by Nietzsche merit mention. Amongst them figures the dandy, which can be seen as prefiguring Nietzsche's notion of the "overman." As Le Rider points out, in one instance Nietzsche translates dandy as "the higher human being" who is not a specialist but "a man of leisure and global education." (*Dandysme. Was der höhere Mensch ist? Das ist kein Spezialist. C'est l'homme de loisir et d'éducation générale.*) (*KSA* XIII 83).

Walter Benjamin has stressed the connection between what he terms Baudelaire's and Nietzsche's "modern heroism" in regard to the experience of the death of God:

> Baudelaire's heroic attitude may be closely related to that of Nietzsche. If Baudelaire still holds on to Catholicism, his experience of the universe is nevertheless associated with the experience Nietzsche formulates in the proposition: God is dead (Benjamin 241).

Indeed, Nietzsche notes: "God is the only being who, in order to reign, does not even have to exist." (*Dieu est le seul être qui, pour régner, n'a même pas besoin d'exister*) (*KSA* XIII 77). Nietzsche shared Baudelaire's disdain for democracy and was certainly intrigued by Baudelaire's social sadism: "In politics, the true saint is he who whips and kills the people for their own good" (*KSA* XIII 79). He notes Baudelaire's apocalyptic predictions with regard to the progression of modern civilization's decline and Baudelaire's demystification of the modern myth of progress. Baudelaire's analysis of love as a taste for prostitution, torture, and the desire to hurt, did not go unnoticed by Nietzsche whose own understanding of love is very close to that of Baudelaire's when he states in *The Case of Wagner*: "But love as fatum, as fatality, cynical, innocent, cruel—and precisely in this [is] a piece of nature. That love which is war in its means, and at bottom the deadly hatred of the sexes!"[25] Many notes also concern Baudelaire's provocative comments on woman and his particular notion of beauty which Nietzsche links to Wagner's: "The beautiful, as Baudelaire understands it (and Richard Wagner). Something glowing and sad, a little vague, giving room for conjecture" (*KSA* XIII 79). Baudelaire's taste for artificiality, as an essential quality in woman and as a factor constituting her beauty, attracts Nietzsche's curiosity as well:

> What bewitches in woman and comprises her beauty: her blasé attitude, her annoyed attitude, an attitude of evanescence, haughtiness, coldness, . . . domination, determination, mischievousness, sickliness, felinity, playfulness, nonchalance, and maliciousness all mingled together.
> *(Was am Weibe bezaubert und die Schönheit ausmacht:*
> *l'air blasé, l'air ennuyé, l'air évaporé, l'air impudent, l'air froid, . . . l'air de*
> *domination, l'air de volonté, l'air méchant, l'air malade, l'air chat, enfantillage,*
> *nonchalence et malice mêlées) (KSA* XIII 80).

The value of all these themes and investigations lies in their establishment of a definitive relationship between Nietzsche and Baudelaire. It seems, however, that the question of Nietzsche's identification with Baudelaire predominates to such an extent that it overshadows the larger concerns both authors shared independently of one another. Nevertheless, the above-mentioned studies, by concentrating on the specific textual evidence of Nietzsche's reception of Baudelaire, lay the groundwork for a broader investigation of the correspondences between the two authors.

More recent discussions of the connection between Nietzsche and Baudelaire have begun to move away from reception in favor of a freer association of their common concerns. This is germane to current debates in the realms of literary theory and art criticism.[26] Beyond Nietzsche's attitude toward Baudelaire, there exists a *correspondance* between the two authors which can be seen dramatically in their separate projects of redefining, reevaluating, and reformulating the character and interrelationships of romanticism, modernity, and decadence.

It is from this perspective that the present study operates, concentrating on Nietzsche's texts which address the question of art and Baudelaire's texts on art and literature. The investigation is not a comparison in the traditional sense, but takes the form of a parallel reading focusing on these three central and ever-timely concepts, which have been challenged by both authors in such a way that their relevance to today's understanding of these terms cannot be underestimated.

Notes

[1] See Mazzino Montinari, "Aufgaben der Nietzsche Forschung heute: Nietzsches Auseinandersetzung mit der französischen Literatur des 19. Jahrhunderts," *Nietzsche Heute: Die Rezeption seines Werkes nach 1968* (Bern: Francke Verlag, 1988), 137–148. Earlier texts: W. D. Williams, *Nietzsche and the French. A study of the influence of Nietzsche's French reading on his thought and writing.* (Oxford: Oxford University Press, 1952) and Pierre Champromis, *"Nietzsche devant la culture française,"* Romanische *Forschungen* 68 (1956): 74–115.

[2] Friedrich Nietzsche, *The Twilight of the Idols*, trans. R. J. Hollingdale (London: Penguin, 1968), 69.

[3] Friedrich Nietzsche, *Ecce Homo*, trans. W. Kaufmann (New York: Vintage, 1969), 248.

[4] The earliest text referring to Nietzsche and Baudelaire is Charles Andler, *Nietzsche, sa vie et sa pensée*, 6. vols. (Paris: 1920–31). See also Georges Blin, *Baudelaire* (Paris: Gallimard, 1939) and Marcel Raymond, *De Baudelaire au surréalisme* (Paris: J. Corti, 1940). In English: *From Baudelaire to Surrealism*, (London: Methuen, 1970).

[5] Walter Benjamin, "Zentralpark," in *Illuminationen* (Frankfurt a. M.: Suhrkamp, 1977). References to this text appear with the author's name.

[6] Albert Camus, *The Rebel* (New York: Vintage, 1960).

[7] George Bataille, *Literature and Evil* (New York: Urizen, 1973).

[8] Paul de Man, *Blindness and Insight* (Minneapolis: University of Minnesota Press, 1971).

[9] The first to bring to attention Nietzsche's notes on Baudelaire was Henri Thomas, "Les Notes de Nietzsche sur Baudelaire," *Nouvelle Revue Française*, (Oct.-Dec. 1953): 1124–1127. He is followed by Geneviève Bianquis, *"Nietzsche lecteur de Baudelaire,"* Bulletin de la société française d'études nietzschéennes 1, (Nov. 1961).

[10] Karl Pestalozzi, "Nietzsches Baudelaire-Rezeption," *Nietzsche-Studien* 7 (Berlin: de Gruyter, 1978): 158–178. References to this text appear with the author's name in the text.

[11] See Jacques Le Rider, "Nietzsche et Baudelaire," *Littérature* 86 (1992): 85–101. References to this text appear with the author's name.

[12] Friedrich Nietzsche, *Beyond Good and Evil*, trans. W. Kaufmann (New York: Vintage, 1966), 197. Original text in *Sämtliche Werke. Kritische Studienausgabe*, ed. Giorgio Colli and Mazzino Montinari, (Berlin: dtv/de Gruyter, 1980), 203. References to this text are designated *KSA*.

[13] Stéphane Michaud, "Nietzsche et Baudelaire," *Le surnaturalisme français, Actes du colloque organisé à l'Université de Vanderbilt,* W. T. Bandy Center for Baudelaire Studies, A la Baconnière (1979), 133–161.

[14] Friedrich Nietzsche, *The Birth of Tragedy*, in *Basic Writings of Nietzsche*, trans. W. Kaufmann (New York: The Modern Library, 1968), 122. Original text in *KSA* I 130.

[15] Charles Baudelaire, "Le Salon de 1859," *Selected Writings on Art and Literature*, trans. P. E. Charvet (London: Penguin, 1992), 287,294. The original text in *Oeuvres Complètes*, 2 vols., ed. Claude Pichois (Paris: Gallimard La Pléiade, 1976), 610, 616. References to this text are designated *PL2*.

[16] Friedrich Nietzsche, *The Twilight of the Idols*, trans. R. J. Hollingdale (London: Penguin Classics, 1969), 81. *KSA* VI 127.

[17] Théophile Gautier, "Preface" in *Mademoiselle de Maupin*, trans. Joanna Richardson (Harmondsworth: Penguin, 1981).

[18] Charles Baudelaire, *Selected Writings on Art and Literature* (London: Penguin Books, 1992), 113. References to this text are designated *SW*.

[19] Marcel Ruff, *Baudelaire*, trans. Agnes Kertesz (New York: New York University Press, 1966), 61.

[20] Friedrich Nietzsche, "Posthumous Fragments," *Kritische Studienausgabe*, eds. G. Colli and M. Montinari, 15 vols. (Berlin: de Gruyter, 1980), XI 600–601. References to these posthumous fragments are indicated in the text by *KSA*. Since no translations of these fragments are yet available, the present translations are my own.

[21] Friedrich Nietzsche, *Sämtliche Briefe. Kritische Studienausgabe*, eds. Giorgio Colli and Mazzino Montinari, 8 vols. (Berlin: de Gruyter, 1984), VIII 263. References to this text are designated *SB*. Translations are mine.

[22] Philip Rippel, *"Die Geburt des Uebermenschen aus dem Geiste der Décadence,"* Der Sturz der Idole. Nietzsches Umwertung von Kultur und Subjekt, ed. Philipp Rippel (Tübingen: Konkursbuchverlag, 1985), 30.

[23] Robert Kopp, "Nietzsche, Baudelaire, Wagner. A propos d'une définition de la décadence," *Travaux de littérature*, vol.1 (Paris: Klincksiek, 1988), 203–216.

[24] Friedrich Nietzsche, *Ecce Homo*, trans. W. Kaufmann (New York: Viking Press, 1969), 217. *KSA* VI 257.

[25] Friedrich Nietzsche, "The Case of Wagner," *Basic Writings of Nietzsche*, trans. W. Kaufmann (New York: The Modern Library, 1968), 615.

[26] See Geoff White, "Nietzsche's Baudelaire, or the Sublime Proleptic Spin of His Politico-Economic Thought," *Representations* 50 (Spring 1995) and Antoine Compagnon, *The Five Paradoxes of Modernity*, trans. Franklin Philip (New York: Columbia University Press, 1994). Originally published in French: *Les Cinq Paradoxes de la Modernité* (Paris: Le Seuil, 1990).

BAUDELAIRE

Chapter 1

ROMANTICISM AND MODERNITY

I.   "The Salon of 1845" *and the Search for Originality*

Baudelaire's aesthetic program—the reformulation of romanticism and his theory of modernity—develops gradually from his first review of "The Salon of 1845" to his essay "The Painter of Modern Life." When the twenty-three-year old Baudelaire reviews his first *Salon*, he is essentially a poet whose foremost concern is to have his voice heard and to define his place in the literary world dominated by writers such as Lamartine, Hugo, Musset, and Vigny. Paul Valéry describes his situation as follows:

> Place yourselves in the situation of a young man who came to the writing age in 1840. He has been brought up on the authors whom his instinct imperiously orders him to wipe out. His literary existence provoked and nourished by them, thrilled by their fame, determined by their works, is, however, necessarily dependent upon negation, upon the overthrow and replacement of those men who seemed to him to fill all fame's niches and to deny him: one, the world of forms; another, that of sentiments; a third the picturesque; a fourth, profundity. . . In short, he is led, constrained, by the state of his soul and its environment, more and more clearly to oppose the system, or the absence of system, called romanticism.[1]

"The Salon of 1845" was Baudelaire's debut in art criticism. The reviews of *Salons* had been a hundred-year long tradition and gone through many stages of popularity. The first account of the *Salon* in 1747 by La Font de Saint-Yenne provoked irritation amongst the artists against the critics and therefore prevented the review of the next *Salon* in 1749. With Diderot's *Salon* in 1759 the genre gained popularity again until the early nineteenth century, when the *Salon* became an established literary genre and was continued by Baudelaire's predecessors, professional critics such as Gustave Planche, Théophile Gautier, Théophile Thoré, and Jules Champfleury. Most of the criticisms of these reviewers, however, are judged today as either too "technical," "honest but narrow," or "picturesque and often overenthusiastic," "utilitarian," or "anecdotal."[2]

The idea behind the review of a *Salon* in the nineteenth century was foremost a practical one. The reviewer, giving his opinions on hundreds of paintings, sculptures, and etchings, helped orient prospective buyers of art works and to guide them through the yearly exhibit in order to promote consumption. Hence its composition into small chapters was arranged according to various genres, e. g., portraits, historical paintings, landscapes, or according to artists.

In his first *Salon*, Baudelaire respects this traditional arrangement while at the same time imposing his individual vision with a tone of firmness and authority. Aligning himself with the visiting crowd, who in his eyes has so often been underestimated, misled, or disgusted even by previous reviews, Baudelaire sees it as his duty to "speak of everything that attracts the eyes of crowd and artists alike" *(. . . nous parlerons de tout ce qui attire les yeux de la foule et des artistes)*.[3] To the contempt with which previous reviewers have alienated the layman, e.g., the bourgeois, Baudelaire opposes his method of selection of artists, which is based on the amount of pleasure their work of art can provide and arranged "according to the order and rating assigned them by public favor" *(suivant l'ordre et le grade que leur a assignés l'éstime public) (SW* 35, *PL2* 353).

His claim, however, to base his criticism on the judgment of the public suggests that Baudelaire's review is substantially based on his personal ideas. The key word of this *Salon* is originality, an essential quality an artist must have in order to be an artist and to distinguish himself from other artists. Above all, the artist has to be himself, regardless of and independent from the expectations or requirements of selection panels, juries, or in short, the academy. Already in this *Salon*, Baudelaire chooses Eugène Delacroix as the artist par excellence, for he is "decidedly the most original painter of both ancient and modern times" *(décidément le peintre le plus original des temps anciens et des temps modernes) (SW* 35, *PL2* 353). With this remark, Baudelaire already points to the importance of the opposition of ancient and modern in regard to his own definition of the modern as it will be developed in the next *Salon*. The merit of Delacroix lies, according to Baudelaire, in the artist's capability to render historical (ancient) subjects in the most modern manner. Through his relentless will to give form to his personal vision of ancient themes which over the ages had been painted again and again, Delacroix reveals another quality important for Baudelaire which is called *naïveté*. In Baudelaire's vocabulary, originality and *naïveté* are closely related and somewhat difficult to distinguish. According to Gilman, originality "stresses the unlikeness of the artist to other artists, naïf [is] his own peculiar quality" (Gilman 23). In the context of this particular *Salon*, these terms seem to be employed by Baudelaire mainly to distinguish between artists who are so in spite of themselves (like Delacroix, sometimes Ingres, and Daumier) and the many others whose personal vision is obstructed by either too much erudition, a tendency toward imitation or overbearing technical skills.

For the present study, the most interesting part of this *Salon* remains Baudelaire's discussion of Delacroix. This painter's qualities are already present here and later *Salons* will serve Baudelaire to establish his theory of modern art. Delacroix the master of harmony between colors, Delacroix the artist who draws with color, Delacroix the poet-painter whose works inspire in the viewer "feelings of intimate, mysterious and romantic poetry" *(poésie intime, mystérieuse et romantique) (SW* 36, *PL2* 354), and finally Delacroix the musician-painter who succeeds "in making colors on a canvas sing ever more capricious melodies, in finding ever more prodigious, new, unknown, delicate, delightful chords of tones" *(Fit-on jamais chanter sur une toile de plus capricieuses mélodies? Un plus prodigieux accord de tons nouveaux, inconnus, délicats et charmants) (SW* 39, *PL2* 357).

In spite of the praise Baudelaire lavishes on Delacroix and his appreciation of a few other artists, however, the *Salon* in Baudelaire's opinion, generally lacks innovative vigor. It resembles too many previous *Salons* and, despite progress in technical skills, it does not testify to a necessary awareness of what the poet calls "modern heroism." Thus the *Salon* ends with an invitation for future artists to focus their artistic energies on the beauty of present times:

> No one is cocking his ear to to-morrow's wind; and yet the heroism of modern life surrounds us and presses upon us . . . The painter, the true painter for whom we are looking, will be he who can snatch its epic quality from the life of today and can make us see and understand, with brush or with pencil, how great and poetic we are in our cravats and our patent-leather boots. Next year let us hope that the true seekers may grant us the extraordinary delight of celebrating the advent of the new![4]
> *(Au vent qui soufflera demain nul ne tend l'oreille; et pourtant l'héroisme de la vie moderne nous entoure et nous presse. . . Celui-là sera le peintre, le vrai peintre, qui saura arracher à la vie actuelle son côté épique, et nous faire voire et comprendre, avec de la couleur ou du dessin, combien nous sommes grands et poétiques dans nos cravates et nos bottes vernies. —Puissent les vrais chercheurs nous donner l'année prochaine cette joie singulière de célébrer l'avènement du neuf!) (PL2* 407).

Margaret Gilman, the first American scholar to investigate Baudelaire's *Salons* and essays on literature, argues that for today's discussion of Baudelaire's art criticism, "The Salon of 1845" is the least elaborate and maybe the weakest in that it remains rather on a level of suggestion and sketch than on the development of critical principles. Furthermore, "the large number of artists mentioned, the pages of brief comments on names now completely unknown to us, end by tiring our minds just as walking through room after room of pictures tires our feet" (Gilman 23). Baudelaire might have agreed, for he was not satisfied with his work. It has been suggested that while aware of the fact that his indebtedness to Diderot and Stendhal might show in his first *Salon,* he feared not having been original enough himself. The seventy two pages on which he reviewed 102 artists went practically unnoticed by the public, except for one favorable note by Champfleury on his *Salon* in the *Revue de Paris*: "M. Baudelaire-Dufays is as bold as Diderot, less the paradox".[5] The following note was written by Champfleury in response to a demand made to him by Baudelaire: "If you would like to write a joking article about me, go ahead as long as it doesn't hurt me too much. But if you would like to please me, write a few serious lines and speak of Diderot's Salons. The best would probably be to combine both" (Pichois 206). Champfleury's line can be considered an ambiguous compliment: on the one hand he concedes Baudelaire boldness in tone and judgment, a quality Baudelaire highly esteemed, on the other, however, he withholds paradoxicalness, another quality which Baudelaire certainly would not wish to lack. According to Timothy Raser, such a compliment might have been one reason for Baudelaire's discontent with his *Salon* and his subsequent decision to depart—formally and philosophically—from the traditional genre of the *Salon* in his next review, which would be "as bold and as paradoxical as Diderot's."[6]

II.   "The Salon of 1846" *and Poetic Criticism*

To this day, Baudelaire's introductory chapter to "The Salon of 1846" dedicated and entitled "To the Bourgeois" provokes contradictory interpretations. The main issue of these arguments is Baudelaire's true position at this point in time regarding the ruling class of France. Considering his later trenchant remarks against the bourgeois, some critics see this text as an ironic curtsy. Others take it as an honest alignment with the majority this class represents. Still others recognize in it the premises of his political engagement of 1848. Gilman argues that Baudelaire, "young, enthusiastic, and filled with an apostolic zeal" essentially meant what he wrote, all the more so because, in line with Stendhal, he rejected old-fashioned, anti-bourgeois romanticism. At the same time, Gilman continues, a certain pleasure in surprising and startling his fellow critics by expressing ideas contrary to the current ones as well as a rising bourgeois liberalism prompted Baudelaire to take a stand for the bourgeois (Gilman 28). Yet another interpretation, probably the very first, is given by Baudelaire's close friend and journalist Charles Asselineau:

> Baudelaire addressed himself deliberately to the most public party of the public . . . not out of love for the paradox as one might think, but rather out of hatred and opposition to the demi-bourgeois and the false artist whom the author qualifies as 'monopolizers' and 'pharisees' . . . What seems to me rather obvious, is that in dealing directly with the bourgeois, Baudelaire found a way to pass over the heads of his confreres and established himself by adopting an affirmative and dogmatic tone he liked and spared himself useless discussions (Pichois 227).

Baudelaire's address to the bourgeois is not merely praise, acceptance, or alignment. His attitude is more that of a mediator between the art world and the beholders of wealth and thus power. Instead of alienating the bourgeois further, Baudelaire condescends to teach them a lesson with the implied promise of a reward if the lesson is well-learned. While conceding them the power to govern, he at the same time reminds them that this power is only legitimate insofar as it is complemented by an appreciation of art:

> The governance of the state is yours, and that is as it should be, because you have the power. But you must also be capable of feeling beauty, for just as one has no right to forgo power, equally no one of you has the right to forgo poetry. You can live three days without bread; without poetry, never; and those of you who maintain the contrary are mistaken; you do not know yourselves.
> *(Vous possédez le gouvernement de la cité, et cela est juste, car vous êtes la force. Mais il faut que vous soyez aptes à sentir la beauté; car comme aucun d'entre vous ne peut aujourd'hui se passer de puissance, nul n'a le droit de se passer de poésie. Vous pouvez vivre trois jours sans pain;—sans poésie, jamais; et ceux d'entre vous qui disent le contraire se trompent: ils ne se connaissent pas) (SW 47, PL2 415).*

Baudelaire sets himself apart from the "monopolists" *(accapareurs)* who so far have denied the money-making, loan-giving, industry-promot-

ing, company-forming bourgeois, who nevertheless "have established col-
lections, museums, galleries," access to aesthetic enjoyment despite their
lack of "the technological knowledge of the arts." As Richard Burton, who
investigates Baudelaire's political position during the years before 1848,
states:

> He [Baudelaire] is not, like the *accapareurs*, saying that the bourgeois can never
> and will never appreciate and purchase authentic art. He is saying rather that the
> bourgeois needs to be educated in artistic appreciation and brought to a position
> where it will be natural for him to prefer a Delacroix to a Vernet. It need hardly be
> added that the key role in this formation of an artistically aware bourgeois public
> will be played by serious art critics like himself.[7]

Baudelaire also appeals to the importance of feeling as the sine qua non for
the understanding of art. It is this very notion of feeling—as opposed to
knowledge, erudition or academism—which stands at the center of
Baudelaire's subsequent development of the new romanticism which is
called modernity. In his address, Baudelaire in fact gives the bourgeois a
chance to be worthy of the task to hold the power "in a city where the
public is cosmopolitan." To make himself understood, Baudelaire presents art as a nourishing commodity the bourgeois cannot do without: "Art
is an infinitely precious possession, a refreshing and warming drink that
restores the stomach and the mind to the natural balance of the ideal."
*(L'art est un bien infiniment précieux, un breuvage rafraîchissant, qui
rétablit l'estomac et l'esprit dans l'équilibre naturel de l'idéal) (SW* 47,
PL2 416). Baudelaire's gesture towards the bourgeois is interpreted in a
study by Felix Leakey who argues that while in "The Salon of 1845,"
Baudelaire was still content with a small audience ("We know we shall be
understood only by a few number of people but that is enough"), in 1846, he
envisaged and thus addressed a larger one albeit wishing it to be comprised
of professionals. It is apparent from the text of the *Salon*, Leakey argues,
that Baudelaire's "primary motive throughout the *Salon* is to expound certain aesthetic ideas and preferences." And since "his arguments are often
highly specialized and technical" it is "aimed over the heads of the bourgeois readers whose support he would certainly be glad to enlist, as a further and more knowledgeable audience—that of artists, critics, and friends."[8]
    Indeed, Baudelaire's attitude toward the bourgeois is marked by
an ambiguity which according to Burton results from the serious artist's
precarious situation within the repressive regime of the Bourgeois Monar-

chy in general. Burton rightfully stresses the fact that Baudelaire's position is one of weakness insofar as he has to deal with the fact that the artist, as the antithesis of the bourgeois, nevertheless needs the bourgeois if he is to be able to live and survive at all. Baudelaire's concern to educate the bourgeois stems from his realization that there is no concrete alternative to the bourgeois' power. His address to the bourgeois thus reflects this dilemma. Burton states:

> Baudelaire . . . despises the bourgeois as he is but considers his power in politics, the economy, society, thought, and culture to be an unchallengeable fact of mid-nineteenth century life. His only hope—and it is a slender one—is that the bourgeois' sensitivity to authentic art might be enhanced through education, whence the genuine attempt to gain its sympathy and interest—, or at the very least, not to antagonize him by the knee-jerk bourgeois-ophobia of *les accapareurs* and their like in the art world (Burton 37).

"The Salon of 1846" serves Baudelaire to establish the foundation of his aesthetic program. One main idea underlies his review: the definition of romanticism out of modernity. But before Baudelaire begins his discussion, he addresses the question of criticism itself. He begins by exposing a paradox: while the artists hold a grudge against a futile criticism, which pretends to teach the bourgeois his art without a chance of success, they nevertheless "owe to it their poor little reputations!" *(doivent à elle seule leur pauvre renommée!) (SW* 50, *PL2* 418). The artist is thus dependent on what he abhors. The artists' grudge against criticism is partially understandable for Baudelaire because it is directed against a certain criticism based on the pretense of objectivity and excludes personal perspective and artistic sensitivity. Thus Baudelaire opposes two types of criticism:

> I sincerely believe that the best criticism is the criticism that is entertaining and poetic; not a cold analytical type of criticism, which, claiming to explain everything, is devoid of hatred and love, and deliberately rids itself of any trace of feeling, but, since a fine painting is nature reflected by an artist, the best critical study, I repeat, will be the one that is that painting reflected by an intelligent and sensitive mind. Thus the best accounts of a picture may well be a sonnet or an elegy.
> *(Je crois sincèrement que la meilleure critique est celle qui est amusante et poétique; non pas celle-ci, froide et algébrique, qui, sous prétexte de tout expliquer, n'a ni haine ni amour, et se dépouille volontairement de toute espèce de tempérament; mais—un beau tableau étant la nature réfléchie par un artiste,— celle qui sera ce tableau réfléchi par un esprit intelligent et sensible. Ainsi le*

meilleur compte rendu d'un tableau pourra être un sonnet ou une élégie) (SW 50, PL2 418).

Baudelaire here justifies his own critical endeavor by suggesting the idea, reiterated fifteen years later in his essay on Richard Wagner's *Tannhäuser* in Paris, that the ideal critic and even the only valuable critic is in fact the artist himself. Whereas a poet by nature has critical abilities, a critic does not necessarily possess poetic faculties.

> Critic into poet—that would indeed be a wholly new event in the history of the arts, a reversal of all psychical laws, a monstrosity; on the contrary, all great poets naturally, inevitably become critics . . . for a critic to become a poet would be miraculous, whereas for a poet not to have a critic within him is impossible . . . I regard the poet as the best critic.
> *(Ce serait un évènement tout nouveau dans l'histoire des arts qu'un critique se faisant poète, un renversement de toutes les lois psychiques, une monstruosité; au contraire, tous les grands poètes deviennent naturellement, fatalement critiques . . . Il serait prodigieux qu'un critique devînt poète, et il est impossible qu'un poète ne contienne pas un critique) (SW 340, PL2 793).*

Having established a distinction between the cold analytical criticism and an ideal poetic criticism, which has its place in books of poetry and is destined for readers of poetry, Baudelaire introduces a third possibility: "As to criticism proper . . . [it] must be partial, passionate, political, that is to say it must adopt an exclusive point of view, provided always the one adopted opens up the widest horizons." *(Quant à la critique proprement dite, . . . [elle] doit être partiale, passionnée, politique, c'est-à-dire faite à un point de vue exclusif, mais à un point de vue qui ouvre le plus d'horizons) (SW 50, PL2 418).* The broadest horizons are opened up by the critic's individuality, "which demands of the artist naïveté and the sincere expression of his temperament, aided by all the means his craft gives him" *(. . . commander à l'artiste la naïveté et l'expression sincère de son tempérament, aidé par tous les moyens que lui fournit son métier) (SW 51, PL2 419).* And again, Baudelaire draws a parallel between the true artist and the good critic. Just as the artist must express his temperament, "the critic must do his duty with passion; for critic though he may be, he is a man nonetheless. . . " *(le critique doit accomplir son devoir avec passion; car pour être critique on n'en est pas moins homme) (SW 51, PL2 419).*

Temperament and passion, however, reflecting the inner nature of the artist and the critic are always combined or rather counterbalanced with technical perfection for the artist and reasoning for the critic. These qualities are essential features of Baudelaire's definition of romanticism which requires of the artist—and the critic himself—to resist conformity to artificial external standards in favor of personal expression combined with skillful mastering of the tools of their trade:

> Since every century, every people has achieved the expression of its own beauty and system of moral values, and if the word romanticism may be defined as the most up to date and the most modern expression of beauty, then, in the eyes of the reasonable and passionate critic, the great artist will be he who combines with the conditions laid down above, namely naïveté, the greatest degree of romanticism possible.
> *(Chaque siècle, chaque peuple ayant possédé l'expression de sa beauté et de sa morale,—si l'on veut entendre par romantisme l'expression la plus récente et la plus moderne de la beauté,—le grand artiste sera donc,—pour le critique raisonnable et passionné,—celui qui unira à la condition demandé ci-dessus, la naïveté,—le plus de romantisme possible) (SW 51, PL2 419).*

III.   Toward a New Romanticism

In the chapter entitled "What is Romanticism" Baudelaire continues to elaborate on the idea that "romanticism and modern art are one and the same thing" for "to call oneself romantic and to fix one's gaze systematically on the past is contradictory" *(qui dit romantisme dit art moderne . . . s'appeler romantique et regarder systématiquement, le passé, c'est se contredire) (SW 52, PL2 421).* The romanticism Baudelaire opposes is the one that deludes itself by giving primacy to choice of subject for lack of temperament, by feigning religious feelings where they do not exist or by judging technical skill higher than feeling. This romanticism is antiquated and no longer reflects the needs of Baudelaire's own time. According to Baudelaire, "romanticism, properly speaking, lies neither in the subjects an artist chooses nor in the exact copying of truth, but in the way he feels" *(Le romantisme n'est précisément ni dans le choix des sujets ni dans la vérité exacte, mais dans la manière de sentir).* Furthermore, "romanticism consists not in technical perfection, but in a view of art, analogous to the moral attitudes of the age" *(le romantisme ne consistera pas dans une exécution parfaite, mais dans une conception analogue à la morale du siècle) (SW 52–53, PL2 420–21).* The "new" romanticism which emerges out of these definitions is "a child of the North" *(fils du Nord).* It has a sense of color expressing dreams "lost in the depths of the infinite" *(les rêves profonds)* and a melancholic feeling inseparable from Baudelaire's definition of beauty. Whereas the South is "brutal" and "naturalistic" because "there nature is so beautiful and clear," the North "in suffering and anxiety, takes comfort in imagination" *(le Nord souffrant et inquiet se console avec l'imagination) (SW* 53, *PL2* 421). The comparison between the impressionistic quality of the northern "atmosphere" with its infinite shades of color versus the naturalistic and clear cut contours of the southern "light" serve Baudelaire to stress the essentially musical quality inherent in color.

In the next chapter "Of Color," Baudelaire sketches out, for the first time, his theory of correspondences, which is based on the suggestive powers of art. Here, the harmonious arrangement of masses of color and shades is compared to a symphony: "In color we find harmony, melody and counterpoint" *(on trouve dans la couleur l'harmonie, la mélodie et le contrepoint) (SW* 55, *PL2* 423). An effect of unity is the central thought in this chapter as well as in the whole *Salon.* Just as a symphony is a harmonious arrangement of various tones when arranged according to law which rules them, so a painting is—or should be—a constellation of masses of color whose very combination in the limited space of a canvas produces a sense of harmony. In a painting, the detail has to be sacrificed to the whole for this is precisely the law of nature. Nature makes no mistakes in the arrangement of its various elements because of the chemical affinities between those elements. In nature "form and color are one," and if the artist understands the law which underlies this principle he enjoys the freedom of creation: "he may do anything he likes because he knows by instinct the scale of tones, the tone value, the results of mixing, and the whole science of counterpoint, and, as a result, he can create a harmony of twenty different reds" *(tout lui est permis, parce qu'il connaît de naissance la gamme des tons, la force du ton, les résultats des mélanges, et toute la science du contrepoint, et qu'il peut ainsi faire une harmonie de vingt rouges différents) (SW* 56, *PL2* 424). In fact, the true artist can and should be able to correct nature—or reality—by imposing his own vision and skill upon it. As he does in many instances, Baudelaire gives a concrete example for a complex thought:

> If for example some anti-colorist landowner had the notion of repainting his country house in some absurd way and with a discordant scheme of colors, the thick and transparent glaze of the atmosphere and the trained eye of a Veronese would

between them restore harmony and produce a satisfying canvas, conventional no doubt, but logical. That explains why a colorist can be paradoxical in his way of expressing color and why the study of nature often leads to a result quite different from nature . . . Falsehoods are constantly necessary even to get trompe l'oeil effects.

(Si un propriétaire anticoloriste s'avisait de repeindre sa campagne d'une manière absurde et dans un système de couleurs charivariques, le vernis épais et transparent de l'atmosphère et de l'oeil savant de Véronèse redresserait le tout et produiraient sur une toile un ensemble satisfaisant, conventionnel sans doute, mais logique. . .les mensonges sont continuellement nécessaires, même pour arriver au trompe-l'oeuil.) (SW 56–67, PL2 424).

Coming back to the correspondence between color and music, Baudelaire defines the unity of color as melody. The power of melody is such that it provokes in the beholder of the painting an "unforgettable memory" *(souvenir profond)*. This thought links Baudelaire to German romanticism for he offers to illustrate this thought by a passage from E. T. A. Hoffmann who speaks of the correspondence between colors, sounds, and scents.

Not only in dreams and in the free association of ideas (which phenomenon often comes just before sleep) but also when fully awake, listening to music, I find an analogy and a close union between colors, sounds and scents. I have the impression that all things have been created by one and the same light, and that they are destined to unite in a wonderful concert. The scent of brown and red marigolds especially produces a magical effect on my being. I fall into a profound reverie and then hear as though from afar the solemn, deep notes of the oboe.

(Ce n'est pas seulement en rêve, et dans le léger délire qui qui précède le sommeil, c'est encore éveillé, lorsque j'entends de la musique, que je trouve une analogie et une réunion intime entre les couleurs, les sons et les parfums. Il me semble que toutes ces choses ont été engendrées par un même rayon de lumière, et qu'elles doivent se réunir dans un merveilleux concert. L'odeur des soucis bruns et rouges produit surtout un effet magique sur ma personne. Elle me fait tomber dans une profonde rêverie, et j'entends alors comme dans le lointain les sons graves et profonds du hautbois) (SW 58, PL2 425–26).

The unifying principle which makes the perception of these correspondences possible is that of imagination, the "queen of all faculties" *(la reine des facultés)*. In this *Salon*, however, Baudelaire only touches lightly on this notion central to his aesthetics and this in regard to Delacroix who in his works "creates deep avenues for the most adventurous imagination to wander down" *(de profondes avenues à l'imagination la plus voyageuse)*

(SW 64, *PL2* 431).

Delacroix unites all the elements of Baudelaire's new romanticism. The comparison between the painter and Victor Hugo serves Baudelaire to establish the difference between "an outward looking" romanticism and an "inward" directed one. Corresponding to the first category, Hugo is characterized as "a craftsman, much more adroit than inventive, much more formalist than creative" *(un ouvrier beaucoup plus adroit qu'inventif, un travailleur bien plus correct que créateur),* someone who exploits all the tools of his trade "with cold calculation," an academician whose eyes are turned toward success and recognition. Imagination has little space in Hugo's works for it is replaced by performance of skill and focus on detail with the result of a certain superficiality. In short, he "has become a painter in poetry." Delacroix on the other hand is a "poet in painting" and moreover in spite of himself." His works, in contrast, are poems, and great poems naïvely conceived" *(de grands poèmes naïvement conçus).* Baudelaire adds his own definition of naïveté: "By the naïveté of genius we must understand technical mastery combined with the *gnoti seauton* (know thyself), but a technical mastery that is humble and leaves the big part to temperament" *(Il faut entendre par la naïveté du génie la science du métier combinée avec le gnôti séauton, mais la science modeste laissant le beau rôle au tempérament) (SW* 64–65, *PL2* 431). Delacroix's greatness lies in his will and ability to translate his innermost thoughts and feeling (temperament) by drawing from the vast "dictionary" of nature without copying it. Rather he distills from it and recombines the elements which serve best to render his "ideal." This is not at all absolute, but it is his personal vision, understanding, and interpretation of the subject:

> The ideal is not a vague thing, that boring and intangible dream floating on the ceilings of academies; an ideal is the individual modified by the individual, rebuilt and restored by brush or chisel to the dazzling truth of its own essential harmony.
> *(Ainsi l'idéal n'est pas cette chose vague, ce rêve ennuyeux et impalpable qui nage au plafond des académies; un idéal, c'est l'individu redressé par l'individu, reconstruit et rendu par le pinceau ou le ciseau à l'éclatante vérité de son harmonie native) (SW* 78, *PL2* 456).

Harmony is not a preexisting condition, it is the result of a struggle between the individual (the artist) and nature, which, although it has laws of its own, is essentially incomplete and has no meaning in itself. The artist's task is to "complete what is incomplete in nature, and to find the ideal hidden within the real" *(il faut tout compléter, et retrouver chaque idéal) (SW 77, PL2 455).* The process of creation is thus:

> a struggle between nature and the artist and the better the artist understands nature's intentions, the easier will be the triumph over her. For him no question arises of copying; it is a matter of interpreting in a more simple and luminous language.
>
> *(une lutte entre la nature et l'artiste, où l'artiste triomphera d'autant plus facilement qu'il comprendra mieux les intentions de la nature. Il ne s'agit pas pour lui de copier, mais d'interpréter dans une langue plus simple et plus lumineuse) (SW 79, PL2 457).*

True, nature has to be studied closely, but what matters most to Baudelaire is the ensuing work of imaginative transposition and modification. In order to create an impact on the inner mind of the spectator, which is after all the main function of art in the eyes of Baudelaire, the selective process has to be triggered by the artist's memory, and must in turn appeal to the viewer's memory. The intensity of the impact furthermore increases by the distance between the spectator and the canvas. This distance is a crucial factor because it is only through distance that the painting can be perceived and appreciated as a whole. To simplify in order to render complexity is the task of the modern painter according to Baudelaire. In this interpretive process, the artist has "to sacrifice detail to the whole" *(sacrifiant sans cesse le détail à l'ensemble),* he has to be "careful to avoid weakening the vitality of his thought by weariness from neater and more meticulous workmanship" *(craignant d'affaiblir la vitalité de sa pensée par la fatigue d'une exécution plus nette et plus calligraphique).* To compose a painting with sharp contours, straight lines and meticulous attention to the most minute details is to ignore the natural law of movement. Delacroix's bold and energetic brushstrokes and touches of color show complete dedication to "movement, color, and atmosphere" and thus testify to this very modern quality, which is "to render the eternal restlessness of nature" *(palpitations éternelles de la nature).* In Delacroix's paintings, "lines are as in the rainbow, nothing but the intimate fusion of two colors" *(les lignes ne sont jamais, comme dans l'arc-en-ciel, que la fusion intime de deux couleurs) (SW 67, PL2 433–34).*

The idea of restlessness is striking insofar as it expresses the dynamic character of Baudelaire's conception of modernity which breaks with the classical ideal of the absolute. Restlessness guarantees change, variety and flux versus determined standards and fixed structures. Revising the classical theory of beauty which prescribes external rules and pretends to the standard of the absolute, Baudelaire insists on multiplicity, since, as Baudelaire states in the last chapter entitled "Of the Heroism of Modern Life," "absolute and eternal beauty does not exist." The idea of absolute beauty excludes passion and temperament, "it is nothing but an abstract notion, creamed off from the general surface of different types of beauty" *(La beauté absolue et éternelle n'existe pas, ou plutôt elle n'est qu'une abstraction écrémée de la surface générale des beautés diverses)*. An artwork has value only insofar as it reflects the innermost thought of the artist, and since the artist is forcibly a child of his time, the specificity of his time and age has to be expressed as well. For Baudelaire, the nineteenth century is above all "a suffering age" *(époque souffrante)*, a time of "perpetual mourning" *(deuil perpetuel)*, where everybody is "attending some funeral or another" *(nous célébrons tous quelque enterrement) (SW* 105, *PL* 493–94). Thus Delacroix is the painter of the nineteenth century par excellence for his paintings echo "that strange and persistent melancholy which pervades all his work, and which his choice of subject, the expressions on his faces, the gestures and the color key all alike reveal" *(c'est cette mélancolie singulière et opiniâtre qui s'exhale de toutes ses oeuvres, et qui s'exprime et par le choix des sujets, et par l'expression des figures, et par le geste, et par le style de la couleur) (SW* 74, *PL2* 440). The modern aspect of Delacroix lies in his particular manner and style. At the same time, however, he is the "inheritor" and "worthy successor" of "the great tradition" and the "great masters". Modernity and tradition are here not mutually exclusive but rather condition each other. Without knowledge of tradition, no true modernity can arise. Baudelaire's view of the history of art is here still linear for if Delacroix were removed from "the great chain of history" the chain would be broken and would fall to the ground *(ôtez Delacroix, la grande chaîne de l'histoire est rompue et s'écoule à terre) (SW* 75, *PL2* 441). In Delacroix, Baudelaire sees the link between the old and the new, a promise for the future of the arts whose present state Baudelaire deplores.

Baudelaire's defense of tradition as opposed to the present is in fact a defense of character and personality versus characterlessness and affectation. Tradition is linked with strength, faith in the ideal of art and courage of personal conviction and temperament. The old tradition had something which is lost today, a sense for unity and the grandiose: "The splendor of costume, the nobility of movement, often mannered yet grand and haughty, the absence of mean little tricks and contradictory techniques are qualities that are all implied in the expression: the great tradition" *(Cette magnificence de costume, cette noblesse de mouvement, noblesse souvent maniérée, mais grande et hautaine, cette absence des petits moyens et des procédés contradictoires, sont des qualités toutes impliquées dans ce mot: la grande tradition) (SW 102, PL2 491)*. Today "doubt, or the absence of faith and naïveté, is a vice" *(le doute, ou l'absence de foi et de naïveté, est un vice particulier à ce siècle)* which has infiltrated and thus weakened the role of art as such:

Just compare this age with past ages; when you leave the *Salon* or a recently decorated church, go and rest your eyes in a museum and analyse the differences. In the former, conflict and hubbub of styles and colors, cacophony of tones, colossal trivialities, vulgarity of gesture and attitudes, conventional dignity, clichés of every kind, and all this staring you in the face, not only in pictures hung side by side, but even in the same picture; in short a complex lack of unity producing a dreadful feeling of fatigue for the mind and the eyes. In the latter, you find an air of reverence that makes even children take their hats off, and grips the soul, just as the dust of tombs and vaults grips the throat. That is the effect, not of yellow varnish and of the filth of the ages, but of a sense of unity, profound unity.

(Comparez l'époque présente aux époques passées; au sortir du salon ou d'une église nouvellement décorée, allez reposer vos yeux dans un musée ancien, et analysez les différences: Dans l'un, turbulence, tohu-bohu de styles et de couleurs, cacophonie de tons, trivialités énormes, prosaïsme de gestes et d'attitudes, noblesse de convention, poncifs de toutes sortes, et tout cela visible et clair, non seulement dans les tableaux juxtaposés, mais encore dans le même tableau:— bref,—absence complète d'unité, dont le résultat est une fatigue effroyable pour l'esprit et pour les yeux. Dans l'autre, ce respect qui fait ôter leurs chapeaux aux enfants, et vous saisit l'âme, comme la poussière des tombes et des caveaux saisit la gorge, est l'effet, non point du vernis jaune et de la crasse des temps, mais de l'unité, de l'unité profonde) (SW 103, PL2 491).

In directing his scorn against "the apes of sentiment" *(singes du sentiment)* who endeavor to imitate for lack of their own originality and against eclectics who have no personal point of view and paint in a cold and rational manner, Baudelaire claims his right to formulate the role of art anew. His defense of tradition is not so much the expression of his adherence to it as a summons for the modern artist to rise to the level of his own time, which equals former ones in richness of subjects and forms of beauty. The order of things for Baudelaire is in fact, to refuse authority of tradition

over present times for if "every age and every people have had their own
form of beauty, we have inevitably ours" *(puisque tous les siècles et tous
les peuples ont eu leur leur beauté, nous avons inévitablement la nôtre)*
(SW 104, *PL2* 493). To fail to understand or worse, to willingly ignore the
particularity of one's own time is to fail not only to be modern but to be an
artist at all. Michel Foucault has shown, in a very short passage, how
Baudelaire's modernity is more "an attitude of modernity" than a romantic
quest of the self: Baudelaire, or "modern man, for Baudelaire, is not the
man who goes off to discover himself, his secrets and his hidden truth; he
is the man who tries to invent himself."[9] The heroic aspect of modern life,
e.g., the black frock-coat as a symbol for the reigning atmosphere on which
Baudelaire insists in his final chapter of the *Salon*, is therefore to be seen
as a necessary construct, which in spite of its irony testifies to a will to
grasp the underlying preoccupations of his times:

> Baudelaire makes fun of those painters who, finding nineteenth-century dress
> excessively ugly, want to depict nothing but ancient togas. But modernity in paint-
> ing does not consist, for Baudelaire, in introducing black clothing unto canvas.
> The modern painter is the one who can show the dark frock coat as 'the necessary
> costume of our time,' the one who knows how to make manifest, in the fashion of
> the day, the essential, permanent, obsessive relation that our age entertains with
> death . . . To designate this attitude of modernity, Baudelaire sometimes employs
> a litotes that is highly significant because it is presented in the form of a precept:
> 'You have no right to despise the present' (FR 40–41).

It is noteworthy that in the end of his review of the *Salon*, Baudelaire
comes back to the question of the choice of subject matter. Whereas he
had previously stated that the subject matter was of secondary importance
to the truly romantic artist, he now insists on its importance as far as the
depiction of the present is concerned. This depiction of the present is not
to be found in nature, but in the city where "scenes of high life and of the
thousands of uprooted lives that haunt the underworld of a great city . . .
show us that we have only to open our eyes to see and know the heroism of
our day" *(le spectacle de la vie élégante et des milliers d'existences flottantes
qui circulent dans les souterrains d'une grande ville . . . nous prouvent que
nous n'avons qu'à ouvrir les yeux pour connaître notre héroisme) (SW*
106, *PL2* 495). On the one hand, it is not surprising that Baudelaire ends
his *Salon* with praise for Balzac. For Balzac did not fail to see that "Parisian life is rich in poetic and wonderful subjects," that it is the place where
"the marvelous envelops and saturates us like the atmosphere" *(La vie*

parisienne est féconde en sujets poétiques et merveilleux. Le merveilleux nous enveloppe et nous abreuve comme l'atmosphère) (SW 107, PL2 496). On the other hand, the absence of Delacroix in Baudelaire's discussion of modern heroism and beauty leaves to wonder whether Delacroix really is the modern painter par excellence. Indeed, Delacroix's subjects are mostly drawn from ancient history, religion, or classical literature. From this perspective, he stands more in line with tradition and classicism. Furthermore, the urban aspect is entirely absent in Delacroix. The accent of his modernity lies mainly on the imaginative originality with which he interprets and renders classical subjects. In other words, at this point in time, in 1846, Delacroix is the master of the "eternal" *(éternel)* element as opposed to the "variable" *(variable)*, the distinguishing feature of the present for which the master has yet to be found.

IV.   *Capturing Modernity: Some Theories*

The neologism "modernity" was used by most art critics contemporary to Baudelaire. In associating the word modernity with new values and realities, however, Baudelaire creates a new concept whose complexity continues to fuel today's debate. Modernity is related to as well as independent from its correlative adjective "modern," which, in the middle of the nineteenth century, either has a pure chronological sense or refers to the aesthetics of the time, romanticism. It is in the latter sense that Baudelaire uses the term in "The Salon of 1846" when he, equating romanticism with modern art, answers the question "What is Romanticism?" with the following definition: "intimacy, spirituality, color, yearning for the infinite, expressed by all the means the arts possess" *(intimité, spiritualité, couleur, aspiration vers l'infini, exprimées par tous les moyens que contiennent les arts) (SW 53, PL2 421).* This romantic modernity, however, does not exactly overlap with the theory of modernity Baudelaire establishes fifteen years later in his essay "The Painter of Modern Life." As a matter of fact, Margaret Gilman points out that the chapter on romanticism is quite isolated in Baudelaire's body of work. Although many ideas in it remain and are constitutive of Baudelaire's aesthetic program, his endeavor to link them to romanticism, to give the word a new meaning, is confined to "The Salon of 1846" (Gilman 29). Indeed, after 1846, the word takes on an historical rather than an actual meaning as in "The Salon of 1859": "Romanticism is a grace, either from Heaven or Hell to which we owe eternal stigmata" *(Le romantisme est une grâce, céleste ou infernale, à qui nous devons des stigmates éternels) (MA 259, PL2 645).* The equation of romanticism and modern art still holds after 1846, especially through the continuing presence of Delacroix. Modernity, in its Baudelairian sense, however, steps more and more into the foreground.

In order to discuss the significance of Baudelaire's reformulation of modernity, it is useful to examine in which way the term modern was used by his contemporaries as well as by himself. According to Claude Pichois, modernity becomes central to Baudelaire's writings in the years 1859–1860 *(PL2* 1413). In "The Painter of Modern Life," Baudelaire takes up were "The Salon of 1846" ended, namely with the idea of fashion as the spectacle of passions and of the "heroism of modern life " *(l'héroisme de la vie moderne).* At the outset of his essay, Baudelaire states his purpose which is to discuss painting as the representation of contemporary life. Baudelaire's attention focuses thus on fashion, attitudes, and make-up as a valuable source for definition of modern beauty. Fashion appears as the modern expression of the immortal taste of man for the ideal:

> The idea of beauty that man creates for himself affects his whole attire, ruffles or stiffens his coat, gives curves or straight lines to his gestures and even, in process of time, subtly penetrates the very features of his face. Man comes in the end to look like the ideal image of himself.
> *(L'Idée que l'homme se fait du beau s'imprime dans tout son ajustement, chiffonne ou raidit son habit, arrondit ou aligne son geste, et même pénètre subtilement, à la longue, les traits de son visage. L'homme finit par ressembler à ce qu'il voudrait être) (SW 391, PL2 684).*

The study of the past is only of value insofar as one recognizes its own past presentness. The past should not be an absolute standard for the present to be imitated, but only a reminder of one's own present:

> The past is interesting, not only because of the beauty that artists for whom it was the present were able to extract from it, but also as past, for its historical value. The same applies to the present. The pleasure we derive from the representation of the present is due, not only to the beauty it can be clothed in, but rather to its essential quality of being the present.
> *(Le passé est intéressant non seulement par la beauté qu'ont su en extraire les artistes pour qui il était le présent, mais aussi comme le passé, pour sa valeur historique. Il en est de même pour le présent. Le plaisir que nous retirons de la représentation du présent tient non seulement à la beauté dont il peut être revêtu, mais aussi à sa qualité essentielle de présent) (SW 391, PL2 684).*

The inherent paradox of the formula "representation of the present" has been underlined by Paul de Man who sees in this formula "which combines a repetitive with an instantaneous pattern" a will to suppress the past as well as the awareness on the part of Baudelaire of "the necessary experience of any present as a passing experience that makes the past irrevocable and unforgettable, because it is inseparable from any present or future."[10] The term representation points to the duality which defines Baudelaire's modernity as "the transient, the fleeting, the contingent" *(le transitoire, le fugitif, le contingent)* as the half of art, which would be incomplete without its other half, "the eternal and the immovable" *(l'éternel et l'immuable)* (*SW* 403, *PL2* 695). This definition refers back to the "rational and historical theory of beauty" *(une théorie rationnelle et historique du beau)* which stands in willful opposition to "the theory of a unique and absolute beauty" *(la theorie du beau unique et absolu)*. Baudelaire's aim is to show that in spite of "beauty's unity of impression" *(l'unité d'impression)*, beauty is in all ages composed of two elements:

> Beauty is made up, on the one hand, of an element that is eternal and invariable . . . and on the other, of a relative circumstantial element, which we may like to call, successively or at one and the same time, contemporaneity, fashion, morality, passion.
> *(Le beau est fait d'un élément éternel, invariable . . . et d'un élément relatif, circonstanciel, qui sera, si l'on veut tour à tour ou tout ensemble, l'époque, la mode, la morale, la passion)* (*SW* 392, *PL2* 685).

Judging from these definitions, modernity then would be confined to denominate only one half of art, namely the relative and circumstantial part of beauty. Another definition shows, however, that modernity also consists in extracting "from fashion the poetry that resides in its historical envelope, to distill the eternal from the transitory" *(de dégager de la mode ce qu'elle peut contenir de poétique dans l'historique, de tirer l'éternel du transitoire)* (*SW* 402, *PL2* 694).

As Gerald Froidevaux points out in his study on Baudelaire, one of the main difficulties of Baudelaire's texts resides in the equivocal sense they lend to the term "modern." For it is already in "The Salon of 1846," if not before, that Baudelaire conceives the idea of a pictural or poetic quality which he calls modernity. Until the essay "The Painter of Modern Life," he designates the new value of the term "modern" as "a sort of anticipated repercussion of modernity on the modern."[11]

Modernity is a term of praise. Baudelaire uses it to point out the presence of original beauty in an artwork. Yet the term "modern" carries a double ambiguity. On the one hand, Baudelaire uses the term in a purely chronological sense, conforming to the definition given in the dictionary *Littré* which equates "modern" with the contemporary. On the other hand, he invests the term with a qualitative value, where "modern" is connected with the idea of beauty or ugliness. In opposition to the supporters of progress, who gladly attach to the word "modern" a positive value, Baudelaire uses it mostly with a negative connotation. Hostile to the glorification of progress, he associates the chronological sense of modern with the evaluative one of "beautiful" and "ugly."

Yet, considering the new and positive signification that Baudelaire attaches to modernity even before "The Painter of Modern Life," "modern" also carries a positive value. As Froidevaux points out, this double meaning of "modern" does not present a major problem: one understands, in spite of the seeming paradox, that Baudelaire reproaches painters for being "modern," since by their modernity they fail to capture the true beauty of the day (Froidevaux 31).

In his essay "Some French Caricaturists," Baudelaire states that "the word modern applies to the manner, not to the period in time." *(le mot moderne s'applique à la manière et non au temps)* (*SW* 210, *PL2* 545). This is only partly true, however, since modernity and "modern" do not carry an ahistorical value but rather designate a novel beauty connected to the present, to the current morals, to fashion. The true paradox thus resides in the fact that "modern" can signify the ugly of the particular ugliness of modern times as well as the beautiful of the particular beauty of modern times. This paradox seems to sum up Baudelaire's reflection on modernity and his investigation of the relationship the present time entertains with the idea of beauty. In unfolding this paradox, one defines the meaning of the present for Baudelaire. Froidevaux insists on the fact that "modern" and modernity are not to be taken as "innocent neologisms." Baudelaire's modernity is not equivalent with the one, which after him, associates beauty to every artistic expresssion which pathetically claims itself to be the present, e.g., avant-garde movements. Modernity and in turn "modern" designate the original and eternal beauty of the present times, but at the same time they indicate the precarious condition of the present, its alignment with invading vulgarity, "the progressive effacement of that primary confidence which allowed, when confronted with a truly beautiful artwork, to experience the feeling of an eternal present" (Froidevaux 32).

By establishing the concept of modernity in its fullest complexity, Baudelaire stands at the beginning of a new era of aesthetic thought while at the same time resuming the discussion as it was addressed in the famous "Quarrel between the Ancients and the Moderns" at the end of the seventeenth century. Hans Robert Jauss has shown how this dispute, which opposed for the first time again since the Renaissance the proponents of classical art and the defenders of modern art, is exemplary and constitutive of modern aesthetics as it developed in the nineteenth century. Jauss argues that the *Querelle*, seen as an epochal turning point toward Enlightenment, was fundamental for the formation of modern consciousness in the realm of art:

> The dispute that flared up again at the height of French classicism concerning the exemplary character of classical art, brought both sides—the Ancients and the Moderns—ultimately to the same conclusion, which was that ancient and modern art in the long run could not be measured against the same standard of perfection (*Beau absolu*), because each epoch had its own customs, its own tastes, and therefore its own ideas of beauty (*Beau relatif*).[12]

If all epochs have their own standards and values it becomes superfluous to measure them with any ideal that would have to be imitated. Just as the ancients of yesterday were the moderns of their times, the moderns of today are bound to become the ancients of tomorrow. Consequently, being stripped from its historical referent, the word "modern" ceases to oppose itself to "ancient"; its antonym—as will be seen with Baudelaire—becomes "eternal." For the moderns of the eighteenth century, the terms "modern" and "ancient" become obsolete in the debate. The new ideal is termed "romantic" and its oppositional term "classic."

This development in the realm of aesthetics is interrupted during the eighteenth century. As Froidevaux states, "the aesthetic modernism which appears at the horizon of the *Querelle* experiences a kind of eclipse; it will resurface only at the time of Baudelaire" (Froidevaux 32). During the Enlightenment, the superiority of the moderns is no longer questioned in the realm of the sciences. At the same time, however, the term "modern" disappears from the aesthetic realm for the moderns are fervent admirers of the ancients whose superiority in matters of taste they do not question. To be modern is to take into consideration one's historical position all the while maintaining one's right to subscribe to the *bon goût* of the ancients. This attitude of undecidedness is what Ernst Behler terms as "double-edged modernity," defined as "a basic resistance among literary authors and literary critics to being outspokenly and deliberately pro modern."[13] Although this "double-edged modernity" is applied in regard to the moderns of the *Querelle*, it seems that this attitude persists during the eighteenth century until the advent of romanticism as the latest expression of modernity. Furthermore, the new modernity, which understands itself as romantic, describes its opposition to antiquity with the term "classical" borrowed from the Schlegel brothers who defined the term less from a historical perspective but rather "as an image of ideal perfection to which the modern age related in an unsatisfied longing" (Behler 62).

In France, the new opposition of classical and modern/romantic was established later than in Germany, at the beginning of the nineteenth century with Madame de Staël's *De L'Allemagne*. Beforehand, in France the term "classical" referred to the canonized authors of the scholarly tradition. The great authors of the seventeenth century like Molière, Corneille, and Racine, to give the most important examples, become known as classics at the beginning of the nineteenth century. Considered moderns at their time, they become classics from the moment that the adversaries of romanticism "codify the classical doctrine, a doctrine raised up after the fact, in the manner of a theory of a practice which had long since run its course. Now the new quarrel takes place between the classics and the romantics" (Froidevaux 33).

Under the heading of romantic movement, various tendencies manifested themselves: on the one hand an aesthetic feeling and worship of nature and on the other the historical ideal of the Christian Middle Ages, or a progressive self-reflective romanticism based on the ideal of infinite perfectibility in the realm of poetry and the arts in general as it was developed by Friedrich Schlegel. What these romantics share, in spite of their conservative or progressive outlook on the arts or humanity was a feeling of insufficiency in regard to their own present which was experienced in terms of incompleteness. The modern consciousness of the romantics, severed from the tyranny of absolute standards as upheld by the classics, is tinted with a sense of loss and deficiency. Behler notes:

> Looked at from the standpoint of the quarrel between the ancients and the moderns, this status of modernity certainly indicates a victory of the moderns over the ancients, in that no classical standard any longer determines the course of modern

poetry . . . The price to be paid for this independence, however, is the relegation of pure beauty and perfection to a past age of classical harmony and the ascription of alienation, imperfection, and deficiency to the status of modernity. Modernism in this view appears as a post-classical age in which the classical structures of self-possession and identity are lost. However, the modern age appears as yearning for a lost harmony and mourning a unity that belongs to the past. And in this sense of a mournful grieving for losses and deficiencies, we could still speak of a lingering dominance of the ancients over the moderns or, in more theoretical terms, of a delay in the full manifestation of modern consciousness or the consciousness of modernity (62).

The new consciousness of modernity develops in the nineteenth century from a recognition by the moderns of an intrinsic dynamic of the term "modern" itself. According to H. R. Jauss, this modern consciousness wants itself to be yet more modern than the romantics—a unique and unprecedented event in literary history:

While the field of signification (*Bedeutungsumpfang*) of the term modern narrows down, step by step, from the Christian era to just a life-time of a generation and finally shrinks down to a fashionable change within current literary tendencies of taste, the term modernity ceases all together to oppose itself to a precise epochal past. The consciousness of modernity, which separates itself during the nineteenth century from the world view of romanticism, makes itself manifest in the experience that today's romanticism, becoming very quickly yesterday's romanticism, finally may appear as classical again.[14]

From this point of view, the great antithesis between the ancient and the modern gradually looses its validity. The historical opposition of romantic and classical reduces itself to the relative opposition between that which constitutes the immediate present and that same present which for the next generation has become already the past:

It is on the basis of this reflection on the process of an ever accelerating, historical change in the realm of the arts and taste that a consciousness of modernity can develop itself, a modernity which in the end only stands out against itself (Jauss 51).

V.   *The Impact of Stendhal*

It is agreed upon by most literary critics, including Jauss and Froidevaux, that it was Stendhal who first illustrated this significant stage in the development of the consciousness of modernity in France.[15] His understanding of romanticism not as a particular period or specific style but rather as an awareness of contemporary life, of modernity in its immediate sense, makes him one of the most important precursors of Baudelaire's theory of modernity. As Jauss points out, Stendhal's definition of romanticism not only breaks with the then accepted signification of the term but turns it around altogether (Jauss 52). Romanticism, as it is defined in *Racine et Shakespeare*, is no longer the fascination with that which transcends the present but with the present itself, the beauty of the day, which when having become past in its turn, can only be of historical interest:

> Romanticism is the art of presenting to different peoples literary works which, in the existing state of their habits and beliefs, are capable of giving them the greatest possible pleasure. Classicism, on the contrary, presents to them that literature which gave the greatest possible pleasure to their great-grandfathers. . . To imitate Sophocles and Euripides today, and to maintain that these imitations will not cause a Frenchman of the nineteenth century to yawn with boredom, is classicism.[16]

According to Stendhal, all great authors are modern during their own time, but the moderns of today are condemned to be the ancients of tomorrow. This is precisely the reason why the imitation of classics is not only wearisome but detrimental to one's own consciousness of one's contemporaneity. Warning against the dangers of imitation, Baudelaire expresses this idea most clearly in "The Painter of Modern Life":

> Woe betide the man who goes to antiquity for the study of anything other than ideal art, logic and general method! By immersing himself too deeply in it, he will no longer have the present in his mind's eye; he throws away the value and the privileges afforded by circumstance; for nearly all our originality comes from the stamp that time impresses on our sensibility.
> *(Malheur à celui qui étudie dans l'antique autre chose que l'art pur, la logique, la méthode générale! Pour s'y trop plonger, il perd la mémoire du présent; il abdique la valeur et les privilèges fournis par la circonstance; car presque toute notre originalité vient de l'estampille que le temps imprime à nos sensations)* (*SW* 405, *PL2* 696).

Stendhal's impact on Baudelaire and on the development of modern aesthetics and its definition of beauty in general cannot be underestimated. His main contribution was to lay bare the mechanism which underlies the awakening of modern consciousness: by stating that everything classical (past) once was romantic (modern) in its own time, he denies the term classic the power of establishing itself as that which is finite in its perfection, absolute in terms of beauty, and forever exemplary in regard to the present. As Jauss sees it, Stendhal, by establishing the term romantic as an epochal concept (*Epochenbegriff*) contributes to the neutralization of the great historical antithesis between classic and modern. Froidevaux states:

> Before Stendhal, the reign of beauty rested on the solidity of absolute concepts. . .
> After Stendhal, art has no longer the mission to reveal the beautiful but modern
> beauty. Yet, modern beauty is always beautiful and it is so only in terms of a
> present stripped of temporal profundity. There is permanence only in change and
> eternity only in modernity (Froidevaux 35).

Stendhal's influence on Baudelaire has been the subject of several early studies.[17] In *Baudelaire the Critic*, Gilman shows how, in his first two *Salons*, Baudelaire borrows from Stendhal's ideas of beauty, romanticism, and the ideal. She concludes, however, by asserting, that while "the assimilation of romanticism to modernity is Stendhal's, the definition of its qualities is Baudelaire's own" (Gilman 52). This is true, especially in regard to "The Painter of Modern Life" where Baudelaire, shortly after the exposition of "the rational and historical theory of beauty," stresses the idea that "duality of art is an inevitable consequence of the duality of man" *(la dualité de l'art est une conséquence fatale de la dualité de l'homme)*, that is, one "may identify the eternally subsisting portion as the soul of art, and the variable element as its body" *(considérez, si cela vous plaît, la partie éternellement subsistante comme l'âme de l'art, et l'élément variable comme son corps) (SW* 393, *PL2* 686).

Having admitted how difficult it is to determine exactly the quantity of the eternal, invariable element of beauty, Baudelaire concentrates on the variable, that which carries the trace of the present and invalidates objective standards as they are upheld by the academicians. Stendhal's definition: "The beautiful is neither more nor less the promise of happiness" *(le beau n'est que la promesse du bonheur)* therefore has the "great merit of getting away from the mistake of the academicians" *(a le grand mérite de s'éloigner décidément de l'erreur des académiciens).* On the other hand, Baudelaire criticizes this formula, for it "subordinates beauty too much to the infinitely variable ideal of happiness." *(elle soumet beaucoup trop le beau à l'idéal infiniment variable du bonheur).* The idea of happiness, in Baudelaire's eyes, "divests beauty too lightly of its aristocratic character" *(elle dépouille trop lestement le beau de son caractère aristocratique) (SW* 393, *PL2* 686). As Jean Prévost suggests, Baudelaire's own formula would be rather: "The cult of beauty is a promise of greatness." In spite of his correction, says Prévost, Baudelaire recognizes the fundamental value of Stendhal's formula for it makes it possible "to break with the abstract banalities of classical aesthetics . . . and to connect beauty with psychology, to give it a greater chance of variation and a logical consistency."[18] This is precisely what Baudelaire has in mind when he illustrates his theory of modern beauty with Constantin Guys's drawings.

VI.   *The Artist as the Painter of Modern Life*

"The Painter of Modern Life" is one of Baudelaire's most enthusiastic texts and may be the only one in which modernity, as an aesthetic value is celebrated without reserve. This text, which belongs to Baudelaire's last great creative period (1858–1860), can be seen as an elaboration, intensification, or in Pichois's term, "crystallization" of many ideas already formulated in "The Salon of 1846": the importance of memory in the process of creation, the correlation between the rapidity of thought, vision and likewise rapid artistic execution, the critique of nature, and finally the definition of modern beauty. In "The Painter of Modern Life" Baudelaire is able to focus in particular on the "transitory" and "variable" element of art for he has found the artist he was looking for in 1846.

In Constantin Guys, Baudelaire sees an artist who rises to the challenge to capture modernity perceived in its complex and dual conception which is still functioning today. Guys was not a studio artist but a newspaper reporter whose fields of observation were the streets of the city, the theaters, and cafés. As a chronicler of present-day life, an "artist-portrayer of manners" *(l'artiste peintre de moeurs)*, Guys is a "genius of mixed composition" *(un génie d'une nature mixte)*.

In contrast to the "painter of things eternal, or at least things of more permanent nature, of heroic and religious subjects" *(peintre des choses éternelles, ou du moins plus durables, des choses héroiques ou religieuses)* Guys, "observer, idler, philosopher . . . comes close to the novelist or the moralist; he is the painter of the fleeting moment and of all that it suggests of the eternal" *(observateur, flâneur, philosophe . . . il se rapproche du romancier ou du moraliste; il est le peintre de la circonstance et de tout ce qu'elle suggère d'éternel) (SW* 394, *PL2* 687). In many ways, Baudelaire's portrait of Guys as a man and artist resembles that of Delacroix. The qualities are a strong temperament and perfect technical skills combined with a powerful imagination. However, while Delacroix belongs to those artists who form "the great chain of history" in painting, Guys represents through the form of sketches the present moment outside of any consciousness of past or future. As the title of one chapter suggests, Guys is the ideal fusion of "an artist, man of the world, man of crowds, and child" *(L'artiste, homme du monde, homme des foules et enfant)*. Guys, "a great traveler and very cosmopolitan" *(très voyageur et cosmopolite)*, is an artist in the broadest sense of the word, not "a specialist, a man tied to his palette like a serf to the soil" *(spécialiste, homme attaché à sa palette comme le serf à sa glaive)*. He does not belong amongst those artists Baudelaire qualifies as "very skilled brutes, mere manual labourers, village pub talkers with the minds of country bumpkin" *(des brutes très adroites, de purs manoeuvres, des intelligences de village, des cervelles de hameau)*, whose so-called artistic activity is limited to the narrow quarters they live in and whose talk "quickly becomes a bore to the man of the world, to the spiritual citizen of the universe" *(devient très vite insupportable à l'homme du monde, au citoyen spirituel de l'univers)*. Guys is precisely this "man of the world, a man who understands the world and the mysterious and legitimate reasons behind all its customs. . ." *(homme du monde entier, homme qui comprend le monde et les raisons mystérieuses et légitimes de tous ses usages)*. The motivation that lies behind his activity is a childlike curiosity, an inner motor running and fueled by the infinite variety of the world's treasures. "He takes an interest in everything the world over, he wants to know, understand, assess everything that happens on the surface of our spheroid." *(Il s'intéresse au monde entier; il veut savoir, comprendre, apprécier tout ce qui se passe à la surface de notre sphéroïde)*.

Guys's curiosity is defined by the image of the convalescent: "Now imagine an artist perpetually in the spiritual condition of the convalescent, and you will have the key to the character of M. G." *(Supposez un artiste qui serait toujours, spirituellement, à l'état du convalescent, et vous aurez la cléf du caractère de M. G.)* (*SW* 397, *PL2* 689–90). Taking Edgar Allan Poe's story "The Man of the Crowd" as a model, Baudelaire goes on to describe the state of convalescence as follows:

> Sitting in a café, and looking through the shop window, a convalescent is enjoying the sight of the passing crowd, and identifying himself in thought with all the thoughts that are moving around him. He has only recently come back from the

shades of death and breathes in with delight all the spores and odors of life; as he has been on the point of forgetting everything, he remembers and passionately wants to remember everything. In the end he rushes out into the crowd in search of a man unknown to him whose face, which he had caught sight of, had in a flash fascinated him. Curiosity had become a compelling, irresistible passion.

(Derrière la vitre d'un café, un convalescent, contemplant la foule avec jouissance, se mêle, par la pensée, à toutes les pensés qui s'agitent autour de lui. Revenu récemment des ombres de la mort, il aspire avec délices tous les germes et les effluves de la vie; comme il a été sur le point de tout oublier, il se souvient et veut avec ardeur se souvenir de tout. Finalement il se précipite à travers cette foule à la recherche d'un inconnu dont la physionomie entrevue l'a fasciné. La curiosité est devenue une passion fatale, irrésistible) (SW 397, PL2 690).

In her article "The Scene of Convalescence," Barbara Spackman defines convalescence as "a space in-between, a hazy yet paradoxically crystal-clear state between sickness and health. Introduced as a third term in the rhetoric of sickness and health, convalescence becomes the vehicle for a series of in-between states."[19] The convalescent experiences in a positive way, the tension between sickness and health, he dwells between two irreconcilable poles and benefits precisely from this irreconcilability. Moreover, the promise of forgetting releases a shock-like impulse supplying the convalescent with new energy, a curiosity which can be called a will to life. Baudelaire compares this state of convalescence with a return to childhood:

The convalescent, like the child, enjoys to the highest degree the faculty of taking a lively interest in things, even the most trivial in appearance. Let us hark back, if we can, by a retrospective effort of our imagination, to our youngest, our morning impressions, and we shall recognize that they were remarkably akin to the vividly colored impressions that we received later on after a physical illness, provided that illness left our spiritual faculties pure and unimpaired. The child sees everything as a novelty; the child is always 'drunk'.

(Or, la convalescence est comme un retour vers l'enfance. Le convalescent jouit au plus haut degré, comme l'enfant, de la faculté de s'intéresser vivement aux choses, même les plus triviales en apparence. Remontons, s'il se peut, par un effort rétrospectif de l'imagination, vers nos plus jeunes, nos plus matinales impressions, et nous reconnaîtrons qu'elles avaient une singulière parenté avec les impressions, si vivement colorées, que nous reçûmes plus tard, à la suite d'une maladie physique, pourvu que cette maladie ait laissé pures et intactes nos facultés spirituelles. L'enfant voit tout en nouveauté; il est toujours ivre) (SW 398, PL2, 690).

Childhood too is an in-between state: it dwells in the very moment of present having as yet no past to remember and no future to fear. The child which is always "drunk" embodies the ideal of the most intense receptiveness which is called for in Baudelaire's prose poem "Get High" *(Enivrez-vous)*:

> You must always get high. Everything depends on it: it is the only question. So as not to feel the horrible burden of Time wrecking your back and bending you to the ground, you must get high without respite.
> *(Il faut être toujours ivre. Tout est là: c'est l'unique question. Pour ne pas sentir l'horrible fardeau du Temps qui brise vos épaules et vous penche vers la terre, il faut vous enivrer sans trève).*[20]

For the child, this state of invigorating, positive intoxication with life occurs naturally, for the grown man—the artist—it becomes an effort, a necessary act of will. The ideal artist, in this case Constantin Guys, is in fact the embodiment of the fusion of "man of genius" and child:

> The man of genius has strong nerves; those of the child are weak. In the one, reason has assumed an important role; in the other, a sensibility occupies almost the whole being. But genius is no more than childhood recaptured at will, childhood equipped now with a man's physical means to express itself, and with the analytical mind that enables it to bring order into the sum of experience, involuntarily amassed.
> *(L'Homme de génie a les nerfs solides; l'enfant les a faibles. Chez l'un, la raison a pris une place considérable; chez l'autre, la sensibilité occupe presque tout l'être. Mais le génie n'est que l'enfance retrouvée à volonté, l'enfance douée maintenant, pour s'exprimer, d'organes virils et l'esprit analytique qui lui permet d'ordonner la somme de matériaux involontairement amassée) (SW 398, PL2 690).*

The term "genius" from Baudelaire's perspective designates essentially will, energy, and reason used in the service of an inexhaustible imagination. The emphasis on the rational side of genius is constantly maintained in Baudelaire's writings and testifies to Baudelaire's aversion to the romantic tendency to mistake genius for mere inspiration. In his article on Wagner's *Tannhäuser*, which is contemporary to this text, Baudelaire speaks against those who deprive "genius of its rationality" and reduce it to "a purely instinctive and, so to speak, vegetable function" *(. . . qui dépouillent ainsi le génie de sa rationalité, et lui assignent une fonction purement instinctive et pour ainsi dire végétale) (SW 340, PL2 793).*
On the other hand, the same emphasis is given to what one might

call inner drive. Thus genius is defined in the same article from the point of view of passion:

> By his passion, he [Wagner] adds to everything he touches an indefinable superhuman element . . . everything that is implied by the words will, desire, concentration, nervous intensity, explosion, is perceptible, may be apprehended through his works. I do not think I am deceiving myself or anybody else when I say that I see there the main characteristics of the phenomenon we call genius.
> *(Par cette passion il ajoute à chaque chose je ne sais quoi de surhumain . . . Tout ce qu'impliquent les mots: volonté, désir, concentration, intensité nerveuse, explosion, se sent et se fait deviner dans ses oeuvres. Je ne crois pas me faire illusion ni tromper personne en affirmant que je vois là les principales caractéristiques du phénomène que nous appelons génie)* (SW 355, PL2 807).

Like Wagner, and to a certain degree Delacroix, Guys is driven by a passion, a passion for life. Unlike Wagner and Delacroix, whose subject matters bring them close to antiquity, Guys's atelier becomes the here and now of modern life. Baudelaire hesitates to confer to Guys the title of "pure artist" *(pur artiste)* which Guys himself declined out of "modesty tinged with aristocratic restraint" *(modestie nuancée de pudeur aristocratique)*. He would rather compare Guys with the figure of the dandy, the other "hero" of the essay, with whom Guys shares "a quintessence of character and a subtle understanding of all the moral mechanisms of this world" *(une quintessence de caractère et une intelligence subtile de tout le mécanisme moral de ce monde)*. Unlike the dandy, however, who "aspires to cold detachment . . . is blasé, or affects to be" *(aspire à l'insensibilité . . . est blasé ou feint de l'être)*, Guys is "dominated by an insatiable passion, that of seeing and feeling" *(dominé par une passion insatiable, celle de voir et de sentir) (SW 399, PL2* 691). Not a philosopher either, Guys is finally "reduced" to the status of the pure pictorial moralist, like La Bruyère. This "reduction" however, is in fact followed by an "elevation" to the status of "prince" whose domain is the crowd to which he serves as a "mirror, a kaleidoscope endowed with consciousness" *(un miroir, un kaléidoscope doué de conscience)*.

Guys holds a liminal position within the crowd—he occupies the locus of the in-between. His privilege is "to be away from home and yet to feel at home everywhere; to see the world, to be at the very center of the world" *(être hors de chez soi, et pourtant se sentir partout chez soi; voir le monde, être au centre du monde)*, and most importantly "to be unseen of the world" *(rester caché au monde)*. Guys is "an ego athirst for the non-ego. . .a prince enjoying his incognito wherever he goes" *(c'est un moi insatiable du non-moi . . . un prince qui jouit partout de son incognito) (SW 400, PL2 692)*. Guys is neither an outside observer viewing the crowd from a distance, nor is he fully participating in it. He is and remains an outside observer inside the social sphere. What he is looking for is as difficult to define as his own status as painter. He is looking for:

> that indefinable something we may be allowed to call 'modernity,' for want of a better term to express the idea in question. The aim for him is to extract from fashion the poetry that resides in its historical envelope, to distill the eternal from the transitory.
> *(ce quelque chose qu'on nous permettra d'appeler la modernité; car il ne se présente pas de meilleur mot pour exprimer l'idée en question. Il s'agit pour lui, de dégager de la mode ce qu'elle peut contenir de poétique dans l'historique, de tirer l'éternel du transitoire) (SW 402, PL2 694)*.

The accent here lies on the process of distillation by which the artist renders the dual nature of beauty—and art as a whole—as a result of the dual nature of man. Baudelaire equates this dual nature of beauty with modernity defined itself as dual: "Modernity is the transient, the fleeting, the contingent; it is one half of art, the other being the eternal and the immovable" *(La modernité, c'est le transitoire, le fugitif, le contingent, la moitié de l'art, dont l'autre moitié est l'éternel et l'immuable) (SW 403, PL2 695)*.

Having previously equated the eternal element with the soul of man and the variable with the body, modern art would be that which represents the ongoing tension between these two poles—soul and body—modern art would be that which freezes in a flash a moment in time while conferring to it the value of the eternal: "In short, in order that any form of modernity may be worthy of becoming antiquity, the mysterious beauty that human life unintentionally puts into it must have been extracted from it" *(En un mot, pour que toute modernité soit digne de devenir antiquité, il faut que la beauté mystérieuse que la vie humaine y met involontairement en ait été extraite) (SW 404, PL2 695)*. In other words, in order for a modern artwork to become classical in the sense of timeless—that is eternally 'modern'—the artist, not unlike an alchemist or a sorcerer, has to perform what Baudelaire in his essay on "The Universal Exhibition of 1855" calls a "magical operation" *(une opération magique)*. There, Baudelaire already links the question to childhood adding in parentheses: "could we but consult the souls of children about it" *(si nous pouvions consulter là-dessus l'âme des enfants)* (*SW* 120, *PL2* 580). The process of distillation, "the magical operation" is of course not a result of truthful copying of reality but materializes on paper through the synthesis of imagination and memory: "In fact all true draughtsmen draw from the image imprinted in their brain and not from nature" *(En fait, tous les bons et vrais dessinateurs dessinent d'après l'image écrite dans leur cerveau, et non d'après la nature)* (*SW* 407, *PL2* 698).

The quality of a painting or, in Guys's case, a sketch depends on the mnemonic faculties of the artist. The role of memory is a permanent feature in Baudelaire's aesthetics. In "The Salon of 1846" he notes that "memory is the great criterion of art" *(le souvenir était le grand criterion de l'art)* and that "slavish imitation interferes with memory" *(l'imitation exacte gâte le souvenir)* (*SW* 77, *PL2* 455). Guys's method of work is based on memory: he goes out, registers, memorizes, and renders his impressions from memory on paper. For him, as for Delacroix, the immediate presence of a model would be a hindrance to a natural process of selection which is operated best precisely by memory.

The stage of the final execution of a work of art is compared to a struggle "between the determination to see everything, to forget nothing, and the faculty of memory, which has acquired the habit of registering in a flash the general tones and shape, the outline pattern" *(Il s'établit alors un duel entre la volonté de tout voir, de ne rien oublier, et de la faculté de la mémoire qui a pris l'habitude d'absorber vivement la couleur générale et la silhouette, l'arabesque du contour)*. Moreover, the selective process effected by memory assists the artist in achieving the so desired "totality of effect" *(totalité de l'effet)* for confronted with his model (here it is the crowd):

> an artist with a perfect sense of form but particularly accustomed to the exercise of his memory and his imagination, . . . finds himself assailed, as it were, by a riot of details, all of them demanding justice, with the fury of the mob in love with absolute equality.
> *(un artiste ayant le sens parfait de la forme, mais accoutumé à exercer surtout sa mémoire et son imagination, se trouve alors comme assailli par une émeute de détails, qui tous demandent justice avec la furie d'une foule amoureuse d'égalité absolue)* (*SW* 407, *PL2* 698).

The reality of things with which the artist is faced is chaos:

where any form of justice is inevitably infringed; any harmony destroyed, sacrificed; a multitude of trivialities are magnified; a multitude of little things become
usurpers of attention. The more the artist pays impartial attention to detail, the
greater does anarchy become.
*(toute justice se trouve forcément violée; toute harmonie détruite, sacrifiée; mainte
trivialité devient énorme; mainte petitesse usurpatrice. Plus l'artiste se penche
avec impartialité vers le détail, plus l'anarchie augmente)* (*SW* 407, *PL2* 698–
99).

Guys, becoming the interpreter of his own vision concentrates on
the main features of his object, highlighting what seems most intriguing to
him without fear of exaggeration. Thus he testifies to a sense of hierarchy
or subordination of the detail to the whole. There exists a direct relation
between the artist's and the viewer's memory and in the ideal case then
"the imagination of the viewer, undergoing in its turn the influence of this
imperious code" *(l'imagination du spectateur, subissant à son tour cette
mnémonique si despotique)* makes the viewer become "the translator of a
translation, which is always clear and always intoxicating" *(le traducteur
d'une traduction toujours claire et enivrante)* (*SW* 407, *PL2* 698).[21]

The dynamics of modern life, springing from the variable element
and memory's fleeting character require from the artist an adequate swift-
ness of execution. Baudelaire points out two important steps in Guys's
work. On the one hand an "absorbed intenseness of a resurrecting and
evocative memory . . . the second is a fire, an intoxication of pencil or
brush, almost amounting to frenzy" *(une contention de mémoire
résurrectionniste, évocatrice . . . l'autre, un feu, une ivresse de crayon, de
pinceau, ressemblant presque à une fureur)*.

During the moment of creation, the artist finds himself in a state
between extreme concentration and inner agitation, in constant "fear of not
going fast enough, of letting the specter escape before the synthesis has
been extracted and taken possession of. . . " *(la peur de n'aller pas assez
vite, de laisser échapper le fantôme avant que la synthèse ne soit extraite
et saisie)* (*SW* 408, *PL2* 699).

The sketch, by definition "a hasty or undetailed drawing or painting made as a preliminary study"[22] is the expression par excellence of
Baudelaire's definition of modernity. Guys's sketches, while rendering the
constant movement particular to his subject matter, have nevertheless reached
at almost every stage, a sufficient effect of completion: "you may call this a

thumbnail sketch, but it is a perfect one" *(vous nommerez cela une ébauche si vous voulez, mais ébauche parfaite)* (*SW* 409, *PL2* 700).

Baudelaire's predilection for the sketch is a direct consequence of the rapid pace of modern life for which the artist has to find the corresponding medium of expression: "there is in the trivial things of life, in the daily changing of external things, a speed of movement that imposes upon the artist an equal speed of execution" *(il y a dans la vie triviale, dans la métamorphose journalière des choses extérieures, un mouvement rapide qui commande à l'artiste une égale vélocité d'exécution)* (*SW* 394, *PL2* 686).

The necessity of the artist's adaptation to the effects of a world becoming increasingly modernized is one of the main thrusts in "The Painter of Modern Life". This idea of adaptation is problematical, and modernization represents decline. It brings with it a leveling out of cultural and artistic values. It is in the figure of the dandy that Baudelaire expresses most clearly his resistance to this modernization.

Notes

1 Paul Valéry, *Variety: Second Series*, trans. W. A. Bradley, (New York: Harcourt, Brace and Company, 1938), 74–75.

2 Margaret Gilman, *Baudelaire the Critic* (New York: Columbia University Press, 1943), 16. References to this text are indicated with the author's name.

3 Charles Baudelaire, *Selected Writings on Art and Literature* (London:Penguin Books, 1992), 34. References to this text are designated *SW*. The original text from *Oeuvres Complètes*, ed. Claude Pichois, 2 vols. (Paris: Gallimard, Bibliothèque de la Pléiade, 1976). References to this text are designated *PL1* and *PL2*.

4 Charles Baudelaire, *The Mirror of Art*, trans. Jonathan Mayne (New York: Phaidon Publishers, 1955), 38. References to this text are designated MA.

5 Claude Pichois, Jean Ziegler, *Baudelaire* (Paris: Julliard, 1987), 206. All further references to this text appear with the first author's name. Translations are mine.

6 Timothy Raser, *A Poetics of Art Criticism. The Case of Baudelaire* (Chapel Hill: University of North Carolina Press, 1988), 91.

7 Richard D. E. Burton, *Baudelaire and the Second Republic* (Oxford: Clarendon Press, 1991), 35.

8 F. W. Leakey, "A Philosophy of Opportunism," *Baudelaire, Collected Essays, 1953–1988*, ed. Eva Jacobs (Cambridge: Cambridge University Press, 1990), 188.

9 Michel Foucault, "What is Enlightenment," *The Foucault Reader*, ed. Paul Rabinow (New York: Random House, 1984), 40. References to this text are designated *FR*.

10 Paul de Man, "Literary History and Literary Modernity," *Blindness and Insight* (Minneapolis: University of Minnesota Press, 1971), 148.

11 Gérald Froidevaux, *Baudelaire, représentation et modernité* (Paris: José Corti, 1989), 30.

12 Hans Robert Jauss, "Art History and Pragmatic History," *Toward an Aesthetic of Reception* (Minneapolis: University of Minnesota Press, 1982), 47.

[13] Ernst Behler, *Irony and the Discourse of Modernity* (Seattle: University of Washington Press, 1990), 43. References to this text are indicated with the author's name.

[14] Hans Robert Jauss, "Literarische Tradition und gegenwärtiges Bewußtsein der Modernität," *Literaturgeschichte als Provokation* (Frankfurt a. M.: Suhrkamp Verlag, 1970), 50. References to this text are indicated with the author's name.

[15] See also Matei Calinescu, *Five Faces of Modernity* (Durham, NC: Duke University Press, 1987). References to this text are designated with the author's name.

[16] Stendhal, *Racine and Shakespeare*, trans. Guy Daniels (The Crowell-Collier Press, 1962), 38.

[17] Margaret Gilman, "Baudelaire and Stendhal," *PMLA* (March 1939) and J. Pommier, "Un Plagiat de Baudelaire," *Bulletin de la Faculté des Lettres de Strasbourg* (May-June 1937).

[18] Jean Prévost, *Baudelaire, Essai sur l'inspiration et la création poétiques* (Paris: Mercure de France, 1953), 52.

[19] Barbara Spackman, "The Scene of Convalescence," *Decadent Genealogies. The Rhetoric of Sickness from Baudelaire to d'Annunzio* (Ithaca, NY: Cornell University Press, 1989), 42.

[20] Charles Baudelaire, *The Parisian Prowler,* trans. by Edward K. Kaplan (Athens, GA: The University of Georgia Press, 1989), 89. References to this text are designated *PP*. In French: *PL1* 337.

[21] See Michelle Hannoosh, "Painting as Translation in Baudelaire's Art Criticism" *Forum for Modern Language Studies* 22 (January 1986).

[22] *The American Heritage Dictionary* (Boston: Houghton Mifflin Company, 1982), 1146.

Chapter 2

DECADENCE

I.   Dandyism: Baudelaire, Foucault, and Camus

Dandyism had been Baudelaire's constant preoccupation. As Marcel Ruff points out in his study on Baudelaire, he had been planning to write an article on the subject from 1860 until the last moments of his literary activity. In this article, artists such as Joseph de Maistre, the Marquis de Custine, Liszt, Ferrari, Paul de Molènes, Barbey d'Aurevilly, and above all Chateaubriand, whom Baudelaire perceived as the father of all dandies, were to be included as subjects.[1]

The article was never written but Baudelaire's chapter on dandyism in "The Painter of Modern Life" read in connection with certain notes in his *Intimate Journals* brings together the main aspects of this particular style of life. Baudelaire's own position as a writer and his personal attitude towards his times as reflected in all his writings testify to his participation in dandyism, which occurs in periods of transition, such as his own, "when democracy has not yet become all powerful, and when aristocracy is only partially weakened and discredited" *(où la démocratie n'est pas encore toute puissante, où l'aristocratie n'est que partiellement chancellante et avilie) (SW* 421, *PL2* 711). In the context of the present study, the interest in dandyism lies in the tension embodied by the dandy between a resistance to modernity and a radical affirmation of it.

An interesting approach to the subject is provided by Michel Foucault's analysis of Baudelaire's constructive invention of modern man and Albert Camus's assessment of the dandy as one of the last "metaphysical rebels."

Michel Foucault has defined Baudelairian modernity as a conscious attitude:

> a mode of relating to contemporary reality; a voluntary choice made by certain people. . . a way of thinking and feeling . . . a way . . . of acting and behaving that at one and the same time marks a relation of belonging and presents itself as a task. . . Modernity is the attitude that makes it possible to grasp the 'heroic' aspect of the present moment . . . it is the will to 'heroize' the present.[2]

It is in the "character" of the dandy that Baudelaire has crystallized this deliberate attitude which "is tied to an indispensable asceticism." Foucault's insistence on the notion of will lends modernity a dynamics which rests on the need for modern man to invent himself a personae: "To be modern is not to accept oneself as one is in the flux of the passing moments; it is to take oneself as object of a complex elaboration"(*FR* 41). The question of modernity raised in these terms addresses the issue of identity.

The dandy, as the embodiment of such a modern construct, lives from "the burning desire to create a personal form of originality" *(besoin ardent de se faire une originalité)*, which can only be achieved through a permanent effort to cultivate appearance at the expense of his inner temperament or nature. Thus Baudelaire states: "The Dandy may be blasé, he may even suffer pain, but in the latter case he will keep smiling, like the Spartan under the bite of the fox." *(Un Dandy peut être un homme blasé, peut-être un homme souffrant; mais dans ce dernier cas, il sourira comme le Lacédémonien sous la morsure du renard)* (*SW* 420, *PL2* 710). The dandy is not the man of leisure whose sole preoccupation resides in elegant clothes and material wealth: "These things are no more than the symbol of the aristocratic superiority of his mind" *(ces choses ne sont . . . qu'un symbole de la supériorité aristocratique de son esprit)*. He is a rebel for the cause of art, a dream "translated into action" *(traduit en action)* (*SW* 419, *PL2* 710).

His "action" is the gesture of a posture he chooses to cultivate in the midst of an age, where great art, as Baudelaire sees it, is on its way to extinction. As a rebel and opponent to his century, dominated by "the rising tide of democracy, which spreads everywhere and reduces everything to the same level" *(la marée montante de la démocratie, qui envahit tout et qui nivelle tout)*, the dandy affirms a new kind of aristocracy, "a kind of religion" *(une espèce de religion)* whose self-imposed rules he obeys stoically for the sake of difference and taste. In Foucault's words, the dandy "makes of his body, his behavior, his feelings and passions, his very existence, a work of art" (*FR* 41). Finally, without mentioning the term, Foucault's analysis seems to suggest that the dandy is in some respect, the embodiment of the idea of *l'art pour l'art,* in that he has no social or political function:

> This ironic heroization of the present . . . this ascetic elaboration of the self—
> Baudelaire does not imagine that these have any place in society itself, or in the
> body politic. They can only be produced in another, a different place, which
> Baudelaire calls art (*FR* 42).

This statement, however, is not to be interpreted as a criticism of Baudelaire
but rather as an alternative, a countermovement to the Kantian definition
of modernity. In his commentary on Foucault's article, Christopher Norris
explains Foucault's position in the following terms:

> For Baudelaire, as indeed for Kant, modernity is characterized as a break with
> tradition, a sense of discontinuity with time and the lack of those taken-for-granted
> certitudes. . . But where Kant conceived this break as a coming-to-maturity through
> the exercise of autonomous, critical reason, Baudelaire imagines it—in high Ro-
> mantic fashion—as the discovery of evermore-inventive variations on the theme
> of aesthetic self-invention. And Foucault follows Baudelaire, rather than Kant,
> in equating modernity with that spirit of perpetual transformation. . . . [3]

In *The Rebel*, Albert Camus devotes an entire chapter to the figure
of the dandy. In this chapter entitled "The Dandies' Rebellion," Camus
anticipates in some way Foucault's positive assessment of modernity as an
attitude based on an ascetic elaboration of the self. Camus, in turn, addresses the question in terms of nihilism and absence of any existential
values. Camus links dandyism directly with romanticism as a movement
of "metaphysical revolt," which consists in denying any validity to man's
aspiration to unity and justice. It is a protest of modern man against the
whole of his condition and the entire order of the universe.

Romanticism, according to Camus, follows the path laid by the
radical writings of the Marquis de Sade: "Strangely enough, it is Sade who
sets rebellion on the path of literature down which it will be led still farther
by the romantics."[4] Romanticism "Lucifer-like in its rebellion"—satanic—
is characterized in Camus's eyes chiefly by "its preference for evil and the
individual" and "by putting emphasis on its powers of defiance and refusal, rebellion, at this stage, forgets its positive content"(Camus 47).

For Camus, "romanticism, at the source of its inspiration, is chiefly
concerned with defying moral and devine law. That is why its most original creation is . . .the Dandy" (Camus 50). Romantic rebellion, as exemplified by the dandy, is the story of a failure for Camus, since the romantic
rebel's choice is to remain locked in the realm of absolute negation which
becomes its very condition of being.

No longer hoping for the rule or the unity of God, determined to take up arms against an antagonistic destiny, anxious to preserve everything of which the living are still capable in a world dedicated to death, romantic rebellion looked for a solution in the attitude that itself it assumed. The attitude assembled, in aesthetic unity, all mankind who were in the hands of fate and about to be destroyed by divine violence. The human being who is condemned to death is, at last magnificent before he disappears, and his magnificence is his justification (Camus 51).

Camus sees no affirmative content in such an attitude for it is based on pure pride leading ultimately to sterility and isolation. The dandy creating "his own unity by aesthetic means," which are based on "singularity" and "negation," "can only exist by defiance":

Up to now man derived his coherence from his Creator. But from the moment that he consecrates his rupture with Him, he finds himself delivered over to the fleeting moment, to the passing days, and to wasted sensibility. Therefore he must take himself in hand (Camus 51).

According to Camus, however, he does just the opposite, since his existence depends on those he pretends to despise: "He can only be sure of his existence by finding it in the expression of others' faces. Other people are his mirror." He is only coherent as an actor and as such he "plays at life because he is unable to live it . . . for the Dandy to be alone is not to exist" (Camus 52). Considering this rather negative assessment of the dandy, it seems that Camus dismisses the ironical as well as the symbolical aspect of dandyism as it appears throughout Baudelaire's text. Camus reduces the dandy to a "profligate without a rule of life," a rebel for rebellion's sake. Camus seems to regret that the dandy's main preoccupation is not the human condition which in the existentialists' thought of "engagement" becomes the object and goal of true revolt, but appearances: "Romanticism demonstrates, in fact, that rebellion is part and parcel of dandyism: one of its objectives is appearances. In its conventional forms, dandyism admits a nostalgia for ethics. It is only honor degraded as a point of honor." On the other hand, romanticism, or dandyism, contains a positive side and here, Camus seems to come close to Foucault's analysis, for:

at the same time it inaugurates an aesthetic which is still valid in our world, an aesthetic of solitary creators, who are obstinate rivals of a God they condemn. From romanticism onward, the artist's task will not only be to create a world, or to exalt beauty for its own sake, but also define an attitude. Thus the artist becomes a model and offers himself as an example: art is his ethics (Camus 53).

Dandyism, as one of the last forms of romantic revolt, is thus not an adequate attitude toward freedom, which as the true objective of revolt for Camus includes the other. However, and this is an interesting aspect of Camus' discussion, Baudelaire himself is seen already outside—or beyond—the realm of the romantic movement as Camus described it. Baudelaire's "real drama, which made him the greatest poet of his time, was something else. Baudelaire can be mentioned here only to the extent that he was the most profound theoretician of dandyism and gave form to one of the conclusions of romantic revolt" (Camus 53). Unfortunately, Camus never defined that "something else" and thus strikes the readers curiosity. Whereas Camus's severe judgment of the dandy stems from his belief that the dandy chooses exile rather than constructive participation within the larger community, Michel Lemaire points out that the dandy's distancing is in fact not quite as radical as it seems:

> Of course he [the dandy] will take his distances on all levels, but he never breaks away completely; he will attack society's bourgeois structure all the while profiting from the pleasures it provides; he does not care for the salon life but does not leave the salons; he will put the entire world into question, but only in words. And the dandy knows that these are only words: his irony is often turned against himself. To maintain a constant distance, he works to provoke astonishment, scandal even, provided that it not be irremediable.[5]

There is a certain playfulness in the dandy's character which also shows a sense for limitations and boundaries he is careful not to overstep in order to remain in the game he in turn keeps interesting by challenging its order and rules.

Baudelaire's conception of the dandy is an important part of his critique of romanticism (excess of emotion, sentimentality, worship of nature, belief in the perfectibility of man). It also expresses his relation to and understanding of decadence as an aesthetic sensitivity in opposition to nineteenth-century progressive optimism. The dandy is both an end and a beginning. He is an end, since he is "the last flicker of heroism in decadent ages, a setting sun . . . declining star . . . magnificent, without heat and full of melancholy" *(le dernier éclat d'héroisme dans les décadence . . . un soleil couchant . . . l'astre qui décline . . . superbe, sans chaleur et plein de mélancolie) (SW* 421, *PL2* 712). As an artist however, he is also a beginning since he embodies the type of such modern artists as Delacroix and Edgar Allan Poe, "this Byron lost in an evil world" *(le Byron égaré dans un mauvais monde) (SW* 191, *PL2* 322), and to a certain extent Baudelaire himself. In *La Fanfarlo*, Baudelaire makes this parallel between the dandy and the artist when he describes his admittedly autobiographical hero Samuel Cramer as an artist *"dont la poésie brille bien plus dans sa personne que dans ses oeuvres"* (whose poetry gleams far more in his person than in his works) *(PL1* 553).[6]

In 1861, around the time when Baudelaire was planning a work with the revealing title "Le Dandysme littéraire ou la grandeur sans conviction," he wrote his mother about another project he dreamt to realize for two years: "My Heart laid bare, in which would be accumulated all my rage. Oh, if ever that sees the light of day, Jean Jacques's confessions will seem pale." *(Mon coeur mis à nu, et où j'entasserai toutes mes colères. Ah! Si jamais celui-là voit le jour, les Confessions de J[ean]-J[acques] paraîtront pâles).*[7]

The idea and title of this book, which finally remained in form of short notes and was only published after Baudelaire's death as *Intimate Journals*,[8] came from Poe who wrote:

> If any ambitious man has a fancy to revolutionize, at one effort, the universal world of human thought, human opinion, and human sentiment, the opportunity is his own—the road to immortal renown lies straight, open, and unencumbered before him. All that he has to do is to write and publish a very little book. Its title should be simple—a few plain words—'My Heart Laid Bare.' But this little book must be true to its title.[9]

Baudelaire took up the challenge, and his notes are of greatest interest insofar as they allow us to gain a broader perspective and insight into Baudelaire's personal thoughts in relation to the themes developed in the published works. That the figure of the dandy shares certain qualities with the artist as Baudelaire perceives him, namely as a being devoted entirely to beauty and thus rejecting any form of utilitarianism, becomes apparent in the few striking comments on the dandy in "My Heart Laid Bare": "To be a useful person has always appeared to me something particularly horrible" *(Être un homme utile m'a paru toujours quelque chose de bien hideux) (JI* 63, *PL1* 679). This observation makes manifest the connection between dandyism and aestheticism. The true artist, the only one who has the right to this title, is he, who like the dandy and in contrast to the "bourgeois," has no clearly defined function, no goal other than "to glorify the cult of images," Baudelaire's "great," "unique," and "primitive passion."

(Glorifier le culte des images . . . ma grande, mon unique, ma primitive passion) (JI 90, PL1 701). This thought is developed a little further when Baudelaire continues: "The vileness of any sort of employment. A Dandy does nothing. Can you imagine a Dandy addressing the common herd, except to make a game of them?" *(Ce qu'il y a de vil dans une fonction quelconque. Un Dandy ne fait rien. Vous figurez-vous un Dandy parlant au peuple, excepté pour le bafouer?) (JI 69, PL1 684)*.

On the other hand, however, as Patrice Bollon points out in his article *"La Figure du Dandy,"* in Baudelaire, the poet opposes himself constantly to the dandy in that his proclaimed "uselessness" is counterbalanced by an equally strong will to work: "It is when Baudelaire exceeds the figure of the Dandy, with whom he otherwise identifies, that Baudelaire becomes the great writer we know."[10]

The *Intimate Journals*, which apart from "My heart laid bare" contain two other sections entitled "Hygiene" (*"Hygiène"*) and "Squibs and Crackers" (*"Fusées"*) indeed reveal a constant struggle to come to terms with contradictory predispositions toward life: "Since my childhood—the sense of solitude . . . the sense of a destiny eternally solitary. Yet a taste for life and for pleasure which is very keen" *(Sentiment de solitude, dès mon enfance . . . sentiment de destinée éternellement solitaire. Cependant, goût très vif de la vie et du plaisir) (JI 65, PL1 680)*.

Baudelaire, whose heightened time-awareness always threatens to undermine his efforts, sees the will as the only means to overcome what he terms "the abyss," *(le gouffre)*: "A succession of small acts of will achieves a large result. Every rout of the will forms a portion of lost matter." *(Une suite de petites volontés fait un gros résultat. Tout recul de la volonté est une parcelle de substance perdue) (JI 104, PL1 672)*. His comments on the importance of escape from life-threatening feelings such as boredom, nausea and the tyranny of time through the discipline of work abound in every section of his *Intimate Journal*:

> We are weighed down, every moment, by the conception and the sensation of Time. And there are but two means of escaping and forgetting this nightmare: Pleasure and work. Pleasure consumes us. Work strengthens us. Let us choose. *(A chaque minute nous sommes écrasés par l'idée et la sensation du temps. Et il n'y a que deux moyens pour échapper à ce cauchemar,—pour l'oublier: le Plaisir et le Travail. Le Plaisir nous use. Le Travail nous fortifie. Choisissons) (JI 100, PL1 669)*.

Baudelaire's choice is clear. Work has a healing function and is less boring than pleasure:

> To heal all things, wretchedness, disease or melancholy, absolutely nothing is required but an inclination for work. *(Pour guérir de tout, de la misère, de la maladie et de la mélancholie, il ne manque absolument que le goût du travail) (JI 101, PL1 669).*

Not to become the victim of one's despair but to exploit it creatively, to turn it into something useful, is what Baudelaire has in mind when he continues: "One must work, if not from inclination at least from despair, since, as I have fully proved, to work is less wearisome than to amuse oneself" *(Il faut travailler, sinon par goût, au moins par déséspoir, puisque, tout vérifié, travailler est moins ennuyeux que s'amuser) (JI 67, PL1 682).*

    This effort to forge for himself a conduct of life according to almost monastic rules brings to mind again the dandy, whose daily renewed strive to perfect appearance is no less work in regard to "the strengthening of the will" and "the schooling of the soul." It seems from this that it is not so much a question of opposition to dandyism that Baudelaire performs through work but much rather a question of complementarity. The insistence on the part of Baudelaire, on the daily effort of self-overcoming—for the dandy as well as for the "working" artist—effaces the oppositional character of which Bollon speaks. Here then also is the connection between dandyism and asceticism, for the dandy as well as the artist both take pleasure in negating pleasure for the sake of a higher goal.

    Moreover, the dandy is not only an artist in the stricter sense of the term, but rather an artist of life as such. His seemingly cold detachment is a necessary mask to preserve his integrity, which constantly threatens to disintegrate. Underneath this mask burns an ardent passion for art and beauty. His ascetism, reflected in the absolute simplicity of his dress and his own code of rules is his only promise of survival in a society promoting the ethics of "useful" work and money. From this point of view, dandyism is a positive reaction against and a creative resistance to certain beliefs of the nineteenth century, which Baudelaire analyzes with relentless rigor.

II.   Critique of Progress in the Realm of the Arts: "The Universal Exhibition of 1855"

For Baudelaire, one of the great errors of his time is the belief in material progress as the guarantee for a spiritual and moral betterment of man. In "My Heart Laid Bare," he thus writes: "Belief in progress is a doctrine of idlers . . . it is the individual relying upon his neighbors to do his work. There cannot be any Progress (true progress, that is to say, moral) except within the individual" *(La croyance au progrès est une doctrine de paresseux. . . C'est l'individu qui compte sur ses voisins pour faire sa besogne. Il ne peut y avoir de progrès (vrai, c'est-à-dire moral) que dans l'individu lui-même) (JI* 66, *PL1* 681). Indeed, it is always in the name of individual responsibility and not under the guise of a school, institution, or movement that Baudelaire assumes his own position which he characterizes as follows: "To be a great man and a saint by one's own standards, that is all that matters" *(Avant tout, être un grand homme et pour soi-même) (JI* 82, *PL1* 691).

In his review of "The Universal Exhibition of 1855," Baudelaire denounces this doctrine as a symptom of decline, of an obvious decadence, for it confuses the material with the spiritual order of things. Progress, described as:

> this obscure beacon-light, a creation of current pseudo-philosophy . . . a ludicrous idea, which has bloomed on the rubbish dump of modern vanity, has absolved every man of his duty, delivered every soul of its responsibility, released the will from all bonds laid upon it by the love of beauty.
> *(Ce fanal obscur, invention du philosophisme actuel. . . Cette idée grotesque, qui a fleuri sur le terrain pourri de la fatuité moderne, a déchargé chacun de son devoir, délivré toute âme de sa responsabilité, dégagé la volonté de tous les liens que lui imposait l'amour du beau) (SW* 121, *PL2* 581).

Baudelaire's attack on progress stems from his disbelief in a teleological development of history. The promoters of progress are under the illusion that through the inventions of steam, electricity, gas-lighting, and such they are superior to ancient civilizations. Their blind optimism makes them forget that these inventions are by no means a guarantee for the improvement of man as a moral and spiritual being. On the contrary, Baudelaire goes so far as to conclude that if one were to follow the logic of progress, one would discover that progress is in reality the downfall of man. Thus Baudelaire raises the question:

whether, in making humanity more sensitive in proportion as it adds to the sum of possible enjoyment, unending progress would not be humanity's most ingenious and cruel form of torture; whether by this process, which is a stubborn negation of itself, progress would not be a constantly renewed form of suicide, and whether, imprisoned within the flaming circle of divine logic, progress, this eternal desideratum, which is humanity's eternal despair, would not be like the scorpion which stings itself with its own deadly tail?

(si, délicatisant l'humanité en proportion des jouissances nouvelles qu'il lui apporte, le progrès indéfini ne serait pas sa plus ingénieuse et sa plus cruelle torture; si, procédant par une opiniâtre négation de lui-même, il ne serait pas un mode de suicide incessament renouvelé, et si, enfermé dans le cercle de la logique divine, il ne ressemblerait pas au scorpion qui se perce lui-même avec sa terrible queue, cette éternel desiteratum qui fait son éternel désespoir?) (SW 122, PL2 581).

The process described in this passage is that of decline rather than advancement. The final logic of progress is a weakening of vitality through an over-refinement of the senses by accumulation of material commodities. In relying on this process, man abdicates responsibility for the condition of his own being, he becomes a passive subscriber to a false and pernicious doctrine which leads to a spiritual death.

Baudelaire's main criticism is the absurdity of the notion of progress when transplanted into the realm of arts and imagination. There it becomes "a grotesque joke rising to horrific heights" *(une grotesquerie qui monte jusqu'à l'épouvantable)*, for it is Baudelaire's conviction that art lies beyond any process of development in a natural or moral sense.

In the realm of poetry and art, the great discoverers rarely have precursors. Every flowering is spontaneous, individual. The artist owes nothing to anyone but himself. To future ages he holds out no promises but his own work. He is a guarantor for no one but himself. He dies without offspring. He has been his own king, priest and God.

(Dans l'ordre poétique et artistique, tout révélateur a rarement un précurseur. Toute floraison est spontanée, individuelle. L'artiste ne relève que de lui-même. Il ne promet aux siècles à venir que ses propres oeuvres. Il ne cautionne que lui-même. Il meurt sans enfants. Il a été son roi, son prêtre et son Dieu) (SW 122, PL2 581).

In Baudelaire's eyes, the artist can be compared to an event, which occurs and disappears like a star. He is one of "nature's wonders" which escape human calculation or even explanation. There is no guarantee for this event to happen in continuous fashion much less a guarantee for it to last and to develop indefinitely. The same goes for the cultural flowering of a nation, which is assured only for a short period of time. Thus France, for instance, from the point of view of its geographical situation, seems to be in a favorable position to gather all the best ideas and poetic works from the neighboring countries and to pass them on, beautifully transformed to other peoples. This, however, is not necessarily so since, like the individual, a country is subject to the natural cycle of birth, growth, and decline:

> But never let it be forgotten that nations, those vast collective beings, are subject to the same laws as individuals. Like babes they wail, gurgle, fill out and grow. Like youths and mature men they produce works full of boldness and wisdom. Like the aged they fall asleep on their heaped-up riches. Often the very principle of their strength and development brings about their decline, especially when that principle, vitalized by all-conquering zeal, has become a kind of routine for the majority. Then . . . the vital spark moves elsewhere, to other lands and races; nor should we think that newcomers inherit the whole estate from previous generations and that they receive from the latter-made doctrine. It often happens . . . that the loss is total, and a new start has to be made.
>
> *(Mais il ne faut jamais oublier que les nations, vastes êtres collectifs, sont soumises aux mêmes lois que les individus. Comme l'enfance, elles vagissent, balbutient, grossissent, grandissent. Comme la jeunesse et la maturité, elles produisent des oeuvres sages et hardies. Comme la vieillesse, elles s'endorment sur une richesse acquise. Souvent il arrive que c'est le principe même qui a fait leur force et leur developpement qui amène leur décadence, surtout quand ce principe, vivifié jadis par une ardeur conquérante, est devenu pour la majorité une routine. Alors, . . . la vitalité se déplace, elle va visiter d'autres territoires et d'autres races; il ne faut pas croire que les nouveaux venus héritent intégralement des anciens, et qu'ils reçoivent d'eux une doctrine toute faite. Il arrive souvent . . . que, tout étant perdu, tout est à refaire* (SW 123, PL2 582).

It seems from these lines that Baudelaire espouses a traditional view of decadence as a natural and inevitable end-stage of an ever newly repeated cycle. Baudelaire, however, insists that these various stages of development are isolated segments, not members of a series. Youth does not inherit from childhood, nor maturity from youth. And Edgar Allan Poe, as will be seen, is a point in case. The idea of the natural law of decline is not new. As Wolfdietrich Rasch points out in his article "Die Darstellung des Untergangs," the interpretation of historical development by way of organic metaphors is current ever since the decline of the Roman Empire. Up to the nineteenth century, the experience of decline has been viewed and lived in a negative way. With Baudelaire, however, Rasch sees the emergence of positive reevaluation of decline, an artistic exploitation of the theme of decay and decline as such.[11]

If Baudelaire is ready to accept the law of decline as an undeniable fact, he at the same time does not judge the end of this cycle in a negative way. This is however what the promoters of progress who often are at the same time the gatekeepers of classical aesthetics do. To the contrary, Baudelaire claims this stage for himself and those artists he admired most: Delacroix, Poe, and Wagner.

III.   Attempt at a Re-evaluation of Decadence

Baudelaire's reevaluation of decadence in an aesthetic sense has to be seen in the context of a critique of decadence as it was performed by conservative and anti-romantic critics such as Désiré Nisard, Armand de Pontmartin, Jules Janin, and others. According to Matei Calinescu, it is Désiré Nisard who introduced for the first time the theoretical notion of *style de décadence* in his study *Etudes de moeurs et de critique sur les poètes latins de la décadence,* published for the first time in 1834 and reedited in 1849.[12] Nisard, a scholar of late Latin poetry, draws a parallel between the French literature of his time and late Roman literature and finds the same decadence in both, a profuse use of description, the prominence of detail, and above all, the elevation of imaginative power to the detriment of reason:

> In France, a country of practical and reasonable literature, a writer who has only imagination, though it be of the rarest sort, cannot be a great writer... In him, the imagination takes the place of everything; imagination alone conceives and performs: it is a queen who governs unchecked. Reason finds no place in his works. No practical or applicable ideas, nothing or next to nothing of real life; no philosophy, no morals.[13]

Considering the central place imagination holds in Baudelaire's poetics, it is easy to understand Baudelaire's ironical comment on the conservative Nisard, with whom he cannot agree and whom he calls in *La Fanfarlo* "cet honnête M. Nisard"* (La Fanfarlo, PL1* 580).

The critic Pontmartin, whom Baudelaire qualifies in his *Intimate Journals* as a provincial, "a man who has always the air of having just arrived from his country town" *(un homme qui a toujours l'air d'arriver de sa province) (JI* 51, *PL1* 665), and whom he later attacks personally, uses the term of literary decadence in the sense of a literature which is qualitatively inferior to the classical one. Thus Gustave Flaubert's *Madame Bovary,* praised by Baudelaire for its irony and lyricism, is an example for Pontmartin of a manifest decadence.[14] In spite of the recognition of a certain talent, Pontmartin judges Baudelaire's poetry as "more or less bizarre curiosity," his mind dominated by "a sick imagination." He sees Baudelaire as a poet who separates himself from "the great human family," without faith, ideas, or soul.[15]

The choice of subject matter is also a reason for Pontmartin's devaluation of literary decadence. Dumas's *La dame aux camélias* is decadent because its heroine is a courtesan.[16]

It is against this conservative position that Baudelaire argues in "Further Notes on Edgar Allan Poe," the preface to his translation of the American poet's tales. Written two years after the "Universal Exhibition of 1855," this text, in which critique of progress and elaboration of the themes of decadence go hand in hand, is crucial in regard to Baudelaire's reevaluation of decadence:

> A literature of decadence!—empty words we often hear fall with a pompous yawn from the lips of the sphinxes without a riddle that guard the holy portals of classical aesthetics. Each time the irrefutable oracle thunders forth, it may safely be affirmed that the cause is a work more amusing than the Illiad, a poem or a novel, evidently, all parts of which are skillfully arranged with a view to surprise, the style of which is splendidly ornate, where all the resources of language and prosody have been exploited by an impeccable hand.
> *(Littérature de décadence!—Paroles vides que nous entendons souvent tomber, avec la sonorité d'un baillement emphatique, de la bouche de ces sphinx sans enigme qui veillent devant les portes saintes de l'Esthétique classique. À chaque fois que l'irréfutable oracle retentit, on peut affirmer qu'il s'agit d'un ouvrage plus amusant que l'Illiade. Il est évidemment question d'un poème ou d'un roman dont toutes les parties sont habituellement disposées pour la surprise, dont le style est magnifiquement orné, où toutes les ressources du langage et de la prosodie sont utilisées par une main impeccable) (SW 188, PL2 319).*

"A literature of decadence" is for Baudelaire an "empty" formula, used by "pundits" (*professeurs jurés*) whose "schoolboy wisdom" *(sagesse d'écoliers)* is incapable of grasping the aesthetic potential of this new style, which Baudelaire defined as at once decadent, spiritual, and modern. Where Nisard sees decline, Baudelaire recognizes creative spirituality. In a note accompanying his poem *"Franciscae mae laudes"*, Baudelaire connects the spirit of Latin decadence with modern poetry:

> Does not the reader think, as I do, that the Latin decadence—a supreme sigh of a robust person already transformed and prepared for spiritual life—is uniquely

appropriate for expressing passion such as the modern poetic world has understood and felt it?

*(Ne semble-t-il pas au lecteur, comme à moi, que la langue de la dernière décadence
latine,—suprême soupir d'une personne robuste, déjà transformée et préparée
pour la vie spirituelle,—est singulièrement propre à exprimer la passion telle que
l'a comprise et sentie le monde poétique moderne?) (PL1 940).*[17]

The correspondence between Roman decadence and modern poetic perception as Baudelaire establishes it, negates the idea of a presup-
posed "scale of literatures, a literature of infancy, a literature in childhood,
in adolescence, etc." *(une échelle de littératures, une vagissante, une puérile,
une adolescente, etc.) (SW* 189, *PL2* 320). Baudelaire refuses the idea of a
scale because the inevitable and fatalistic aspect of this "mysterious law"
(loi mystérieuse) justifies censorship and serves in reality only to make the
modern late-comers "feel ashamed of obeying this law with pleasure," to
make them feel "guilty of rejoicing in [their] own destiny." *(Tout ce que je
puis comprendre dans la parole académique, c'est qu'il est honteux d'obéir
à cette loi avec plaisir, et que nous sommes coupables de nous réjouir dans
notre destinée) (SW* 205, *PL2* 320). Finally, the establishment of such a
law reveals itself as entirely useless and is bound to become an embarrass-
ment to these theoreticians, argues Baudelaire, when they encounter the
opposite phenomenon—and this is an allusion to Poe, who, as an American does not belong to a late period in history—namely "when a nation
begins in decadence, and starts in fact where others end up" *(où une nation
commence par la décadence, et débute par où les autres finissent) (SW*
189, *PL2* 320).

As Rasch points out, Baudelaire uses the term "literary decadence"
in a new sense, namely as a "value-free designation for a type of literature
which turns itself toward the themes of decline and whose subject matter is
equivalent to classical poetry" (Rasch 421). Pontmartin responded disap-
provingly to Baudelaire's arguments presented in the "Further Notes" in an
essay entitled *"La poésie en 1861."* Baudelaire sent this essay to his mother
and added in a note: "This is an imbecil who forbids the poet to choose his
own subject matter" *(C'est un imbécile qui défend au poète de choisir
lui-même ses sujets) (Corr* 2, 188).

One of the key concepts of literary décadence is for instance the
"dying sun" *(soleil agonisant),* a metaphor of decline and decay. This
metaphor has been used often to describe decadence, but always in the
context of a whole epoch of decline such as the Roman empire or a na-

tional culture. Baudelaire uses this image in a wholly different sense, namely as a summarizing concept for all the single and various subjects and themes referring to decay and decline. The "dying sun," which produces a variety of shades and color stands as a metaphor for decline as a central theme of decadent poetry as such and unfolds into many single and individual motifs:

> That sun which a few hours ago was crushing everything beneath the vertical, white light will soon be flooding the western horizon with varied colors. In the changing splendors of the dying sun, some poetic minds will find new joys; they will discover dazzling colonnades, cascades of molten metal, a paradise of fire, a melancholy splendor, nostalgic ruptures, all the magic of dreams, all the memories of opium. And the sunset will then appear to them as a marvelous allegory of a soul, imbued with life, going down beyond the horizon, with a magnificent wealth of thought and dreams.
> *(Ce soleil qui, il y a quelques heures, écrasait toutes choses de sa lumière droite et blanche, va bientôt inonder l'horizon occidental de couleurs variées. Dans les jeux de ce soleil agonisant, certains esprits poétiques trouveront des délices nouvelles: ils y découvriront des colonnades éblouissantes, des cascades de métal fondu, des paradis de feu, une splendeur triste, la volupté du regret, toutes les magies du rêve, tous les souvenirs de l'opium. Et le coucher du soleil leur apparaîtra en effet comme la merveilleuse allégorie d'une âme chargée de vie, qui descend derrière l'horizon avec une magnifique provision de pensées et de rêves)* (*SW* 189, *PL2* 320).

This passage is central to Baudelaire's reevaluation of decadence. All the motifs of decline are not only as valid as those moments of "ascending life," they not only have the same rights as classical motifs, but they are even richer in aesthetic potential. With Baudelaire, the term "decadence" loses its contemptuous flavor, no longer designates a minor kind of poetry or art in general, but a particular, higher type of modern poetry.

IV.   Against the Grain: Edgar Allen Poe

The relationship between Baudelaire and Edgar Allen Poe has been and continues to be the subject of many studies. Baudelaire discovers Poe's tales for the first time in 1847 and he becomes acquainted with his poetry and theoretical work only in 1952. Baudelaire's reaction to Poe's writings is legendary. In Poe, the man and *poète maudit,* he recognizes aspects of himself and in his work finds an echo of his own ideas which, however, were "vague and confused, badly organized and which Poe knew to combine to perfection."[18] It is thanks to Baudelaire's lifelong translation of Poe's works that the American writer, scorned for the largest part by his fellow citizens, became one of the most celebrated poets of the Symbolist movement in France.

As Jonathan Culler points out in his article "Baudelaire and Poe," Mallarmé, who spoke of Poe as his great master, as *"le cas littéraire absolu,"* focused on Poe's conception of poetry "as musical play of the signifier linked with a radical theory of the universe." And Valéry "admired above all else the theoretician of poetic effects."[19] It is perhaps because of this positive reception of Poe in France that Baudelaire's relationship to Poe is mostly discussed in terms of Poe's influence on Baudelaire. Indeed, for Valéry, Poe represents the main modifying factor in Baudelaire's ideas and art:

> He enlightened him, he enriched him, he determined his opinions on a quantity of subjects: philosophy of composition, theory of the artificial, comprehension and condemnation of the modern, importance of the exceptional and of a certain strangeness, an aristocratic attitude, mysticism, a taste for elegance and precision, even politics . . . Baudelaire was impregnated, inspired and deepened by them.[20]

The subjects here enumerated are indubitably common to Poe and Baudelaire, but the question of definitive influence remains questionable. Lloyd Austin, in his *Univers Poétique de Baudelaire* comes to the conclusion that the influence of Poe on Baudelaire has been less great than it has been so often asserted.[21] And Marcel Ruff maintains that although Baudelaire was deeply moved by Poe, in whose writings he found a "strangely fraternal spirit," he expressed numerous reservations about the particular writings supposed to have influenced him (Ruff 67–75).

Baudelaire himself denies this overstated influence in a letter, written in 1864, to Théophile Thoré where he gives the main reason for his interest in Poe:

> Well, I myself am accused of imitating Edgar Poe! Do you know why I've translated Poe so patiently? Because he was like me. The first time I opened one of his books, I saw, with horror and delight, not only topics I'd dreamt of, but sentences I'd thought of, and that he had written 20 years before.
> *(Eh bien! On m'accuse, moi, d'imiter Edgar Poe! Savez-vous pourquoi j'ai si patiemment traduit Poe? Parce qu'il me ressemblait. La première fois que j'ai ouvert un livre de lui, j'ai vu, avec épouvante et ravissement, non seulement des sujets rêvés par moi, mais des phrases pensées par moi, et écrites par lui vingt ans auparavant) (SL 204, Corr 2, 386).*

It is thus in the light of a spiritual affinity that the relationship between Baudelaire and Poe has to be approached. What is of interest in the context of the present study is that Baudelaire saw Poe, like himself, as an exception, a *force résistante* in the midst of a "world enamored of material progress."[22] Baudelaire defended precisely the themes and motives in Poe's work which were labeled as decadent by others but in which Baudelaire found the expression of a modern sensitivity akin to his own and also to that of Delacroix.

A passage of Baudelaire's first essay on Poe entitled "Edgar Poe, his Life and Works," where Baudelaire links Poe and Delacroix together by highlighting the suggestive faculties of their respective mediums—poetry and painting respond each other—he also gives his own interpretation of decadence as an infinite reservoir of new forms and supernatural adventures:

Like our own Eugène Delacroix, who has raised his art to the height of great poetry, Edgar Poe loves to have his characters live and move against lurid backgrounds of mingled purple and green, which reveal the phosphorescence of decay and the smell of storm. So-called inanimate nature participates in the nature of the living beings, and, like them, is seized with a supernatural and galvanic shuddering. Space is extended by opium; opium confers a magical meaning on every tint, and gives a more significant resonance to every sound. Sometimes the landscapes open up and reveal magnificent horizons, full of light and color, where, sparkling in the sun's golden rain, oriental cities and diverse buildings appear in the distant haze.
(Comme notre Eugène Delacroix, qui a élevé son art à la hauteur de la grande poésie, Edgar Poe aime à agiter ses figures sur des fonds violâtres et verdâtres où se révèlent la phosphorescence de la pourriture et la senteur de l'orage. La nature dite inanimée participe de la nature des êtres vivants, et, comme eux, frissonne d'un frisson surnaturel et galvanique. L'espace est approfondi par l'opium; l'opium y donne un sens magique à toutes les teintes, et fait vibrer tous les bruits avec une plus significative sonorité. Quelquefois des échappées magnifiques, gorgées de lumière et de couleur, s'ouvrent soudainement dans les paysages, et l'on voit apparaître au fond de leurs horizons des villes orientales et des architectures, vaporisées par la distance, où le soleil jette des pluies d'or) (*SW* 186, *PL2* 318).

As Ernst Behler points out, the special interest of Baudelaire's writings on Poe lies in the fact that they transcend the historical-critical presentation of Poe's life and work and express, through the figure of Poe, the spirit of a new conception of art. Baudelaire's method introduces a new style of representation which consists in concentrating on "exceptional beings" *(ces âmes d'élite)* such as Delacroix, Poe and Wagner, who stand concretely in the place of abstract aesthetic principles. This method has been carried out in the most radical way later by Nietzsche in the figures of Richard Wagner and Socrates. Poe thus turns out to be for Baudelaire an occasion to define the relationship of the modern poet toward society and state and to highlight the melancholy tendency provoked by modern life through artistic discipline or a certain style of writing, which reflects the condition of the modern "man of nerves".[23]

It is perhaps in *"Le poème du Haschisch"* that Baudelaire draws together the most characteristic features of the modern sensitive man in a portrait which fits Poe particularly well but also other artists Baudelaire admired and supported in his writings:

> A temperament that mixes nervousness equally with passion . . . let us add a cultivated mind, trained by study of form and color; a tender heart, worn out by misery, but ever ready to be renewed . . . a few old failings . . . an easily excitable nature . . . a regret for misspent and badly occupied time. A taste for metaphysics, and a knowledge of the various philosophical hypotheses about human destiny . . . to add a great refinement of the senses . . . I believe that I would then have assembled all the most common universal elements of the modern homme sensible, the creature that could be called the commonplace form of the unusual.[24]
> *(Un tempérament à moitié nerveux, moitié bilieux . . . ajoutons un esprit cultivé, exercé aux études de la forme et de la couleur; un coeur tendre, fatigué par la douleur . . . des fautes anciennes . . . une nature facilement excitable . . . le regret du temps profané et mal rempli . . . Le goût de la métaphysique, la connaissance des différentes hypothèses de la philosophie sur la destinée humaine . . . Une grande finesse de sens . . . je crois que j'ai rassemblé les éléments généraux les plus communs de l'homme sensible moderne, de ce qu'on pourrait appeler la forme banale de l'originalité) (PL1 429).*

Baudelaire admires the double gesture with which Poe, not unlike him, responds to the hostile conditions the artist is forced to cope with. The author who "releases floods of scorn and disgust over democracy, progress and so-called civilization" *(lâche à torrents son mépris et son dégoût sur la démocratie, le progrès et la civilisation)* is also the same "hoaxer" *(farceur)* who leads the proud and credulous modern men by the nose, seemingly flattering them but in reality scoffing at their gullibility. Baudelaire insists: Poe was never a dupe. His ability to see through the lie of "all these flatterers of humanity, of all these mollycoddlers and opiate-peddlers" *(ces complimenteurs de l'humanité, tout ces dorloteurs et endormeurs)* who keep preaching the idea of the inherent goodness of man, make him the great exception as which Baudelaire saw him. For Poe, himself "the product of a self-infatuated age, the child of a nation more full of its own importance than any other, has seen clearly, has calmly proclaimed the natural wickedness of man" *(produit d'un siècle infatué de lui-même, enfant d'une nation plus infatuée d'elle-même qu'aucune autre, a vu clairement, a imperturbablement affirmé la méchanceté naturelle de l'Homme)*. It is this "primeval perversity of man" *(la perversité primordiale de l'homme)* which makes him "at one and the same time, homicidal and suicidal, murderer and executioner" *(à la fois homicide et suicide, assassin et bourreau)*. Like Baudelaire, Poe ridiculed the idea of progress, "that grand heresy of decrepitude" *(cette grande hérésie de la décrépitude)*, which has been invented by modern "civilized" man "to console himself for his abdication and decline" *(pour se consoler de son abdication et de sa déchéance)*. Here again, the logic of progress reverting to decadence, developed in "The Universal Exhibition of 1855" comes to the fore:

> Is it not a matter of astonishment that this oh! so simple notion does not flash in every brainbox, namely that progress (in so far as it exists) sharpens suffering in proportion as it refines sensual pleasure, and that if the skins of peoples get ever more delicate, they are evidently pursuing nothing but an Italiam fugientem, a conquest lost again at every minute, a form of progress that is a constant negation of itself?
> *(N'est-ce pas un sujet d'étonnement que cette idée si simple n'éclate pas dans tous les cerveaux: que le Progrès [en tant que progrès il y ait] perfectionne la douleur à proportion qu'il raffine la volupté, et que, si l'épiderme des peuples va se délicatisant, ils ne poursuivent évidemment qu'une Italiam fugientem, une conquète à chaque minute perdue, un progrès toujours négateur de lui-même?)* (*SW* 194, *PL2* 325).

Seemingly in line with the Rousseauistic idea that civilized man is a "depraved animal" in contrast to "natural" man, the "savage," Baudelaire gives this thought, however, a crucial twist. Yes, he argues, civilized man is a "depraved animal," but he is so by nature. Therefore he is entitled to reproach Rousseau "for having invoked simple nature" which "creates only monsters." (*SW* 195 *PL2* 325) The idea that nature teaches nothing but evil is intimately related to Baudelaire's preoccupation with original sin, which lies at the bottom of the human condition and which gives a strange coloring to all human experience. For Baudelaire, true civilization is obviously not the one based on material wealth but one which engenders spiritual refinement, artistic productivity, and inventiveness. A short passage in "My Heart Laid Bare" illustrates Baudelaire's "theory of true civilization:"

Theory of the true civilization. It has nothing to do with gas or steam or table-turning. It consists in the diminution of the traces of original sin. Nomad peoples, shepherds, hunters, farmers and even cannibals, may all be by virtue of energy and personal dignity, the superiors of our races of the West.
(Théorie de la vraie civilisation. Elle n'est pas dans le gaz, ni dans la vapeur, ni dans les tables tournantes, elle est dans la diminution des traces du péché originel. Peuples nomades, pasteurs, agricoles, et mêmes anthropophages, tous peuvent être supérieurs, par l'énergie, par la dignité personnelles, à nos races d'Occident) (*JI* 85, *PL1* 697).

Baudelaire's comparison between the savage and the "modern" man is thus not to be understood as an invitation to a return to a natural, more innocent state of being but rather a *tour de force* to debunk the illusory belief of modern, "progressive" man in his superiority over more "primitive" but in Baudelaire's eyes more spiritual civilizations.

The savage "by his nature, of necessity, even, is encyclopedic." Modern man having abdicated his own responsibility to the illusion of progress, has become a narrow minded specialist who no longer cultivates any higher ideal other than his comfort. In Baudelaire's eyes, he is the decadent, whereas the savage, not unlike the dandy, comes closer to "the borders of the ideal" *(rase de plus près la lisière de l'idéal)* and is compared to a "feared and respected husband, a warrior forced to be individually brave" *(époux redouté et respecté, guerrier contraint à la bravoure personnelle)* and as a man who accepts his fate without flinching: "a poet in moments of melancholy, when the declining sun incites him to sing of the past and of his ancestors" *(poète aux heures mélancholiques où le soleil déclinant invite à chanter le passé et les ancêtres)*. The universe of the savage, with its rituals and sense of beauty (their priests, sorcerers and medicine men are indeed compared to the dandy whose "clothes, adornment, weapons and pipe all display an inventive faculty that we have long since lost") is depicted polemically by Baudelaire in order to highlight the flatness and mediocrity of "a century dedicated to materialism" *(d'un siècle voué à la matière)*. Thus the cruelty of human sacrifices as they were performed by the savage priest seems to Baudelaire "quite gentle and humane" in comparison with the deceptive practices of the modern "financier who sacrifices populations solely to his personal interest" *(financier qui n'immole les populations qu'à son intérêt propre)*. The poet is not made for this environment consisting of a "mob of buyers and sellers." And to show the degree of degenerescence in which the poet is forced to live, Baudelaire compares the classical conception of a *Salon* as it used to flourish formerly in Europe as "a republic of cultured minds, where beauty held sway" with the American saloon, "a vast drinking saloon, thronged with consumers doing their business at dirty tables, against a hubbub of coarse talk" *(un vaste cabaret, où le consommateur afflue et traîte d'affaires sur les tables souillées, au tintamarre des vilains propos)* *(SW* 197, *PL2* 327).

It comes as no surprise then that in such surroundings, "where the utilitarian idea, the most hostile in the world to the idea of beauty, takes first place and dominates all other considerations" *(où l'idée d'utilité, la plus hostile du monde à l'idée de beauté, prime et domine toute chose)*, literary errors are committed against which Poe battled with all his might. In discussing Poe's "Poetic Principle" and largely quoting from the original text interspersed with his own comments, Baudelaire draws particular attention to the importance given by Poe to the imagination, his attack on the "heresy of the didactic," his critique of inspiration, the musical quality of the poem, and the introduction of strangeness as an enhancing element for beauty.

In the *"Salon* of 1859" Baudelaire defines imagination as "analysis" and "synthesis" at the same time and states that "the man who has mere skill is a fathead, and the man with imagination who tries to do without skill is a lunatic" *(celui qui ne possède que l'habileté est une bête, et l'imagination qui veut s'en passer est une folle)* *(SW* 290, *PL2* 612).

Poe's merit lies in that in his work, he gives equal importance to both. Dividing the world of the spirit into "pure intellect, taste and moral sense" *(intellect pur, goût et sens moral)*, Poe confers to the imagination the role of "queen of all faculties" *(la reine des facultés)*, the main ordering principle of all poetic creation. Imagination is more than "fantasy" *(fantaisie)*, it is not mere "sensibility" *(sensibilité)* either, it is "a virtually divine faculty that apprehends immediately, by means lying outside philosophical methods, the intimate and secret relation of things, the correspondences and analogies" *(une faculté quasi divine qui perçoit tout d'abord, en dehors des méthodes philosophiques, les rapports intimes et secrets des choses, les correspondances et les analogies)* *(SW* 199, *PL2* 329).

The lengths of a literary work is of great importance as to the deployment of the imagination. For Poe, it is the short story where imagination can achieve the best results, for "its brevity adds to the intensity of its effects" *(sa briéveté ajoute à l'intensité de l'effet)*. Baudelaire sees the short story as a creative challenge for, if the totality of effect be achieved, the author is required to yield to a preconceived plan where nothing is left to chance and every element willfully planted in its right place. The first sentence must contain the logic of the final sentence and "not a single word must be allowed to slip in that is not loaded with intention, that does not tend, directly or indirectly, to complete the premeditated design" *(pas un seul mot qui ne soit une intention, qui ne tende directement ou indirectement, à parfaire le dessein prémédité) (SW* 200, *PL2* 329).

Jonathan Culler sees Poe's "aesthetics of compression" as one of the main inspirations for Baudelaire to write prose poems (Culler 66). In a letter to his mother, Baudelaire expresses the hope that with his prose poems he succeeds *"à produire un ouvrage singulier, plus singulier, plus volontaire du moins, que* Les Fleurs du Mal," where he would combine *"l'effrayant avec le bouffon" (Corr2* 473). Short prose is thus an exercise in discipline and has advantages over poetry in that "the author . . . has at his disposal a multitude of tones, shades of language, the reasoning tone, the sarcastic, the humorous, all of which poetry eschews and which are like discords, affronts to the idea of pure beauty" *(l'auteur d'une nouvelle a à sa disposition une multitude de tons, de nuances de language, le ton raisonneur, le sarcastique, l'humoristique que répudie la poésie, et qui sont comme des dissonances, des outrages à l'idée de beauté pure) (SW* 200, *PL2* 329).

The idea of discipline, which Baudelaire defines as the subjugation of inspiration to "the strictest method and analysis" and the importance of length and size of a literary work, is continued in Baudelaire's discussion of Poe's poetic theory. In agreement with Poe, Baudelaire states that "a poem deserves its name only insofar as it excites, ravishes the soul" *(un poème ne mérite son titre qu'autant qu'il excite, qu'il enlève l'âme).* Like a short story, a poem should neither be too long nor too short. If it is too long, a poem loses its "totality of effect" and "unity of impression." If it is too short, its effect is neither profound nor lasting.

One of the main errors which obstruct the true function of literary activity, however, is that of the "heresy of didactism," *(hérésie de l'enseignement)* by which it is believed that poetry should be useful to the improvement of conscience and social behavior, that it should teach a moral lesson. This error is not only fostered in America but flourishes as well in France. Against this false assumption, Baudelaire affirms with Poe, that after an honest introspection of one's soul, "poetry will be seen to have no other aim but itself" *(que la poésie n'a d'autre but qu'elle même).* Baudelaire goes further than Poe, however, by feeling compelled to elaborate on this idea, which Poe does not. To prevent any misunderstanding, Baudelaire concedes a certain degree of usefulness to poetry, but only in so far as it ennobles manners and "raises man above squalid interests" *(élever l'homme au dessus du niveau des intérêts vulgaires)*. Any intention or pretense on the part of the author to convey a moral lesson is a guarantee for failure: "Poetry cannot, except at the price of death or decay, assume the mantle of science and morality; the pursuit of truth is not its aim, it has nothing outside itself" *(la poésie ne peut pas, sous peine de mort ou de défaillance, s'assimiler à la science ou à la morale; elle n'a pas la Vérité pour objet, elle n'a que elle-même) (SW* 203, *PL2* 333). This statement is in line with Baudelaire's earlier arguments brought forth in an essay written in 1851, entitled "Of Virtuous Plays and Novels," against various literary schools *(l'école du bon sens, the bourgeois school, the socialist school)*, which, in reaction to "the puerile excesses of the so-called romantic school" *(débordements puérils de l'école dite romantique)* have become moralizing institutions "with the feverish ardor of missionaries" for whom "art is a mere question of propaganda"*(SW* 111, *PL2* 41). The main question in this essay revolves around the idea of virtue as the ultimate value for a literary work of art. Baudelaire uncovers this "humanitarian ideal" as a lie, a hypocritical scheme for the sake of success. Art is used to justify and redeem the bourgeois's greed and vice disguised under the mantle of virtue. The "so-called virtuous writers" deliver to the public what they want to read and see on the stage. They produce "the poetry of the heart" *(la poésie du coeur)*, a perversion of poetry, which not only destroys the precision of the French language but also pretends to ignore the darker and no less beautiful side of the human condition. Baudelaire's statement is powerful:

> Is art useful? Yes. Why? Because it is art. Is there such a thing as a pernicious form of art? Yes! The form that distorts the underlying conditions of life. Vice is alluring; then show it as alluring; but it brings in its train peculiar moral maladies and suffering; then describe them. Study all the sores, like a doctor in the course of his hospital duties, and the good-sense school, the school dedicated exclusively to morality, will find nothing to bite on. Is crime always punished? No; and yet if your novel, if your play is well put together, no one will take it into his head to break the laws of nature. The first necessary condition for the creation of a vigorous art form is the belief in underlying unity. I defy anyone to find a single work of imagination that satisfies the condition of beauty and is at the same time a pernicious work.
>
> *(L'Art est-il utile? Oui. Pourquoi? Parce qu'il est l'art. Y a-t-il un art pernicieux?*

Oui. C'est celui qui dérange les conditions de la vie. Le vice est séduisant, il faut
le peindre séduisant; mais il traîne avec lui des maladies et des douleurs morales
singulières; il faut les décrire. Etudiez toutes les plaies comme un médecin qui
fait son service dans un hôpital, et l'école du bon sens, l'école exclusivement
morale, ne trouvera plus où mordre. Le crime est-il toujours chatié, la vertu
gratifié? Non; mais cependant, si votre roman, si votre drame est bien fait, il ne
prendra envie à personne de violer les lois de la nature. La première condition
nécessaire pour faire un art sain est la croyance à l'unité intégrale. Je défie
qu'on me trouve un seul ouvrage d'imagination qui réunisse toutes les condi-
tions du beau et qui soit un ouvrage pernicieux) (SW 112, *PL2* 41).

  This passage leads back to Baudelaire's discussion of Poe's poetic
theory since it implies that a superior form of beauty lies beyond any moral
truth. The "dissonances" and "deformities" of vice, for instance, might
indeed hurt the poetic spirit of the "man of taste" *(l'homme de goût)* but
they are also part of the spectacle of this world and in their "strangeness"
(l'étrangeté) an "indispensible condiment of all beauty" *(le condiment in-*
dispensable de toute beauté). Therefore, it seems almost to be an under-
statement when Baudelaire does not consider it "shocking to regard any
infringement of morality, of moral beauty, as a kind of offense against universal rhythm and prosody" *(qu'il soit scandalisant de considérer toute*
infraction à la morale, au beau moral, comme une espèce de faute contre
le rythme et la prosodie universels) (SW 204, *PL2* 334).

  The sense of the beautiful is not moral but "instinctive." It corresponds to "our unquenchable thirst for all that lies beyond." *(notre soif*
insatiable de tout ce qui est au-delà). And it is through the medium of
poetry and music that the human soul takes flight from the consciousness
of natural imperfection and gains but brief glimpses of a "revealed paradise" *(paradis révélé).* The poetic principle is thus "strictly and simply the
human longing for a superior form of beauty," a form of beauty which,
according to Baudelaire's conception, cannot be found in nature. "Superior beauty" is therefore "independent of passion . . . for passion is natural,
too natural not to introduce a hurtful, jarring note into the realm of pure
beauty. . . " *(indépendant de la passion . . . car la passion est naturelle, trop*
naturelle pour ne pas introduire un ton blessant, discordant, dans le domaine
de la beauté pure. . .). This quest for the ethereal in the form of "supernal"
and in Baudelaire's terms "supernatural beauty" *(beauté surnaturelle),* is
not conducted under the spell of inspiration, but with a controlled mind
and skillful employment of all the stylistic means the poet has at his disposal: "Just as some writers make a parade of negligence, aiming at a

masterpiece with their eyes shut . . . so Edgar Poe . . . prided himself on hiding spontaneity, on simulating cold deliberation." *(Autant certains écrivains affectent l'abandon, visant au chef-d'oeuvre les yeux fermés, plein de confiance dans le désordre . . . autant Edgar Poe . . . a mis d'affectation à cacher la spontanéité, à simuler le sang froid et la délibération) (SW 206, PL2 335).*

Not unlike the dandy, Poe affects an attitude which may shock the proponents of inspiration but is necessary to create what Baudelaire terms in his preface to the translation of Poe's poem "The Raven" this "object of luxury," *(objet de luxe)*, the perfect poem. Even though Baudelaire recognizes underneath Poe's affected coolness "one of the most inspired men" known to him *(l'un des hommes les plus inspirés que je connaisse)*, he nevertheless understands the motive behind such an attitude.[25] Therefore it is not surprising when he adds that "a little charlatanism is always permitted to genius . . . it is, like rouge on the cheeks of a naturally beautiful woman, an additional stimulus to the mind"[26] *(un peu de charlatanerie est toujours permis au génie . . . c'est comme le fard sur les pommettes d'une femme naturellement belle, un assaisonnement nouveau pour l'esprit) (PL2 344).*

Finally, it seems safe to conclude, that the two main points which Baudelaire stresses in Poe and which most forcefully captivate his attention are Poe's quest for supernal beauty and his resourceful ingenuity, his painstaking craftsmanship. Both ideas become synonymous with artificiality, which lies at the center of the aesthetics of decadence. Baudelaire formulates this aesthetics of artificiality in regard to Poe's work and introduces it with perhaps one of the most forceful images susceptible to reflect decadent sensitivity as opposed to the "naturalness" apparently desired by those who oppose this "decadent" sensitivity and literary form of expression. Baudelaire, brushing his opponents against the grain, addresses them as follows:

> Do you take me for a barbarian like yourself, and do you think I can take my pleasures as dismally as you do? Grotesque comparisons then begin to dance in my brain; I have the impression that two women are being introduced to me, one a rustic matron, bursting with rude health and virtuousness, with no style or expression, in short 'owing nothing but to nature unadorned'; the other, one of those beautiful women who dominate and oppress our memories, adding to her own profound native charm the eloquent appeal of dress, knowing exactly how to walk with grace, aware of her regal poise, with a speaking voice like a well-tuned

instrument and thoughtful eyes that reveal only what they want to.

(Me prenez-vous pour un barbare comme vous, et me croyez-vous capable de me divertir aussi tristement que vous faites? Des comparaisons grotesques s'agitent alors dans mon cerveau; il me semble que deux femmes me sont présentées: l'une, matrone rustique, répugnante de santé et de vertu, sans allure et sans regard, bref, ne devant rien qu'à la simple nature; l'autre, une de ces beautés qui dominent et oppriment le souvenir, unissant à son charme profond et originel toute l'éloquence de sa toilette, maîtresse de sa démarche, consciente et reine d'elle-même,—une voix parlant comme un instrument bien accordé, et des regards chargés de pensée et n'en laissant couler que ce qu'ils veulent) (SW 188, PL2 319).

Baudelaire's preference is doubtless the latter type in which is reflected an aesthetics based on artificiality as opposed to a natural, organic view of art as it was promoted in the eighteenth century. This passage, which sets the tone of Baudelaire's defense of Poe's so-called "literature of decadence" already prepares the terrain for the fusion of the artificial and the modern as it appears in "The Painter of Modern Life" (especially in the corresponding chapter "In Praise of Make-up") in the form of the dandy.

V.   *Artificiality*

In this text Baudelaire performs the most rigorous attack against traditional aesthetics yet: its misunderstanding of nature, and the resulting misconceptions of beauty. The polemical character of this very short but intense chapter has not gone unnoticed by Baudelairian scholars. Some interpret Baudelaire's theory of the artificial expressed through make-up as the highest degree of supreme art for Baudelaire.[27] Others focus on the relative character and contradictory aspects of Baudelaire's argumentation and place this theory within the context of a complex attitude on the part of Baudelaire towards nature.[28]

In the context of the present study, the interest lies precisely in the provocative tone adopted by Baudelaire, whose concern it is to formulate an aesthetics based on the transgression of limits imposed by nature and also by man himself. Baudelaire begins this chapter with a refutation of an aesthetic credo which is based on the assumption that "nature embellishes beauty" *(la nature embellit la beauté)* and which is derived from what Baudelaire sees as "false" naturalistic ethic of the eighteenth-century philosophers, with the denial of original sin and the supremacy of nature "as a basis, source and prototype of all possible forms of good and beauty" *(la nature . . . comme base, source et type de tout bien et de tout beau possible)* (*SW* 424, *PL2* 715). However, considering the facts as they occur in history, as they are reported in the daily newspapers, Baudelaire is prompted to protest. Nature "teaches" man nothing from a moral perspective, it merely "compels man to sleep, drink, eat and protect himself" *(contraint l'homme à boire, à manger, et à se garantir, tant bien que mal, contre les hostilités de l'atmosphère).*

Under Baudelaire's pen, nature becomes an active and negatively-productive agent of need and evil, since it "drives man" to kill, torture, imprison, and even eat his fellow men, in brief "nature can do nothing but counsel crime" *(la nature ne peut conseiller que le crime).* The logic that follows is a radical reversal of this value system. If crime is committed naturally, effortlessly, he argues, virtue, that is "everything that is beautiful and noble" *(tout ce qui est beau et noble)* can only be "artificial, supernatural" *(artificiel et surnaturel)* and thus is always "the product of an art" *(le produit d'un art).* The term "art" allows Baudelaire to transfer his argument from the moral to the aesthetic sphere: if nature is "a bad counselor in matters of ethics," art has to take its place, apply its "veil" as a surface over nature's imperfection and vileness in an endless reformative effort. Baudelaire's argument for man's need of art as a corrective surface is first substantiated by the savage's and baby's instinctive and primitive taste for the arts of adornment and finally by fashion, which becomes the ever-changing expression for man's unrelenting effort to correct nature:

> Fashion must therefore be thought of as a symptom of the taste for the ideal that
> floats on the surface of the human brain, above all the coarse, earthy and disgust-
> ing things that life according to nature accumulates, as a sublime distortion of
> nature, or rather as a permanent effort to reform nature.
> *(La mode doit donc être considérée comme un symptome du goût de l'idéal
> surnageant dans le cerveau humain au-dessus de tout ce que la vie naturelle y
> accumule de grossier, de terrestre, d'immonde, comme une déformation sublime
> de la nature, ou plutôt comme un essai permanent et successif de réformation de
> la nature)* (*SW* 426, *PL2* 716).

The idea of permanent effort guaranties a dynamics of creativity which underlies Baudelaire's entire argumentation. In choosing cosmetics as the ultimate means to beauty, Baudelaire stretches his theory of art as artifice to the extreme. It is not the place here to investigate Baudelaire's complex attitude towards women, but in the context of "artifice," where she takes a central place next to the dandy—first in opposition to him, and then, through cosmetics, the "ruse" par excellence, becoming his equal.[29] One of the most controversial comments by Baudelaire on woman is to be found in "My Heart Laid Bare" where she is reduced to a "natural animal":

> Woman is the opposite of the Dandy. Therefore she should inspire horror. Woman is hungry, and she wants to eat; thirsty, and she wants to drink. She is in rut and she wants to get laid. What admirable qualities! Woman is natural, that is to say abominable. Thus she is always vulgar; the opposite, in fact, of the Dandy.
> *(La femme est le contraire du Dandy. Donc elle doit faire horreur. La femme a faim elle veut manger. Soif, et elle veut boire. Elle est en rute et elle veut être foutue. Le beau mérite! La femme est naturelle, c'est-à-dire abominable. Aussi est-elle toujours vulgaire, c'est-à-dire le contraire du Dandy)* (*JI* 61, *PL1* 677).

This passage, shocking and revolting if taken out of the general context of Baudelaire's other views on women,[30] is however of importance to highlight the decadent's horror of the underlying forces of nature. Camille Paglia explains this passage in such terms. Why indeed, should woman inspire horror,

> an oddly intense word in the context of the dandy. The answer is that the mineral flesh of Baudelaire's vampires restricts and confines nature's chtonian liquidity. Woman is the dandy's opposite because she lacks spiritual contour and inhabits the procreative realm of fluids where objects dissolve. All art, as a cult of the autonomous object, is a flight from liquidity. The Decadent swerve from sexual experience is identical with the Decadent creation of a world of glittering art objects. Both are responses to the horror of the female liquid realm. The Baudelairian woman is mentally and physically impenetrable.[31]

The image of fertile liquidity versus frozen sterility is striking and can be seen as a metaphor for the artistic transformation of nature into art. Baudelaire's praise of make-up constitutes a reversal of nature's and art's essence: nature in its limitations becomes sterile. Art, in its infinite possibility of combination becomes fertile in the realm of the imagination. Woman can and must become artist and artwork at the same time:

> Woman is well within her rights, we may even say she carries out a kind of duty, in devoting herself to the task of fostering a magic and supernatural aura about her appearance; she must create a sense of surprise; she must fascinate; idol that she is, she must adorn herself, to be adored . . . she must borrow, from all the arts, the means of rising above nature. . . It matters very little that the ruse and artifice be known of all, if their success is certain, and the effect always irresistible.

(La femme est bien dans son droit, et même elle accomplit une espèce de devoir en s'appliquant à paraître magique et surnaturelle; il faut qu'elle étonne, qu'elle charme; idole, elle doit se dorer pour être adorée. Elle doit donc emprunter à tous les arts les moyens de s'élever au-dessus de la nature pour mieux subjuguer les coeurs et frapper les esprits. Il importe fort peu que la ruse et l'artifice soient connus de tous, si le succès est certain et l'effet toujours irrésistible) (SW 427, PL2 717).

The accent lies here on the unconditional employment of "ruse" and "artifice" for the sake of "totality of effect" which Baudelaire had already recognized with pleasure in Poe and Delacroix and which he doesn't cease to legitimize. What is "commonly called make up" *(vulgairement appelé maquillage)* is for Baudelaire not only a "corrective" of nature but a creative device to suggest divine spirituality as well as sensuality: on the one hand, the application of rice powder provides a screen from nature's imperfections bestowed "outrageously" *(outrageusement)* on the human face, and creates, like a masque, "an abstract unity of texture and color" *(une unité abstraite dans le grain et la couleur)* approximating the human being to a "divine and superior being" *(d'un être divin et supérieur)*. On the other hand, as for black eyeliner and rouge, although their use stems from the desire to surpass nature, their color suggests refined sensuality: "Red and black represent life . . . an excessive life." *(Le rouge et le noir représentent la vie, une vie . . . excessive)*. The black around the eyes gives the appearance of "a window open to the infinite" *(une fenêtre sur l'infini)*, whereas the rouge confers an intense glow on the woman's face, which adds to it "the mysterious passion of a priestess" *(la passion mystérieuse de la prêtresse) (SW 427, PL2 717)*.

The decorative function of make-up is thus not completely dismissed by Baudelaire but relegated to a secondary level. What is at stake here is the dethronement of all imitative art:

Thus, if I have been properly understood, painting the face is not to be used with the vulgar, unavowable intention of imitating the fair face of nature, or competing with youth. It has, moreover, been observed that artifice does not embellish ugliness, and can only serve beauty. Who would dare assign to art the sterile function of imitating nature?
(Ainsi, si je suis bien compris, la peinture du visage ne doit pas être employée dans le but vulgaire, inavouable, d'imiter la belle nature et de rivaliser avec la jeunesse. On a d'ailleurs observé que l'artifice n'embellissait pas la laideur et ne pouvait servir que la beauté. Qui oserait assigner à l'art la fonction stérile d'imiter la nature? (SW 428, PL2 717).

A certain paradox cannot be overlooked here and the limitation of artifice are clearly indicated too. While artifice on the one hand constitutes the means par excellence to reform nature, it also has its limits in that it can only serve those—artists and woman alike—who have received "at birth" *(en naissant)* what Baudelaire calls in his final line "a spark of that sacred fire" *(une étincelle de ce feu sacré),* a gift precisely from nature herself. This observation is a far cry from Baudelaire's condemnation of all women as "naturally abominable" and shows Baudelaire's awareness of the limitations of any exclusive point of view. His attempt at a formulation of a theory of artifice therefore cannot only be conceived of as radical "perversion" of the "natural order of things" which in A. E. Carter's terms is the hallmark of decadent aesthetics with Baudelaire as its abettor,[32] but rather as one way to restore art's primal function, which is to create beauty at any price. Artificiality is not an end in itself but a manifestation of willpower to control, to translate, and give form to the underlying abyss upon which rests the human condition. Without that "spark of life," without this natural, inborn quality which Baudelaire defined as "naïveté" and which pertains to the artist's "inner" nature and temperament as the unquestioned and foremost requirement for true art to emerge, artificiality would be nothing but yet another system or "applied technique" unable to render or account for the infinite variety and contradictions which are the fabric out of which art is woven. Baudelaire's own words testify best of his awareness of the limitations of any systematic approach and can be seen as a warning and reminder to the reader and the critic that any one-sided interpretation of aesthetic phenomena lead to an impasse:

> Like all my friends I have tried more than once to lock myself inside a system, so as to be able to pontificate as I liked. But a system is a kind of damnation that condemns us to perpetual backsliding; we are always having to invent another, and this form of fatigue is a cruel punishment. And every time, my system was beautiful, big, spacious, convenient, tidy and polished above all; at least so it seemed to me. And every time, some spontaneous unexpected product of universal vitality would come and give the lie to my puerile and old fashioned wisdom, much-to-be-deplored daughter of Utopia. In vain did I shift or extend the criterion, it . . . was for ever chasing multiform and multicolored beauty, which dwells in the infinite spirals of life. Under the threat of being constantly humiliated by another conversion . . . I arrogantly resigned myself to modesty; I became content to feel; I came back and sought sanctuary in impeccable naiveté.
> *(J'ai essayé plus d'une fois . . . de m'enfermer dans un système pour y prêcher à mon aise. Mais un système est une espèce de damnation qui nous pousse à une*

abjuration perpétuelle; il en faut toujours inventer une autre, et cette fatigue est un cruel châtiment. Et toujours mon système était beau, vaste, spacieux, commode, propre et lisse surtout; du moins il me paraissait tel. Et toujours un produit spontané, inattendu, de la vitalité universelle venait donner un démenti à ma science enfantine et vieillote, fille déplorable de l'utopie. J'avais beau déplacer ou étendre le criterium, il . . . courait sans cesse après le beau multiforme et versicolore, qui se meut dans les spirales infinies de la vie. Condamné sans cesse à l'humiliation d'une conversion nouvelle . . . je me suis orgueilleusement résigné à la modestie; je me suis contenté de sentir; je suis revenu chercher un asile dans l'impeccable naïveté) (SW 118, PL2 578).

It is with this passage in mind that all of Baudelaire's criticism and aesthetic judgment should be approached. In the context of the theory of artificiality, this statement puts into question any final assessment as to Baudelaire's complete adherence to the theory, for the very nature of a system lies in its artificiality and by that proves insufficient and prevents the artist and critic alike to let his fingers "run nimbly up and down the vast keyboard of [precisely] nature's correspondences" *(courir avec agilité sur l'immense clavier des correspondances) (SW* 117, *PL2* 577).

84

Notes

[1] M. A. Ruff, *Baudelaire*, trans. Agnes Kertesz (New York: NYU Press, 1966), 143.

[2] Michel Foucault, "What is Enlightenment" *The Foucault Reader*, ed. Paul Rabinow (New York: Random House, 1984), 39. References to this text are designated *FR*.

[3] Christopher Norris, "What is Enlightenment?": Kant according to Foucault," *The Cambridge Companion to Foucault*, ed. G. Gutting (Cambridge: Cambridge University Press, 1994), 174.

[4] Albert Camus, *The Rebel*, trans. Anthony Bower (New York: Vintage, 1960), 46. Further references to this text are indicated with the author's name.

[5] Michel Lemaire, *Le Dandysme de Baudelaire à Mallarmé* (Paris: Klincksiek, 1978), 46. Translation is mine.

[6] Charles Baudelaire, *The Prose Poems and La Fanfarlo,* trans. Rosemary Lloyd (Oxford: Oxford University Press, 1991), 1.

[7] Charles Baudelaire, *Correspondance*, 2 vols. ed. Claude Pichois (Paris: Bibliothèque de la Pléiade, 1966), vol. 2, 141. All further references to this text are indicated by *Corr*. In English: Rosemary Lloyd, *Selected Letters of Charles Baudelaire* (Chicago: The University of Chicago Press, 1986), 166. All further references to this text are indicated by *SL*.

[8] Charles Baudelaire, *Intimate Journals*, trans. Ch. Isherwood (Westport: Hyperion Press, 1930). All references to this text are indicated *JI*.

[9] Edgar Allen Poe, *Essays and Reviews* (New York: Library of America, 1984), 1423.

[10] Patrice Bollon, *"La figure du Dandy" Magazine Littéraire* 273 (jan. 1990): 42–44.

[11] Wolfdietrich Rasch, *"Die Darstellung des Untergangs," Jahrbuch der deutschen Schiller Gesellschaft* XXV (1981): 414–434.

[12] Matei Calinescu, "The Idea of Decadence," *Five Faces of Modernity* (Durham: Duke University Press, 1987), 157.

[13] Désiré Nisard, *Essais sur L'école romantique* (Paris: Calman Lévy, 1891), 245, 248.

[14] *Armand de Pontmartin, Nouvelles Causeries de Samedi, Paris 1865, 291.*

[15] Armand de Pontmartin, *Nouvelles Semaines Littéraires*, Paris 1865, 236.

[16] Armand de Pontmartin, *Nouvelles Causeries Littéraires*, Paris 1885, 283.

[17] Translation mine.

[18] Claude Pichois, Jean Ziegler, *Baudelaire* (Paris: Julliard, 1987), 237.

[19] Jonathan Culler, "Baudelaire and Poe", *Zeitschrift für französische Sprache und Literatur* 100 (1989), 63. References to this text are indicated with the author's name.

[20] Paul Valéry, "The Position of Baudelaire," *Variety: Second Series,* trans. W. A. Bradley (New York: Harcourt, Brace and Company, 1938), 89. References to this text are indicated with the author's name.

[21] Lloyd Austin, *L'Univers Poétique de Baudelaire*, (Paris, Mercure de France, 1956), 9.

[22] If not indicated otherwise, the following quotations are from "Further Notes on Edgar Poe," *SW* 188–208 (*PL2* 319–337).

[23] Ernst Behler, *"'Eine Kunst für Künstler, nur für Künstler: Poe, Baudelaire, Nietzsche,"* *Athenäum* (Paderborn: Ferdinand Schöningh, 1994), 19.

[24] Charles Baudelaire, *Artificial Paradise*, trans. Ellen Fox (New York: Herder and Herder, 1971), 67.

[25] Baudelaire's definition of inspiration, however, contrasts with the romantic notion of inspiration when he writes in *"La Genèse d'un poème:"* " By inspiration one understands energy, intellectual enthusiasm, and a permanent alertness of one's faculties" *(par inspiration on entend l'énergie, l'enthousiasme intellectuel, et la faculté de tenir ses facultés en éveil) (PL2* 343).

[26] *Baudelaire on Poe*, trans. and ed., Lois and Francis E. Hyslop, Jr. (State College, PA: Bald Eagle Press, 1952), 156.

[27] Albert Cassagne, *La théorie de l'art pour l'art en France* (Paris: Lucien Dorbon, 1959), 326.

²⁸ Felix Leakey, *Baudelaire and Nature* (Manchester: University of Manchester Press, 1969), 140.

²⁹ Marcel Ruff in his *Baudelaire*, would not agree with this point, arguing that women, although they rehabilitate themselves through cosmetics, nevertheless are "incapable of ascending to the heights of dandyism" (Ruff 142). As will be noted, however, cosmetics can be seen as a literal metaphor for spirituality, which is a key notion for dandyism and feminine beauty alike.

³⁰ The opposite is affirmed in the chapter "Woman" in "The Painter of Modern Life," where she is "the source of the most lively . . . the most lasting joys; the being towards or for whom all [men's] efforts tend." *(L'être qui est la source des plus vives . . . des plus durables jouissances; l'être vers qui ou au profit de qui {les hommes] tendent tous leurs efforts) (SW* 423, *PL2* 713).

³¹ Camille Paglia, *Sexual Personae* (New York: Vintage Books, 1991), 430.

³² A. E. Carter, *The Idea of Decadence in French Literature* (Toronto: University of Toronto Press, 1958).

Chapter 3

RICHARD WAGNER

I.   *Wagner's Situation in France in 1860*

At the end of his essay on Wagner, Baudelaire gives a striking general statement which can be seen as an astonishingly acute characterization of Wagner himself:[1]

> In matters of art, I confess I am not opposed to excess; moderation has never appeared to me the hall-mark of a vigorous artistic nature. I like those excesses of robust health, this overflowing of will-power, which stamp themselves on a work like burning lava in the crater of a volcano, and which, in ordinary life, often accompany the phase, so full of exquisite delight, that comes after a great moral or physical crisis.
>
> *(En matière d'art, j'avoue que je ne hais pas l'outrance; la moderation ne m'a jamais semblé le signe d'une nature artistique vigoureuse. J'aime ces excès de santé, ces débordements de volonté qui s'inscrivent dans les oeuvres comme le bitume enflammé dans le sol d'un volcan, et qui, dans la vie ordinaire, marquent souvent la phase, plein de délice, succédant à une grande crise morale ou physique) (SW 355, PL2 807).*

Baudelaire's article on Richard Wagner's *Tannhäuser* in Paris is his first and only attempt at musical criticism and perhaps should not be viewed as such alone but as an opportunity, once more, for Baudelaire to develop and illustrate his own vision of aesthetic performance. With Wagner, as with Delacroix and Poe before, Baudelaire takes up the challenge to defend and discuss the work of an innovative and consequently controversial artist struggling for proper recognition of his works. In spite of Delacroix's rather reserved attitude toward him, Baudelaire never ceased to praise the painter's greatness. To this day, he is and remains Delacroix's most recognized critic. As for Poe, his impact on French symbolism and his worldwide reputation might never have happened if it hadn't been for Baudelaire. Baudelaire studied Delacroix and Poe a great deal. His preoccupation with Delacroix was lifelong, and his translations of Poe's tales, poems, and other writings occupied the last fifteen years of his life. Considering his passion for painting and for his own profession, the alchemy of words, this tenacity is not astonishing. However, because music was not a main preoccupation in his life, as he himself admits, it is all the more impressive that his essay on Wagner remains an important landmark for Wagner scholars, as well as for critics interested in theories of representation and the relation between music and literature.

Baudelaire admired Wagner for years before he actually made contact with him. He first mentions Wagner in a letter in 1849, wherein Baudelaire urges a friend to help a German critic who wants to publish a study on the *Tannhäuser* and says to his friend in prophetic terms *"vous servirez la cause de celui que l'avenir consacrera le plus illustre parmi les maîtres"* (you will be serving the cause of the one whom the future will single out as the most illustrious among all masters).[2]

The next document is a letter Baudelaire wrote to Wagner a few weeks after his much-disputed concert on January 25, 1860, at the *Théâtre des Italiens*. As André Ferran points out in his extensive study on Wagner's experience in France, this occurred at a time when Wagner, rejected by the Germans, returned to Paris in order to try his fortune there again. Wagner had already lived in Paris in 1839, 1842, and 1859 without achieving the success he had anticipated. Now, in 1860, a small group of admirers of Wagner—amongst others, Baudelaire's friends Jules François Champfleury and Théophile Gautier—was fighting to adapt and establish this "music of the future" so misunderstood and mocked. "Baudelaire was the most fervent militant of the group and combated, like always, with an impartial ardor."[3] Wagner had hoped that this concert would wipe out the humiliations he had endured during his previous performances between 1839 and 1859, but such was not the case. Before the concert had even begun, there were two camps of critics. One camp, from the *"Gazette Musicale,"* was hostile to the German composer in principle, declaring that he was devoid of talent and ideas. The other camp, composed of critics who were not actually hostile, but who went with the general attitude, was condescending and smug. The musician came to conduct in person and although there was no show of real enthusiasm, the audience was intent on being courteous. At the first intermission, there was some applause but the result was far from what Wagner had hoped for and even predicted. The main criticism targeted the length and the monotony of the pieces chosen.[4] Baudelaire's letter to Wagner precedes his essay by one year and deserves close attention since it already contains the main themes developed in detail in the later essay.

II.   *Baudelaire's Letter*

Baudelaire, outraged by the indifference with which most critics received the concert, wrote to Wagner to express his own pleasure and sense of revelation, which according to Lloyd Austin, turns out to have been more of a confirmation of Baudelaire's own ideas rather than a revelation of novelty. At this point in time most of Baudelaire's poetry had been written, and his poetics and his general aesthetic credo had already found expression. He does not see in Wagner a possible rival for poetry, nor a model to follow. According to Austin, it is only the next generation which will deal intensely with the relationship music/poetry.[5] Thus the general tone is that of an artist speaking to his equal:

> Above all, I want to say that I owe you the greatest musical pleasure I've ever experienced. I've reached an age where one hardly enjoys writing to famous men anymore and I would have hesitated much longer . . . had I not day after day set eyes on unworthy, ridiculous articles where all possible efforts are made to defame your glory. Yours is not the first case where my country has caused me suffering and shame. In short, it's indignation that has led me to express my gratitude. I said to myself: I want to be distinguished from all those jackasses.
> *(Avant tout je veux vous dire que je vous dois la plus grande jouissance musicale que j'aie jamais éprouvée. Je suis d'un âge où on ne s'amuse plus guère à écrire aux hommes célèbres, et j'aurais hésité longtemps encore . . . si tous les jours mes yeux ne tombaient sur des articles indignes, ridicules, où on fait tous les efforts possibles pour diffamer votre génie. Vous n'êtes pas le premier homme, Monsieur, à l'occasion duquel j'ai eu à souffrir et à rougir de mon pays. Enfin l'indignation m'a poussé à vous témoigner ma reconnaissance; je me suis dit: je veux être distingué de tous ces imbéciles)[6]* (SL 145, Corr1 673).

Admitting that he too had shared certain prejudices of those who mistrusted Wagner and explaining this mistrust by having been often "duped" by the music of so many "charlatans making great claims" *(charlatans à grandes prétentions)*, Baudelaire then affirms the seductive effect of Wagner's music as a shock not unlike the one he experienced reading Poe, a recognition of himself in the work of another:

> I was instantly won over. What I felt is beyond description, but if you'll deign not to laugh, I'll try to convey my feelings to you. At first it seemed to me that I knew your music already, and later . . . I understood what caused this illusion. It seemed to me that the music was my own, and I recognized it, as any man recognizes those things he is destined to love. For anyone who isn't a man of intelligence such a claim would seem ridiculous in the extreme, above all when it's written by

someone who, like me, does not know music and whose entire musical education
extends no further than listening (with great pleasure admittedly) to a few fine
pieces by Weber and Beethoven.
*(Par vous, j'ai été vaincu tout de suite. Ce que j'ai éprouvé est indescriptible, et
si vous daignez ne pas rire, j'essaierai de vous le traduire. D'abord il m'a semblé
que je connaissais cette musique, et plus tard . . . j'ai compris d'où venait ce
mirage; il me semblait que cette musique était la mienne, et je la reconnaissais
comme tout homme reconnaît les choses qu'il est destiné à aimer. Pour tout autre
que pour un homme d'esprit, cette phrase serait immensément ridicule, surtout
écrite par quelqu'un qui comme moi, ne sait pas la musique, et dont toute
l'éducation se borne à avoir entendu [avec grand plaisir, il est vrai] quelque
beaux morceaux de Weber et de Beethoven) (Corr1 673).*

Baudelaire's critique will thus not be based on "knowledge," but
on his experience of Wagner's music, and on the feelings which are produced in him by the music. He will not speak as a technician but as an
artist, a poet who translates a translation (Wagner's work) into his own
poetic language. Wagner's music becomes his music which in the final
instance is poetry.[7] Leaving aside the quarrels between the various anti-
Wagnerian camps, Baudelaire focuses—as with Delacroix and Poe—on
the power of the effect and the suggestiveness of a higher, spiritual sphere,
which confers the work a greatness and novelty ("a new musical emotion")
and instantly involves the listener, who is swept away, mind and senses
alike:

Then the element that struck me above all was the grandeur of your music. It
represents the heights, and it drives the listener to the heights . . . One instantly
feels swept up and subjugated . . . I felt all the majesty of a life greater than the
one we lead . . . I frequently experienced a rather odd emotion . . . the pride and
joy of comprehension, of allowing myself to be penetrated and invaded—a truly
sensual pleasure, recalling that of floating through the air or rolling on the sea.
*(Ensuite, le caractère qui m'a principalement frappé, ç'a été la grandeur. Cela
représente le grand, et cela pousse au grand . . . On se sent tout de suite enlevé
et subjugué . . . J'ai senti toute la majesté d'une vie plus large que la nôtre . . .
j'ai éprouvé souvent un sentiment d'une nature assez bizarre, c'est l'orgeuil et la
jouissance de comprendre, de me laisser pénétrer, envahir, volupté vraiment
sensuelle, et qui ressemble à celle de monter dans l'air ou de rouler sur la mer)
(Corr1 673).*

Here comes to light what Baudelaire considers the great achievement of an artist, namely to create "the totality of effect," which is to combine and convey to the spectator—whether reader or listener—intellectual
understanding, sensuality, and emotion all at once. This sensation of ex-

pansion, of upward movement towards a realm in which one's whole being
is filled with luminous energy and understanding of all that surrounds it, is
evoked throughout Baudelaire's entire work but comes to light particularly
strongly in regard to Wagner's music which makes him apprehend the idea
of "a soul floating in light, of an ecstasy compounded of joy and insight,
hovering above and far removed from the natural world" *(l'idée d'une âme
se mouvant dans un milieu lumineux, d'une extase faite de volupté et de
connaissance, et planant au-dessus et bien loin du monde naturel) (SW
331, PL2 785).* And in the final important passage, Baudelaire comes to
speak of what is going to constitute one of his main arguments in the essay,
namely the correspondence between sound and color:

> Finally, I experienced in addition—and I beg you not to laugh—feelings that
> probably stem from my particular cast of mind and my frequent preoccupations.
> Your music is full of something that is both uplifted and uplifting, something that
> longs to climb higher, something excessive and superlative. To illustrate this, let
> me use a comparison borrowed from painting. I imagine a vast expanse of deep
> red spreading before my eyes. If this red represents passion, I see it change gradu-
> ally, through all the shades of red and pink, until it reaches the incandescence of
> a furnace. It would seem difficult, even impossible, to render something more
> intensely hot, and yet a final flash traces a whiter furrow on the white that pro-
> vides its background. That, if you will, is the final cry of a soul that has soared to
> a paroxysm of ecstasy.
> *(Enfin, j'ai éprouvé aussi, et je vous supplie de ne pas rire, des sensations qui
> dérivent probablement de la tournure de mon esprit et de mes préoccupations
> fréquentes. Il y a partout quelque chose d'enlevé et d'enlevant, quelquechose
> d'excessif et de superlatif. Par exemple, pour me servir de comparaisons
> empruntés à la peinture, je suppose devant mes yeux une vaste étendue d'un
> rouge sombre. Si ce rouge représente la passion, je le vois arriver graduellement,
> par toutes les transitions de rouge et de rose, à l'incandescence de la fournaise.
> Il semblerait difficile, impossible même d'arriver à quelquechose de plus ardent;
> et cependant une dernière fusée vient tracer un sillon plus blanc sur le blanc qui
> lui sert de fond. Ce sera, si vous voulez, le cri suprême de l'âme montée à son
> paroxisme) (CorrI 673–74).*

The sensuous and quasi-sexual intensity of Wagner's music, which
Baudelaire, while experiencing, translates into a mental painting, is such
that it lifts the listener to the limits of sensation. It is difficult to imagine a
more eloquent compliment on the part of Baudelaire, who introduces himself at the beginning of the letter as "a man poorly suited to outbursts of
enthusiasm." At the end of the letter, Baudelaire mentions that he does has
not included his address so that Wagner would not think he may be asking

something of him, leaving it up to Wagner to respond or not. The composer's favorable reaction to Baudelaire's letter appears in Wagner's memoirs, and according to Ferran and Starkie,[8] Baudelaire soon became a frequent guest at Wagner's musical soirées.

III.   The Essay on the Tannhäuser

Baudelaire's article on Wagner was published on April 1, 1861, in *La Revue Européenne.* Although it is entitled "Richard Wagner and Tannhäuser in Paris," and appeared only a week after the fiasco of Wagner's first performance of his opera *Tannhäuser*, the essay only treats the concert Wagner gave in March 1860. Nevertheless Baudelaire forges a timely defense of Wagner in general by trying to "circumscribe as sweepingly as possible the domain of Wagner's music, as if his essay were a panoramic view over the whole Wagnerian landscape."[9] This is indeed how Baudelaire views the task he has given himself, believing that it is "more convenient, for certain types of mind, to judge of the beauty of a landscape by standing on a height, rather than by following in turn all the paths that run through it" *(plus commode, pour certains esprits, de juger de la beauté d'un paysage en se plaçant sur une hauteur, qu'en parcourant successivement tous les sentiers qui le sillonnent) (SW* 344, *PL2* 796).

At the beginning of the essay, Baudelaire, setting himself apart from all the other critics, makes a point of basing his criticism on a very personal basis: "That 'I' justly taxed with impertinence in many cases, implies however, a high degree of modesty; it imprisons the writer within the strictest limits of sincerity." *(Ce 'Je' accusé justement d'impertinence dans beaucoup de cas, implique cependant une grande modestie; il enferme l'écrivain dans les limites les plus strictes de la sincérité) (SW* 325, *PL2* 779). Recalling the thirteen months preceding the *Tannhäuser* concert, Baudelaire notes one positive aspect of the controversy surrounding Wagner, and which is entirely to Wagner's credit. His concerts provoked, even before they were performed, "a veritable battle of doctrines, like one of those solemn crises in art, beneficial crises which show a state of health and abundance in the intellectual life of a nation" *(une véritable bataille de doctrines, comme une de ces solennelles crises de l'art . . . crises heureuses qui dénotent la santé et la richesse dans la vie intellectuelle d'une nation) (SW* 326, *PL2* 780).

Wagner, shunning the expectations of the public "fond above all of virtuosos and their vocal feats" *(un public amoureux de virtuoses et de leurs tours de force)* shows his audacity by offering a program composed solely of choral and orchestral extracts. In spite of the public's general resistance, some people could not help but be enthusiastic about "those irresistible pieces" *(irrésistibles morceaux)* like the overtures of *Tannhäuser* and *Lohengrin*, including the *Wedding Music* and the *Epithalamium*. Even if some parts seemed obscure, the more intelligent critics were willing to postpone their judgment until the works were produced within their proper setting, the stage. Until then, Baudelaire notes, "as a symphonist, as an artist expressing, by means of innumerable combinations of sound, the tumults of the human soul, Richard Wagner was the equal of the most exalted and certainly as great as the greatest" *(comme symphoniste, comme artiste traduisant par les milles combinaisons du son les tumultes de l'âme humaine, Richard Wagner était à la hauteur de ce qu'il y a de plus élevé, aussi grand, certes, que les plus grands) (SW 328, PL2 781)*. In short, Baudelaire considers Wagner a romantic, but a romantic in the modern sense—one who knows how to combine, to build, consciously and willfully, a piece of art capable of reflecting an underlying idea which, ideally, should be recaptured in the listener's imagination: "Music conveys things in its own way and by means peculiar to itself. In music, as in painting, and even in the written word, which, when all is said and done, is the most positive of the arts, there is always a gap, bridged by the imagination of the hearer." *(La musique traduit à sa manière, et par les moyens qui lui sont propres. Dans la musique, comme dans la peinture et même dans la parole écrite, qui est cependant le plus positif des arts, il y a toujours une lacune complétée par l'imagination de l'auditeur) (SW 328, PL2 782)*.

What Baudelaire recognizes in Wagner immediately and which attracts him most clearly, as in Poe, is a reflective power dominating inspirational drives. His "musical rhetoric" is "worked out so thoroughly" that even without the libretto at hand, the listener would be able to grasp the ideas conveyed through Wagner's music alone:

> Yes, indeed, without the poetry Wagner's music would still be a poetic work, endowed as it is with all the qualities that go to make a well organized poem; self-explanatory, so well are its component parts united, integrated, mutually adapted, and, if I may invent a word to express the superlative of a quality, prudently

concatenated.
(En effet, sans poésie, la musique de Wagner serait encore une oeuvre poétique,
étant douée de toutes les qualités qui constituent une poésie bien faite; explicative
par elle-même, tant toute choses y sont bien unies, conjointes, réciproquement
adaptées, et, s'il est permis de faire un barbarisme pour exprimer le superlatif
d'une qualité, prudemment concatenées (SW 351, PL2 803).

This trait in Wagner has also been stressed by Thomas Mann, who relates that "sheer staying power often had to take the place of spontaneous inspiration with him; that on his own admission he was able to do his best work only with the aid of reflection" (Mann 132). The idea of Wagner as an artist in full control of his work is reiterated throughout the essay. Baudelaire detects and approves of Wagner's "overriding despotic taste for a dramatic ideal . . . where every single detail must contribute to a total effect" *(ce goût absolu, despotique, d'un idéal dramatique, . . . où tous les détails doivent sans cesse concourir à une totalité d'effet) (SW 337, PL2 790).* Wagner, through his "excellent construction technique," his "spirit of order and distribution" recalls "the structure of ancient tragedies." But he only recalls them, he does not attempt to recreate them and at this point, Wagner proves to be classical and romantic at the same time, i.e., modern in the Baudelairian sense.

As Baudelaire explains, and this explanation brings to mind the complementarity of the pair eternal/variable used in his definition of modernity, "phenomena and ideas that come back periodically down through the ages always borrow, at every reappearance, something distinctive from variants and from circumstance" *(les phénomènes et les idées qui se produisent périodiquement à travers les ages empruntent toujours à chaque résurrection le caractère complémentaire de la variante et de la circonstance).* Wagner's representation of the mythical Venus of antiquity, for example, (as Baudelaire imagines it) proves to be of a modern kind: Venus has not "traveled" through the "horrific shades of the Middle-Ages" *(les horrifiques ténèbres du Moyen-age)* unruffled. Nor does she dwell any longer in Olympus or on "the shores of some sweet-smelling archipelago" *(les rives d'un archipel parfumé)* but in going underground, "Venus has come nearer to hell, and she goes and pays regular homage to the Archdemon, prince of the flesh and lord of sin" *(Vénus s'est rapprochée de l'enfer et elle va rendre regulièrement hommage à l'Archidémon, prince de la chair et seigneur du péché) (SW 337, PL2 790).*
Wagner's Venus resembles Delacroix's women, "mysterious" beau-

ties, classical and statuesque, yet with the stamp of time and experience engraved on their traits, which makes them modern and recall the first modern one of all, Eve—after the Fall.[10] Also in his poetry, Wagner shows "a genuine liking and a perfect understanding for classical beauty" *(un goût sincère et une parfaite intelligence de la beauté classique)* combined with "a strong admixture of the romantic spirit" *(une forte dose de l'esprit romantique)*. It is this fusion of the classical and the romantic which above all stirs Baudelaire's curiosity when he states that the Wagnerian poems "may suggest to us the majesty of Sophocles and Aeschylus" *(font rêver à la majesté de Sophocle et d'Echyle),* while at the same time they "forcibly recall to our minds the mystery plays of the period when Catholicism was dominant in plastic arts" *(ils contraignent . . . l'esprit à se souvenir des Mystères de l'époque la plus plastiquement catholique).* Wagner's poems "are like those great visions that the Middle Ages spread out on the walls of its churches or wove into its magnificent tapestries" *(ces grandes visions que le Moyen Age étalait sur les murs de ses églises ou tissait dans ses magnifiques tapisseries) (SW* 338, *PL2* 791).

The idea of a giant fresco and woven tapestries as metaphors for Wagner's symphonies leads back to Baudelaire's pursuit, "namely to show that true music suggests similar ideas in different minds" *(démontrer que la véritable musique suggère des idées analogues dans des cerveaux différents).* He insists that even if one were to take away "the help provided by plastic art, scenery, the embodiment in live actors of characters created by the imagination of the dramatist and even song" *(le secours de la plastique, du décor, de l'incorporation des types rêvés dans des comédiens vivants et même de la parole chantée),* the music alone would be all the stronger, purer even to suggest analogous ideas in different minds. It seems almost as if these aforementioned "helpers" are more of a hindrance than enhancement for he states that "the more eloquent the music is, the quicker and the more clear cut will be the suggestions conveyed, the greater the chances that sensitive natures will conceive ideas akin to those that inspired the artist" *(plus la musique est éloquente, plus la suggestion est rapide et juste, et plus il y a de chances pour que les hommes sensibles conçoivent des idées en rapport avec celles qui inspiraient l'artiste) (SW* 328, *PL2* 782). To justify this hypothesis, Baudelaire compares three different interpretations of the overture to *Lohengrin*: Wagner's own program handed out at the concert, Franz Liszt's interpretation of the piece and finally Baudelaire's own "reading" of the music.

In all three texts, Baudelaire uses numerous italics, whose purpose, he says, the reader will soon understand. Baudelaire never comes back to the question of italics but has awakened the reader's curiosity. The most obvious reason for its abundant use seems to be to show the similarities and corresponding ideas among the texts. Margaret Miner, however, adds another level of meaning to the question of italics. After close scrutiny of all the italics from the point of view of grammar and context, she discovers that Baudelaire's use of them is "erratic" and finally concludes that they are "less a riddle to be solved intellectually than as an effect to be experienced sensually." This is an interesting point because it addresses the very musicality inherent in poetry:

> It is as if the italics are meant to bring the musical motif of the Prelude directly into the text of the programs. The italics would thus demonstrate that 'the written word' can translate Wagner's original in a manner that is just as musical . . . the italics aim to transpose the musical movement of the Prelude's motif directly onto the pages of Baudelaire's essay (Miner 395).

It seems doubtful, however, that Baudelaire's use of italics is indeed erratic. As Baudelaire readily concedes, there are differences between the texts. His own text especially stands out, since it is "vaguer and more abstract" *(plus vague et plus abstrait),* that is to say more suggestive. The poet's focus, however, rests on the similarities rather than on the differences, since he is convinced and would like to convince the reader as well, that "all things always have been expressed by reciprocal analogies" *(les choses s'étant toujours exprimées par une analogie réciproque)* ever since the world was created "as a complex indivisible totality" *(comme une complexe et indivisible totalité) (SW* 330, *PL2* 784). In line with his thought that ideal criticism should above all be poetic,[11] Baudelaire proceeds to strengthen his argument by inserting his poem *"Correspondances"* in lieu of further theoretical elaborations. Furthermore, in weaving together certain italicized expressions from each text, one finds a certain atmosphere taking shape in the form of a painting or a symphony. Wagner speaks of "infinite spaces" and "depths of space," Liszt of "the ineffable beauty of the sanctuary," Baudelaire of "rare joy that dwells in high places." Wagner speaks of a "luminous apparition," Liszt of the colors "gold," "greenish chrysolyte," "opal," and "cymophane," Baudelaire of "diffused light" as well as "light growing in intensity." Space and light are perceived by all three writers in a similar fashion. Wagner is thus the master "in depicting space and depth, material and spiritual" *(à peindre l'espace et la profondeur, matériels et spirituels)*; he is a virtuoso for "he has the art of rendering by subtle gradations all that is excessive, immense, ambitious in both spiritual and natural man" *(il possède l'art de traduire, par des gradations subtiles, tous ce qu'il y a d'excessif, d'immense, d'ambitieux, dans l'homme spirituel et naturel)* (*SW* 329–330, *PL2* 783–784). At last Wagner comes close to the snake-charmer in that "the sound of that ardent, despotic music seems to recapture for the listener, against the background of shadow torn asunder by reverie, the vertiginous imaginings of the opium smoker" *(il semble parfois, en écoutant cette musique ardente et despotique, qu'on retrouve peintes sur le fond des ténèbres, déchiré par la rêverie, les vertigineuses conceptions de l'opium)* (*SW* 332, *PL2* 785).

Baudelaire states that from this first concert, it seemed to him that he had undergone "a spiritual operation" *(une opération spirituelle)*, "a revelation" *(une révélation)*, that he had discovered something new which he found himself powerless to define. Feeling annoyed and challenged by this powerlessness and spurred on by curiosity to understand Wagner's "mysterious intentions" *(intentions mystérieuses)* and a "technique" unknown to him, Baudelaire decides to "exchange [his] sensuous pleasure for knowledge" *(de transformer ma volupté en connaissance)* before it is too late, that is "before a performance on the stage brought complete enlightenment" *(avant qu'une représentation scénique vînt me fournir une élucidation parfaite)* (*SW* 333, *PL2* 786).

Yet with this last remark, Baudelaire seems to implicitly reject the idea of a "complete" knowledge, or of "concrete revelation" which he thinks could be furnished by a an actual performance (which might even reveal itself to be disappointing); instead, in addition to quoting from texts by and about Wagner, Baudelaire seems to prefer to use his imagination combined with his knowledge of the librettos, rather than to risk being disturbed by the memory of a stage performance. It is therefore less the "technical knowledge" than the confirmation of his own ideas about Wagner the man, the artist and art in general, that Baudelaire is seeking in these texts. As Baudelaire states, amongst the documents "I propose to select only those that seem to me the most appropriate for illuminating and defining the nature and character of the master" *(je ne veux extraire que ceux qui me paraissent plus propres à éclairer et à définir la nature et le caractère du maître)* (*SW* 334, *PL2* 787).

The two main points Baudelaire sorts out are first Wagner's "capacity for suffering" *(facilité de souffrir)*, which is a common and even necessary trait in all good artists because it is a result of their acute and overdeveloped "sense of justice and beauty" *(instinct du juste et du beau)*. Then Baudelaire notes Wagner's early love for the theater and music, which instilled in him the capacity of thinking on two levels at the same time: the musical and the poetical. Since myth is at the center of any discussion about Wagner, Baudelaire quotes extensively from Wagner himself:

> The myth is the primitive and anonymous poetry of the people, and we find it taken up again in every age, remodeled constantly by the great poets of cultivated ages. In the myth, indeed, human relations discard almost completely their conventional form, intelligible only to abstract reason; they show what is really human in life, what can be understood in any age, and show it in that concrete form, exclusive of all imitation, that confers upon all true myths their individual character, which is recognizable at the first glance *(SW* 339).

Wagner's definition of myth and the role it plays in the creative process of representation corresponds and responds to Baudelaire's own conception of art—modern art—namely the combination of the eternal, that which is eternally human and occurs over and over again, and the circumstantial, the individual, original, and particular form in which this purely human element presents itself and is presented differently at every epoch according to the artist's spirit and temperament. It is particularly the universality of the myth which Baudelaire highlights in his own definition of myth as:

> a tree that grows everywhere, in every climate under the sun, spontaneously and without propagation. The religions and the poetry of the four corners of the globe provide us with abundant evidence on this subject. Just as sin is everywhere, so is redemption everywhere, so is myth everywhere. What is more cosmopolitan than the Eternal?
> *(le mythe est un arbre qui croit partout, en tout climat, sous tout soleil, spontanément et sans boutures. Les religions et les poésies des quatre parties du monde nous fournissent sur ce sujet des preuves surabondantes. Comme le péché est partout, la rédemption est partout, le mythe partout. Rien de plus cosmopolite que l'Eternel) (SW* 348, *PL2* 800).[12]

Each of the three overtures represents for Baudelaire different aspects of eternally human themes of which the one in *Tannhäuser* probably comes closest to Baudelaire's own preoccupations.

Tannhäuser echoes Baudelaire's famous double postulation voiced in "My Heart Laid Bare," according to which "there are in every man, always, two simultaneous allegiances, one to God, the other to Satan" *(il y a dans toute homme, à toute heure, deux postulations simultanées, l'une vers Dieu, l'autre vers Satan) (JI 67, PL1 682). Tannhäuser* is the musical and poetic representation of this idea. It "represents the struggle between the two principles . . . the flesh and the spirit, hell and heaven, Satan and God" *(représente le lutte des deux principes . . . la chair avec l'esprit, l'enfer avec le ciel, Satan avec Dieu).* Each of these two principles is expressed by two thematic melodies—one "religious," the other "sensual," which according to a formula Baudelaire borrows from Liszt "are established here like the terms of an equation, which are resolved in the finale." Baudelaire illustrates the "equation" as follows:

> The Pilgrim's Chorus appears first with all the authority of the supreme law, as though emphasizing at once the true meaning of life, the goal of the universal pilgrimage, God, in other words. But as the inner sense of the divine is soon smothered in every conscience, by the lusts of he flesh, so is the melody symbolizing holiness gradually submerged by the sounds of pleasure. The true, the terrible, the universal Venus already emerges in every imagination.
> *(Le Chant des pèlerins apparaît le premier, avec l'autorité de la loi suprême, comme marquant tout de suite le véritable sens de la vie, le but essentiel de l'universel pèlerinage, c'est-à-dire Dieu. Mais comme le sens intime de Dieu est bientôt noyé dans toute conscience par les concupiscences de la chair, le chant représentatif de la sainteté est peu à peu submergé par les soupirs de la volupté. La vraie, la terrible, l'universelle Vénus se dresse déjà dans toutes les imaginations) (SW 341, PL2 794).*

From this passage and others in this text, it seems that Baudelaire's attention is not held so much by the idea of a final resolution which consists of a feeling of "redemptive beatitude" but rather by a relentless intensity, produced by the balanced alternation of these principles, "a power of contrast that makes an irresistible impact on our minds" *(une puissance de contraste qui agit irrésistiblement sur l'esprit) (SW 343, PL2 795).*

Furthermore, a closer look at Baudelaire's own "representation," which is both translation and interpretation, allows the reader to recognize that greater emphasis is given to the "sensual" melodies which are, after all the ones that not only save Wagner's love-theme from triviality but also confer greatness to his music. Baudelaire emphasizes more than once that in the *Tannhäuser* it is not the question of "a ditty of commonplace lovers trying to kill time in cool arbors" *(un chant d'amoureux vulgaires, essayant de tuer le temps sous les tonnelles),* but something not only "truer and more sinister" *(plus vrai et plus sinistre)* but simply more stimulating: "Languorous delights, lust at fever heat, moments of anguish, and a constant returning towards pleasure, which holds out hope of quenching thirst but never does; raging palpitations of heart and senses, imperious demands of the flesh, the whole onomatopoeic dictionary of love is to be heard here." *(Langueurs, délices mêlées de fièvre et coupées d'angoisses, retours incessants vers une volupté qui promet d'éteindre, mais n'éteint jamais la soif; palpitations furieuses du coeur et des sens, ordres impérieux de la chair, tout le dictionnaire des onomatopées de l'amour se fait entendre ici)* (*SW* 324, *PL2* 794).

Although the religious melody follows the turbulence of the senses and establishes a certain state of balance by throwing a calming veil over the "sickly and disordered" *(maladif et désordonné)* outbursts, it seems that Baudelaire increasingly concentrates on the "sensual," that is the more "diabolical" expressions of Wagner's music. He thereby draws Wagner closer into his own "moral universe," which is marked by an unresolvable tension between the two principles, with a marked predilection, however, for the overabundance of energy expressed in the sensual as opposed to the "peaceful" grounds of the religious. "Whence," asks Baudelaire, "has the master drawn this frenzied song of the flesh, this total knowledge of the diabolical element in man" *(où donc le maître a-t-il puisé ce chant furieux de la chair, cette connaissance absolue de la partie diabolique de l'homme)* if not from his awareness, like Baudelaire's, that "every well-ordered brain has within it two infinities, heaven and hell" *(tout cerveau bien conformé porte en lui deux infinis, le ciel et l'enfer),* and that "in any image of one of these it suddenly recognizes the half of itself" *(dans toute l'image de l'un de ces infinis il reconnaît subitement la moitié de lui-même).* And Baudelaire insists again: "there is nothing trivial here" in this sensual part of the overture, "rather is it the overflowing of a powerful nature, pouring into evil all the strength it should devote to the cultivation of good; it is love, unbridled, vast, chaotic, raised to the height of an anti-religion, a satanic religion." *(c'est plutôt le débordement d'une nature énergique, qui verse dans le mal toutes les forces dues à la culture du bien; c'est l'amour effréné, immense, chaotique, élevé jusqu'à la hauteur d'une contre-religion, d'une religion satanique)* (*SW* 343, *PL2* 796).

Wagner's merit is all the greater since he has the courage to choose to emphasize the more problematical, and for Baudelaire undoubtedly the more intriguing side of human nature. By expressing "the overabundance of desire and energy, the indomitable, unrestrained ambition of a delicate soul that has taken the wrong road" *(l'excès dans le désir et dans l'énergie, l'ambition indomptable, immodérée, d'une âme sensible qui s'est trompée de voie)*, Wagner avoids the "vulgarity" *(vulgarité)* which so often accompanies the depiction of love, this "most popular" *(le plus populaire)* of feelings, which Baudelaire is tempted to call feeling of "the populace" *(populacier)*. Also, and this is a point which he again shares with Poe and Delacroix, Wagner always favors simplicity to increase the intensity of effect and convey the idea that lies behind;

> In the plastic representation of the idea, he wisely discarded the irksome crowd of victims, the Elviras by the dozen. The pure idea, personified by the one and only Venus, conveys a clearer, more eloquent message. Here is no ordinary libertine, flitting from beauty to beauty, but man in general, universal man, living morganatically with the absolute ideal of love, with the queen of all the she-devils, the female fauns and female-satyrs, banished below ground since the death of the great Pan . . .
> *(Dans la représentation plastique de l'idée, il s'est dégagé heureusement de la fastidieuse foule des victimes, des Elvires innombrables. L'idée pure, incarnée dans l'unique Vénus, parle bien plus haut et avec plus d'éloquence. Nous ne voyons pas ici un libertin ordinaire, voltigeant de belle en belle, mais l'homme général, universel, vivant morganatiquement avec l'idéal absolu de la volupté, avec la reine de toutes les diablesses, de toutes les faunesses et de toutes les satyresses, reléguées sous terre depuis la mort du grand Pan. . .) (SW* 344, *PL2* 796).

Finally, it is not with a feeling of "redemptive beatitude" that *Tannhäuser* ends in Baudelaire's narrative. In accordance with Wagner's predilection for the "heroic style," Tannhäuser "the sinner," when realizing the irreparable nature of his crime, not only accepts his fate but experiences a "feeling almost ineffable by its very terror" *(le sentiment presque ineffable, tant il est terrible)*, namely "joy in damnation" *(la joie dans la damnation)*. Be it damnation or salvation, it ultimately doesn't matter as much as the power and energy of one's aspirations. "Come from Satan, come from God—who cares" *(De Satan ou de Dieu, qu'importe)*[13]—if only a chance of a glimpse of the infinite is revealed to the human, all too human, being. As André Ferran concludes, "What matters to Baudelaire is a certain human—or rather superhuman—quality in man. Baudelaire announces the Nietzschean superman" (Ferran 278).

Richard Wagner amply meets Baudelaire's foremost requirement by which an artist "a man really worthy of that great name, must surely have in him something essentially *sui generis,* by the grace of which he is himself and not someone else" *(un homme vraiment digne de ce grand nom, doit posséder quelque chose d'essentiellement sui generis, par la grâce de quoi il est lui et non un autre) (SW* 355, *PL2* 806). Like Delacroix and Poe, Wagner is an artist in spite of himself, that is, he can't escape his temperament, his "ardent personality" which is precisely what saves him from being trivial and confers on him a creative power expressed by "nervous intensity, violence in passion and in will-power" *(intensité nerveuse, la violence dans la passion et dans la volonté).* It is also this passionate element which adds to everything Wagner touches "a superhuman element" *(un je ne sais quoi de surhumain),* which in turn is the unmistakable sign for his modernity. Like Delacroix, Wagner is modern not by the choice of his subjects, but by his temperament: "if by the choice of his subjects and his dramatic method, Wagner comes close to antiquity, by the passionate energy of his expression he is in our day the most genuine representative of modern man" *(si, par le choix de ses sujets et sa méthode dramatique, Wagner se rapproche de l'antiquité, par l'énergie passionnée de son expression il est actuellement le représentant le plus vrai de la nature moderne) (SW* 355, *PL2* 806).

As soon as Baudelaire had finished his article, he send a copy to Wagner who replied with the following letter:

> I have on several occasions been to your house, without finding you in. You can imagine how anxious I am to tell you the tremendous pleasure you have given me by your article, which honors and encourages me more than anything that has ever been said about my poor talent. Will it be possible for me to tell you soon, in person, how transported I felt as I read those beautiful pages which explain to me, just as the finest poem might, the impressions which I am proud to have awakened in so highly sensitive a temperament as yours? A thousand thanks for all your good favors to me, and believe me I am proud to be able to count you among my friends (Starkie, 422).

Notes

1 Thomas Mann, "The Sorrows and Grandeur of Richard Wagner" *Pro and Contra Wagner,* trans. Allan Blunden (Boston: Faber and Faber, 1985), 91–148. Wagner appears in Mann's portrait as a split personality, oscillating between health and spiritual crisis: "He was endowed with vast resources of good temper and inexhaustible resilience, this dispirited melancholic, whose illness was simply a socially unconventional form of health" (119).

2 *Correspondances,* 2 vols., Claude Pichois, ed. Paris: Gallimard, La Pléiade, 1966 (vol. 1, 157). Subsequent references to this text will appear as *Corr* followed by volume number and page reference. Translations of the text are my own.

3 André Ferran, *L'Esthétique de Baudelaire* (Paris: Hachette, 1933), 278. Further references to this text appear with the author's name.

4 Enid Starkie, *Baudelaire* (Norfolk, CT: New Directions, 1958), 418. Further references to this text appear with the author's name.

5 Lloyd Austin, *L'univers poétique de Baudelaire* (Paris: Mercure de France, 1956), 264.

6 Letter of 17 February, 1860, in *Selected Letters,* 145–146, and *Correspondances* vol. 1, 672–674. This discussion represents the entire letter.

7 Philippe Lacoue-Labarthe, "Baudelaire contra Wagner," *Etudes françaises* 17.3–4 (1991): 23–52. In this article, the author argues that in his letter and subsequent essay, Baudelaire does not simply submit to the superiority of Wagner's music but in fact *writes* Wagner and thus, from the point of view of the confrontation between music and poetry, Baudelaire goes on to show that music is in itself writing: "Music is poetry only insofar as it is, by nature and function scripture, system. That is, in Baudelairian terms, book."

8 Ferran, André. *L'Esthétique de Baudelaire* (Paris: Hachette, 1933), 317, and Enid Starkie, *Baudelaire* (Norfolk: New Directions, 1958), 410.

9 Margaret Miner, "Putting the Emphasis on Music: Baudelaire and the Lohengrin Prelude," *Nineteenth Century French Studies* 21.3–4 (1993): 384. Further references to this text appear with the author's name.

10 "The Painter of Modern Life," *SW* 403, *PL2* 695.

[11] This theme is developed in Chapter 1.

[12] C. Pichois's note to this passsage (*PL2* 1466) suggests that here, Baudelaire founds, a long time before C. G. Jung, a poetic science of myths and archetypes. See Bettina L. Knapp, "Baudelaire and Wagner's Archetypal Operas," *Nineteenth Century French Studies* 17 (Fall-Winter 1988–89): 56–69.

[13] Charles Baudelaire, "Hymne à la Beauté," *Les Fleurs du mal,* trans. R. Howard (Boston: D. Godine, 1983), 207. French: p.28.

NIETZSCHE

Chapter 4

ROMANTICISM AND MODERNITY

I.   The Question of Romanticism in Nietzsche

Nietzsche's relationship to romanticism is characterized by ambivalence from the first to the last. In general, it is Nietzsche's negative assessment of romanticism, as a product of pessimism and decadence, which stands in the foreground of scholarly attention. And it is true that most of the time Nietzsche uses his efforts to invent ever more "spiritual cures" *(eine geistige Kur)*, that he calls "anti-romantic self-treatment" *(antiromantische Selbstbehandlung)* against the physical "attacks" *(Erkrankung)* that he literally feels as "the danger of romanticism" *(die Gefahr der Romantik)*.[1] That he continually feels compelled to lead a campaign against "the danger of romanticism" suggests that he is well aware of certain romantic traits in his own nature—to which he refuses to yield, however, after *The Birth of Tragedy.*

Nietzsche always addresses the question of romanticism (decadence and pessimism) in terms of awareness: to be a romantic is less a problem than not to know that one is a romantic. As Adrian del Caro puts it, for Nietzsche, "the trick is to know one's weakness."[2] Furthermore, since romanticism is also defined by Nietzsche as a psychological condition, an essentially life-negating attitude, it has to be overcome. Failure to do so betrays one's surrender to the force behind this self-negating attitude: the Christian cross.

Nietzsche's understanding of romanticism as a historical, philosophical, and aesthetic world-view is formed by a European perspective which is German and French. Rousseau represents for Nietzsche one of the initial and most unnerving proponents of romanticism. And it is through Rousseau and Kant (and his philosophical investigations of the subjectivity of truth) that romanticism—"passion" and "spiritual sensuality"—prevailed in the decisive battle in the eighteenth century between romanticism and enlightenment. For Nietzsche, the romantic movement continued full force through the first half of the nineteenth century, reaching its most refined form and expression in the late French romanticism of Eugène Delacroix and George Sand.

Such authors as Shelley, Stendhal, Leopardi, Heine, and Emerson, who in literary history are generally considered as romantics, were not considered so by Nietzsche.[3] Alongside Richard Wagner and Arthur Schopenhauer, who he considers the two main representatives of romanticism, appear Victor Hugo, Brahms, Berlioz, even Ingres—and with certain reservations, Baudelaire.

In his article "Nietzsche und die Frühromantische Schule," Ernst Behler highlights certain correspondences between Nietzsche and the more theoretically minded German romantics, in particular, the Schlegel brothers, and suggests that Nietzsche's general understanding of romanticism is composed of three elements. Although coming dangerously close to cliché, they have become the dominant conceptions of romanticism in the nineteenth century, and continue to influence our understanding of it today.[4]

The first common characterization of romanticism comes from Goethe's famous metaphor equating the classical with health and the romantic with illness, Novalis being the prototype of the death-yearning romantic. Without recourse to Novalis, Nietzsche takes this equation and intensifies the opposition sick/healthy and romantic/classical to the utmost.

The second characterization, developed by Hegel, depicts romanticism as the disintegration of reason in favor of a free-floating, unattached, and irresponsible subjectivity. From the early 1880s on, Nietzsche sees late French romanticism in this light, and is particularly attentive to its "capacity for artistic passion" *(die Fähigkeit zu artistischen Leidenschaften)*, and "that devotion to form, for which the phrase *l'art pour l'art* has been invented, along with a thousand others" *(zu Hingebungen an die Form, für welche das Wort l'art pour l'art, neben tausend anderen, erfunden ist).*[5] *(KSA* V 199) *(L'art pour l'art* easily passes into *tout pour rien).*

His third characterization of romanticism goes back to Heinrich Heine's thesis, which defines romanticism as a movement exclusively oriented towards the past and entirely absorbed by a Catholic clericalism, not to mention an anti-progressive even reactionary sensibility that causes the neglect of more pressing questions and matters (Behler 69). It is late German romanticism that Nietzsche has in mind when he speaks about the romantic movement, which "brings into honor older, primitive sensibilities and especially Christianity, the folk-soul, folk-lore, folk-speech, the medieval world, oriental estheticism, the world of India"[6] *(ältere, primitive*

*Empfindungen und namentlich das Christenthum, die Volksseele,
Volkssage, Volkssprache, die Mittelalterlichkeit, die orientalische
Aesthetik, das Indertum zu Ehren bringen) (KSA* III 171). The reactionary tendencies of romanticism thus accentuated by Heine are interpreted
by Nietzsche as "a furious resolve against everything that is 'now'" *(eine
wütende Entschlossenheit gegen Alles,was 'jetzt' ist).* That the romantics frequently reverted to the Christian faith, Nietzsche sees as the "usual
romantic finale," *(das übliche Romantiker-Finale),* namely, as a "break-
down, return, collapse before an old faith, before the old God"[7] *(Bruch,
Zusammenbruch, Rückkehr und Niedersturz vor einem alten Glauben,
vor dem alten Gotte) (KSA* I 21).

He turns his attack on romanticism against himself in "An Attempt
at a Self-Criticism," a short but radical preface which he added later to an
edition of his first book, *The Birth of Tragedy* (1872). In this preface,
composed in 1886 when he was writing *Beyond Good and Evil*, Nietzsche
reexamines his first book, written under the romantic spell of Schopenhauer's
philosophy and conceived in honor of Richard Wagner. Retrospectively
Nietzsche attempts to shift certain accents of this "impossible" but also
"audacious" book, whose main flaw for Nietzsche is that it naively established an analogy between the "grandiose Greek problem" and the hope for
the revival of the "German spirit" through Richard Wagner's musical
Gesamtkunstwerk.

Fourteen years after the book's appearance and ten years after his
break with Wagner, Nietzsche tries to "salvage" the good points of his book
and to point out, if not correct, its shortcomings, which he attributes to his
youthful and optimistic attitude at the time. Apart from the fact that it is
"constructed from a lot of immature, over green personal experiences,"
(aufgebaut aus lauter vorzeitigen, übergrünen Selbsterlebnissen) it is
a book for and from "an exceptional type of artist for whom one might have
to look far and wide . . . a book full of psychological innovations and artists'
secrets," *(für eine Ausnahme-Art von Künstlern, nach denen man
suchen muß . . . voller psychologischen Neuerungen und Artisten-
Heimlichkeiten)* and above all "with an artists' metaphysics in the background" *(mit einer Artisten-Metaphysik im Hintergrunde).* Nietzsche attempts to explain his earlier impulse to construct this artists' metaphysics,
which implies the idea of art as a religion, a consolation, a redeeming force,
and a promise of some better realm "beyond" life itself:

What found expression here was . . . a strange voice, the disciple of a still 'unknown God,' one who concealed himself for the time being under the scholar's
hood, under the gravity and dialectical ill-humor of the German, even under the bad
manners of the Wagnerian . . . a mystical, almost maenadic soul that stammered
with difficulty . . . in a strange tongue, almost undecided whether it should commu-
nicate or conceal itself. It should have sung, this 'new soul'—and not spoken.
(Hier redete . . . eine fremde Stimme, der Jünger eines noch 'unbekannten Gottes,'
der sich einstweilen unter die Kapuze des Gelehrten, unter die Schwere und
dialektische Unlustigkeit des Deutschen, selbst unter die schlechten Manieren des
Wagnerianers versteckt hat . . . wie eine mystische und beinahe mänadische Seele
die mit Mühsal . . . in einer fremden Zunge stammelt . . . fast unschlüssig darüber
ob sie sich mittheilen oder verbergen wolle . . . Sie hätte singen sollen, diese 'neue
Seele'—und nicht reden) (BT 20, KSA I 15).

The most interesting point in this passage is the notion of concealment, which Nietzsche seems to condemn. The "true" author of this book,
it seems, had not yet reached the stage of the self-critical author now speaking. Disguised as a "disciple," a "scholar," a "Wagnerian," only a "strange
voice" could be heard, a voice prevented from singing because it tried "to
express by means of Schopenhauerian and Kantian formulas strange and
new valuations" *(dass ich mühselig mit Schopenhauerischen und*
Kantischen Formeln fremde und neue Werthschätzngen auszudrücken
suchte). Apparently what he had been trying to express was "a valuation
of life—purely artistic and anti-Christian . . . called Dionysian" *(eine*
Gegenwerthung des Lebens, eine rein artistische, eine antichristliche .
. . die dionysische).

Nietzsche, definitely marked by romanticism while endeavoring to
break away from it, seems to remain, as shall be seen, in that very state
which he characterizes in the passage above as the undecidedness between communication and concealment. He was torn between direct condemnation of and hopeless entanglement in romanticism. Even while writing *Human, All Too Human* and apparently freed from Wagner's and
Schopenauer's bonds, Nietzsche feels compelled to condemn romanticism,
and by that protestation reveals his lingering, unwanted but real feeling for
romanticism.

At the point Nietzsche was writing his "Attempt at a Self-Criticism," he looked at his book with a "much older, a hundred times more
demanding, but by no means a colder eye which has become a stranger"
(älteren, hundert Mal verwöhnterem, aber keineswegs kälter
gewordenem Auge, das auch jener Aufgabe nicht fremder wurde) to

the main task of this otherwise "sentimental" *(gefühlsam)*, sharp-edged book. What he was attempting was "to look at science from the perspective of the artist, but at art from the perspective of life" *(die Wissenschaft unter der Optik des Künstlers zu sehn, die Kunst aber unter der des Lebens) (BT 19, KSA I 14)*. Life, art, and science, three key words in Nietzsche's philosophy of the future: art as a form of science, science as an art form and both always in the service of life. This seems to be the main thrust of his work from *The Birth of Tragedy* on, though always with a different shift of perspective or a displacement of accent.

In the last aphorism of the "Attempt," Nietzsche addresses the question of romanticism directly in an indirect way. Making use of a stylistic method dear to him, he invents a fictional party, the critical reader, who voices his reservations about the reactionary tendency of romanticism:

> But my dear Sir, what in the world is romantic if your book isn't? Can deep hatred against 'the Now' against 'reality' and 'modern ideas' be pushed further than you pushed it in your artists' metaphysics? Believing sooner in the Nothing, sooner in the devil than in 'the Now'? Is it not a deep bass of wrath and the lust for destruction that we hear humming underneath all of your contrapuntal vocal art and seduction of the ear . . . Isn't this the typical creed of the romantic of 1830, masked by the pessimism of 1850? . . . Is your pessimist's book not itself a piece of anti-Hellenism and romanticism . . . in any case a narcotic, even a piece of music, German music?
>
> *(Aber, mein Herr, was in aller Welt ist Romantik, wenn nicht Ihr Buch Romantik ist? Lässt sich der tiefe Hass gegen 'Jetztzeit,' 'Wirklichkeit' und 'moderne Ideen' weiter treiben, als es in Ihrer Artisten-Metaphysik geschehen ist?-welcher lieber noch an das Nichts, lieber noch an den Teufel, als an das 'Jetzt' glaubt? Brummt nicht ein Grundbass von Zorn und Vernichtungslust unter aller Ihrer contrapunktischen Stimmen-Kunst und Ohren-Verführerei hinweg . . . ist das nicht das ächte rechte Romantiker-Bekenntnis von 1830, unter der Maske des Pesssimismus von 1850? . . . Wie? ist Ihr Pessimisten-Buch nicht selbst ein Stück Antigriechenthum und Romantik . . . ein Narkotikum jedenfalls, ein Stück Musik sogar, deutscher Musik?) (BT 25, KSA I 21).*

II.   The Birth of Tragedy: *Communication and Concealment*

Nietzsche's answer to this question moves restlessly between affirmation and negation, between communication and concealment. Although *The Birth of Tragedy* is considered to be a deeply romantic book, the term romanticism, oddly enough, is nowhere to be found in the text. Clearly, enthusiasm, daring, and passionate, ornate linguistic verve, all attributes of a romantic nature, are at work here. Dialectical opposition on the one hand and complex and incomplete developments on the other, imaginative schematization and philological elaborations are all mixed together in this text so resistant to summarization. Julian Young's extremely brief abstract addresses the most important issue, namely art as the healing force for a human condition anchored in suffering:

> If one attempted to summarize the essence of its complex argument the following might be offered: we stand in need of a 'solution' to the suffering and absurdity of life. The Greeks found such a solution in the art of their great tragedians. Our only hope for a solution—given the untenability of Christianity in the modern age—lies in the rebirth of such art in the music-dramas of Richard Wagner.[8]

Young's perspective is that in *The Birth of Tragedy*, Nietzsche's solution represents an entirely Schopenhauerian world-view, a flight from and denial of life. For Young, there is a definitive break in Nietzsche's thought between his first (and in his eyes most pessimistic) work, and the later works—beginning with his "positivistic phase" of *Human, All Too Human,* published in 1876. Young disagrees with scholars who seek to incorporate *The Birth of Tragedy* into the body of Nietzsche's work "by driving a wedge between Schopenhauer's 'sick' philosophy and the healthier turn taken, even at the beginning, by Nietzsche's" (Young 27). Nietzsche's foremost translator, Walter Kaufmann, is one of the main scholars to take such a position:

> Instead of proving himself in his first book as an unswerving follower of Schopenhauer—as has so often been taken for granted—Nietzsche discovered in Greek art a bulwark against Schopenhauer's pessimism. One can oppose the shallow optimism of so many Western thinkers and yet refuse to negate life. Schopenhauer's negative pessimism is rejected along with the superficial optimism of the popular Hegelians and Darwinists: one can face the terrors of history and nature with unbroken courage and say 'yes' to life.[9]

Whether Nietzsche really was a pessimist—in his words a romantic—at the time of *The Birth of Tragedy,* or whether he was always already in the process of overcoming it, is likely to remain an open question. To compound the difficulty, one must add that Nietzsche also differentiates between "pessimism of weakness" and "pessimism of strength." His own retrospective claims, far from giving a straightforward answer, oscillate between communication and concealment, and thus elude the very notion of a "solution" as propounded by Young.

One of the most revealing statements, which forms the basic thought of the book, appears in the preface to Richard Wagner, where Nietzsche affirms "that art represents the highest task and the truly metaphysical activity of this life" *(dass ich von der Kunst als der höchsten Aufgabe und der eigentlich metaphysischen Thätigkeit dieses Lebens . . . überzeugt bin) (BT 32, KSA I 24)*.

In *The Birth* he describes the ideal version of this metaphysical activity as the dialectical and harmonious interplay of the two Greek mythological deities—Apollo and Dionysos. Nietzsche makes clear from the beginning that he only "borrows" their names for want of a better designation, in order to illustrate his very personal idea of what he proposes as the highest form of art—Greek tragedy. This art form, which came into being "by a metaphysical miracle of the Hellenic will" *(durch einen metaphysischen Wunderakt)*, represents in a certain way the ideal archetype for Richard Wagner's musical dramas.

It is not so much the static portrait of two deities that Nietzsche draws but rather the inherent tendencies these two figures embody:

> as artistic energies which burst forth from nature herself, without the mediation of the human artist—energies in which nature's art impulses are satisfied in the most immediate and direct way—first in the image world of dreams . . . then as intoxicated reality.
> *(als künstlerische Mächte betrachtet, die aus der Natur selbst, ohne Vermittelung des menschlichen Künstlers, hervorbrechen, und in denen sich ihre Kunsttriebe zunächst und auf directem Wege befriedigen: einmal als Bilderwelt des Traumes . . . andererseits als rauschvolle Wirklichkeit) (BT 38, KSA I 30)*.

The dehumanization of the artist, who becomes the medium of nature's two most powerful drives, is at the same time a deification of art. Art becomes the ultimate interplay and expression of appearance and reality, form and content, dreams, and ecstasy, the Apollonian and Dionysian.

Nietzsche makes an interesting equation between the philosophical/Schopenhauerian man, who has the "presentiment that the reality in which we live and have our being is also mere appearance" *(das Vorgefühl, dass auch unter dieser Wirklichkeit, in der wir leben und sind, eine zweite ganz andere verborgen liege)*, and the position of the "esthetically sensitive man," *(der künstlerisch erregbare Mensch)* who stands in the same relation to the reality of dreams as the philosopher does to the reality of existence, and who "is a close and willing observer, for these images afford him an interpretation of life, and by reflecting on these processes he trains himself for life" *(er sieht genau und gerne zu: denn aus diesen Bildern deutet er sich das Leben, an diesen Vorgängen übt er sich für das Leben).*

Apollonian dream images are by no means all simply "agreeable and friendly" *(angenehm und freundlich)*, not made of a shining surface alone. They gain their depth in the reality and company of "the serious, the troubled, the sad, the gloomy, the sudden restraints, the tricks of accident, anxious expectations, in short, the whole divine comedy of life, including the inferno" *(das Ernste, Trübe, Traurige, Finstere, die plötzlichen Hemmungen, die Neckereien des Zufalls, die bänglichen Erwartungen, kurz die ganze "göttliche Komödie" des Lebens, mit dem Inferno).*

Life is possible and worth living because man, usually dwelling in an "incompletely intelligible everyday world" *(lückenhaft verständlichen Tageswelt),* gains from the "soothsaying" *(wahrsagende)* Apollonian, a glimpse into "the higher truth" *(die höhere Wahrheit),* which can be best defined as an "immediate understanding of things" *(alle Formen sprechen zu uns)* or a complete vision of the world in which "nothing [is] unimportant or superfluous" *(es gibt nichts Gleichgültiges oder Unnöthiges)* (*BT*,35, *KSA* I 27).

The Apollonian, as sculptural and verbal form-giving energy, also means the imposition of limits, a necessary "measured restraint," which is liberating since it allows "freedom from the wilder emotions" *(Freiheit von den wilderen Regungen).* Apollo, the sun-god, the deity of light and "ruler over the beautiful illusion of the inner world of fantasy" corresponds to the Schopenhauerian image of "the man wrapped in the veil of Maya" *(der im Schleier der Maja befangene Mensch),* the sailor who sits quietly in his frail bark in the midst of a stormy sea, sustained by and trusting in the "principium individuationis" (principle of individuation), his armor of individuality. It is this very principle of individuation which guarantees beautiful illusions and conceals knowingly and wisely the "tremendous terror" *(das ungeheure Grausen),* as well as the "blissful ecstasy" *(wonnevolle Verzückung)* welling from the depths of nature and man.

It is the Dionysian that commands most of Nietzsche's attention and provokes the most inspired, engaged, enthusiastic passages in *The Birth of Tragedy,* a book whose first subtitle was significantly "out of the spirit of music" *(aus dem Geiste der Musik)* before it was changed to "or Hellenism and Pessimism" *(oder Griechenthum und Pessimismus).*

If the Apollonian is the art of sculpture (in the largest sense of the term, i.e., of solid form-giving), the Dionysian is the art of music (i.e., of fluid-floating). Whereas the Apollonian represents cool self-awareness and intellectual presence, the Dionysian is pure emotion. The intensity of sensory perception and emotional thrill in the Dionysian state of being is so high and dense—intoxicating—that "everything subjective vanishes into complete self-forgetfulness" *(das Subjective zu völliger Selbstvergessenheit hinschwindet) (BT* 36, *KSA I* 29).

The Dionysian impulse represents the most primitive, the most powerful, the most expressive life force in men. In line amazingly with romantic folklore, Nietzsche conjures up an idealized vision of the Middle Ages, with its swelling, singing, dancing crowds, to illustrate the Dionysian impulse. And here is a rare occurrence of Nietzsche's identification with romanticism as the revival and celebration of folk-spirit, an indirect analogy to the Wagnerian Bayreuth festivals. Keeping in mind Nietzsche's later agreement with the Goethean identification of the romantic with the sick, one finds here, the contrary, a complete reversal of the image. Nietzsche contends that those who "from obtuseness or lack of experience" *(aus Mangel an Erfahrung oder aus Stumpfsinn)* judge these Dionysian folk-revelings as "folk-diseases" *(Volkskrankheiten)* are themselves sick precisely because of their "contemptful and pitying" *(spöttisch oder bedauernd)* attitude, defined by Nietzsche as "corpselike and ghostly . . . healthy-mindedness" *(leichenfarbige und gespenstige Gesundheit).*

Before it was Apollo who freed man from the bonds of passion, now it is Dionysos who frees man from all "hostile barriers that necessity, caprice, or 'impudent convention' have fixed between man and man" *(die starren, feindseligen Abgrenzungen, die Noth, Willkür oder 'freche Mode' zwischen den Menschen festgesetzt haben).* In contrast to Apollo, whose principle of individuation is isolating and dividing, Dionysos brings "the gospel of universal harmony" *(Evangelium der Weltharmonie),* revealing to each one not only that he is "united, reconciled, and fused with his neighbor, but as one with him, as if the veil of Maya had been torn aside and were now merely fluttering in tatters before the mysterious primordial unity" *(Jeder mit seinem Nächsten nicht nur vereinigt, versöhnt, verschmolzen, sonderns eins, als ob der Schleier der Maja zerrissen wäre und nur noch in Fetzen vor dem geheimnisvollen Ur-Einen herumflattere) (BT* 37, *KSA* I 30).

The destructive power of the Dionysian goes hand in hand with an unconscious, creative impulse, which wills expression like an irrepressible urge, and uplifts—physically as well as spiritually—anyone under its spell.

> In song and dance man expresses himself as a member of a higher community; he
> has forgotten how to walk and speak and is on the way toward flying into the air,
> dancing. His very gestures express enchantment. Just as the animals now talk,
> and the earth yields milk and honey, supernatural sounds emanate from him too:
> he feels himself a god ... in ecstasy. He is no longer an artist, he has become a work
> of art: in these paroxysms of intoxication the artistic power of all nature reveals
> itself to the highest gratification of primordial unity. The noblest clay, the most
> costly marble, man, is here kneaded and cut, and to the sound of the chisel strokes
> of the Dionysian world-artist rings out the cry of the Eleusinian mysteries: 'Do
> you prostrate yourselves, millions? Do you sense your Maker, world?'
> *(Singend und tanzend äussert sich der Mensch als Mitglied einer höheren
> Gemeinsamkeit: er hat das Gehen und das Sprechen verlernt und ist auf dem
> Wege, tanzend in die Lüfte emporzufliegen. Aus seinen Gebärden spricht die
> Verzauberung. Wie jetzt die Thiere reden, und die Erde Milch und Honig giebt, so
> tönt auch aus ihm etwas Uebernatürliches: als Gott fühlt er sich...so verzückt und
> erhoben. Der Mensch ist nicht mehr Künstler, er ist ein Kunstwerk geworden: die
> Kunstgewalt der ganzen Natur, zur höchsten Wonnebefriedigung des Ur-Einen,
> offenbart sich hier unter den Schauern des Rausches. Der edelste Thon, der
> kostbarste Marmor wird hier geknetet und behauen, der Mensch, und zu den
> Meisselschlägen des dionysischen Weltenkünstlers tönt der eleusinische
> Mysterienruf: 'Ihr stürzt nieder, Millionen? Ahnest du den Schöpfer, Welt?') (BT
> 37, KSA I 30).*

This passage is one of the few which illustrates clearly Nietzsche's affinity with the quasi-religious nature-cult as it flourished during the romantic period. The pastoral image of milk and honey provided by Mother Nature is one strong example. The human being, in the trance-like state of total immersion in nature, becomes the medium through which a godly voice reveals itself as art. Furthermore, one can think of the opposition male/female in terms of the two archetypal deities. Apollo, form-giving authority, appears as a kind of father (*BT* 41, *KSA* I 34). And Dionysus appears closely related to the female principle, since it is through his "triumphant cry ... the spell of individuation is broken, and the way lies open to the Mothers of Being, to the innermost heart of things" *(unter dem mystischen Jubelruf des Dionysus der Bann der Individuation zersprengt wird und der Weg zu den Müttern des Sein's, zu dem innersten Kern der Dinge offen liegt) (BT* 101, *KSA* I 103).

Camille Paglia, whose critical interpretation of the Dionysian and Apollonian is essentially centered around the question of gender, as the title of her book *Sexual Personae* suggests, offers an interesting perspective on the topic. She draws a direct connecting line from the two Greek gods, who continue to operate actively as the "two great Western principles [which] govern sexual personae in life and art," through nineteenth century aesthetics, up to art of the present day.[10] Just as in *The Birth of Tragedy*, which she mentions only in passing, but which seems to have been a source of inspiration, definitions of either principle abound sometimes to the point of confusion. Apollo is presented as the "hard, cold separatism of Western personality and categorical thought . . . " He represents "obsessiveness, voyeurism, idolatry, fascism—frigidity and aggression of the eye, petrification of objects" (Paglia 96). As an Olympian, which Paglia equates with Western civilization, Apollo is aristocratic, and consequently "authoritarian and repressive." And what they repress, these Westerners and Olympians, are nature's impulses, which Paglia elevates to the status of "the monstrous giantism of chtonian nature, that murky night-world from which society must be reclaimed day by day" (Paglia 73). Dionysos, "the heir to the Great Mother of chtonian nature" is:

> the all-embracing totality of mother-cult. Nothing disgusts him, since he contains everything there is. Disgust is an Apollonian response, an aesthetic judgment. Disgust always indicates some misalignment toward or swerving away from the maternal . . . the nineteenth century estheticism, a vision of a glittering crystalline world, is a flight from the chtonian swamp into which nature-loving Wordsworth led Romanticism. Estheticism insists on the Apollonian line, separating objects from each other and from nature. Disgust is Apollonian fear at a melting borderline (Paglia 93).

The notion of disgust is an important one in Nietzsche's thought and gains in importance as his critique of romanticism—and in relation to it, modernism—intensifies. He sees a dominant Apollonian impulse finding expression in late French romanticism and its formalistic obsessions, an aesthetic which becomes synonymous with decadence.

For Nietzsche, disgust, which appears as "nausea" in Kaufmann's translation and as "Ekel" in Nietzsche's text, is the logical outcome of a pessimistic, overly refined, and above all, Christian state of being, against which he fought all his life. His favorite creation and ideal companion Zarathustra is characterized as "the man who overcame the great nausea" *(der Ueberwinder des grossen Ekels)* (*KSA* IV 334).[11] And in *Ecce Homo*, Nietzsche confesses: "Nausea at man is my danger" *(Der Ekel am Menschen ist meine Gefahr)* (*KSA* VI 371).[12] This statement, made in his last published book and written in the present tense, indicates Nietzsche's unresolved struggle against a kind of romanticism whose imperative is form and effect at any price. It seduces him but also threatens his unconditional taste for life, the necessary fabric from which art is woven.

III.   The Tragedy: Classical Versus Romantic

It should not be forgotten, however, that what is aimed at in *The Birth of Tragedy*, and what makes classical Attic Tragedy the ultimate form of art, is a balanced interplay between the two artistic drives. Although Nietzsche makes it clear that the chasm between the two is fundamentally unbridgeable, the interplay of the Apollonian and the Dionysian is nevertheless crucial to capture and express truthfully, i.e., the most artfully, the essence of the world, which for Nietzsche, as for Schopenhauer and the Greeks, is suffering. To illustrate the Greeks' attitude, Nietzsche recounts the legend of Dionysos's companion Silenus telling King Midas that for mankind the best thing would be not to have been born and the second best would be to die soon (*BT* 42, *KSA* I 35). And for Nietzsche it was the Greeks' solution to this conviction, their will to imagination—or illusion— which saved them from pessimism and guaranteed their dignity. The Greeks' invention of the gods and the Olympian world is thus a means to cope with the terrifying reality of being. Thus "out of the original Titanic order of terror, the Olympian divine order of joy gradually evolved through the Apollonian impulse toward beauty, just as roses burst from thorny bushes" *(aus der ursprünglichen titanischen Götterordnung des Schreckens durch jenen apollinischen Schönheitstrieb in langsamen Uebergängen die olympische Götterordnung der Freude entwickelt wurde: wie Rosen aus dornigem Gebüsch hervorbrechen)* (*BT* 43, *KSA* I 36).

This impulse toward beauty is the very impulse "which calls art into being as the complement and consummation of existence, seducing one to a continuation of life" *(der die Kunst ins Leben ruft als die zum Weiterleben verführende Ergänzung und Vollendung des Daseins)*. The Gods become a "a transfiguring mirror" *(ein verklärender Spiegel)*, justifying man's existence by living mankind's passions, which Nietzsche calls the "only satisfactory theodicy" *(die alleingenügende Theodicee)*. Through the Apollonian transformation of Dionysian truth into an "existence under bright sunshine," Silenus's pronouncement is reversed to such a degree that "lamentation itself becomes a song of praise" *(dass selbst die Klage zu seinem Preisliede wird)*—perhaps the shortest formula for the Attic Tragedy.

To arrive at this desirable stage of harmony, which Nietzsche defines with Schiller's term "naive" as "oneness of man with nature," however, is hard work. Harmony is not a given condition, as Rousseau's *Emile* suggests, but a struggle between two forces in which the the Apollonian may win, but not before it must overthrow "Titans and slay monsters" and has "triumphed over an abysmal and terrifying view of the world." The beauty of Greek art expresses great suffering, not some idealistic union with nature.

Homer is the Apollonian Greek, that is the "naive" artist *par excellence*. The artificiality of the Apollonian naïveté cannot be overlooked, for the Apollonian state of being can exist only as long as it is "artificially dammed up" *(künstlich gedämmte Welt)* against the "bewitching" and "alluring" sounds *(lockender Zauberweisen)* of the Dionysian, which in its natural state of "intoxication," *(Rausch)* "self-oblivion," *(Selbstvergessenheit)*, and "excess" *(Uebermaass)* reveals itself as "truth" *(Wahrheit)*. The Greeks' strength lies in their ability to cope with the nausea brought on by Dionysian truth, to overcome it in the desire for wholeness through the willful self-deception of Apollonian illusion:

> The Dionysian man resembles Hamlet: both have once looked truly into the essence of things, they have gained knowledge, and nausea inhibits action; for their action could not change anything in the eternal nature of things; . . . knowledge kills action; action requires the veil of illusion.
>
> *(In diesem Sinne hat der dionysische Mensch Aehnlichkeit mit Hamlet: beide haben einmal einen wahren Blick in das Wesen der Dinge gethan, sie haben erkannt, und es ekelt sie zu handeln; denn ihre Handlung kann nichts am ewigen Wesen der Dinge ändern; . . . die Erkenntnis tötet das Handeln, zum Handeln gehört das Umschleiertsein durch die Illusion) (BT* 60, *KSA* I 57).

The Apollonian, however, is in itself part of the "titanic" and "barbaric." The Apollonian Greek recognized that "despite all its beauty and moderation, his entire existence rested on a hidden substratum of suffering and of knowledge, revealed to him by the Dionysian" *(sein ganzes Dasein mit aller Schönheit und Mässigung ruhte auf einem verhüllten Untergrunde des Leidens und der Erkenntnis, der ihm wieder durch jenes Dionysische aufgedeckt wurde) (BT* 46, *KSA* I 40). The struggle between these forces thus continues *ad infinitum* straight into the modern age. Whenever the Dionysian ("the willing," nature unadorned) wins, "contradiction, the bliss born of pain, [speaks] out from the heart of nature," and the the Apollonian is "destroyed." Whenever the Apollonian wins ("con-

templation," nature artificially adorned) "the authority and majesty" of the
sun god shows itself as more "rigid and menacing" than ever. The sobriety
of Doric art is "explicable only as a permanent military encampment of the
Apollonian" *(ein fortgesetztes Kriegslager des Apollinischen).*

For Nietzsche, however, a point of perfection seems to be reached
in the struggle when both forces meet and reunite in a tragedy composed of
poetry and music. The objective Nietzsche attempts to reach in his investigation of the mystery—or the magic, one might say—surrounding the union
of the Apollonian and the Dionysian is ultimately a romantic ideal in which
the difference between the "objective" (the Apollonian) and the "subjective" (the Dionysian) is canceled out, or as he says in *Ecce Homo* while
reflecting on his earlier book, "in tragedy, this antithesis is sublimated into a
unity" *(in der Tragödie, der Gegensatz zur Einheit aufgehoben)* (*EC*
271, *KSA* VI 310).

Nietzsche starts out with the assumption, taken over from
Schopenhauer, that music is a "repetition and recast of the world" *(eine
Wiederholung der Welt und ein zweiter Abguss derselben).* Since in
ancient lyric poetry, the lyrist is identified with the musician, or in other
words the Dionysian artist, this very same artist, having "identified himself
with the primal unity, its pain and contradiction . . . produces the copy of this
primal unity as music" *(gänzlich mit dem Ur-Einen, seinem Schmerz und
Widerspruch, eins geworden und producirt das Abbild dieses Ur-Einen
als Musik).* Having given up his subjectivity during the Dionysian process,
the artist, touched by Apollo's laurel, perceives the image, which shows him
his identity "with the heart of the world" *(dem Herzen der Welt)* as a
"dream scene" *(Traumszene)* that "embodies the primordial contradiction
and primordial pain, together with the primordial pleasure, of mere appearance" *(die jenen Urwiderspruch und Urschmerz, sammt der Urlust des
Scheines, versinnlicht).* In this mirroring process, the artist becomes a
mere symbol of what Nietzsche calls "the world-genius" *(Weltgenius)* which
is the "one truly existent subject" *(das eine wahrhaft seiende Subject),*
celebrating through the artist become "medium" *(Medium)* his "release in
appearance" *(seine Erlösung im Scheine).* In other words, the artist has
no individual power, he is not even a creative subject but an instrument, an
aesthetic translation at best, through which "the true author" of this world
speaks (*BT* 50, *KSA I* 44).

Nietzsche's portrait of the artistic "genius" is, as Young suggests,
"essentially continuous with the Kant-Schopenhauer conception of the art-

ist as 'genius.'" This is, because "as with Schopenhauer, the artist is portrayed essentially as a bringer of metaphysical and hence (since, for Nietzsche as for Schopenhauer, the domain of the conceptual is confined to the phenomenal world) conceptually unparaphrasable news" (Young 37). Nietzsche later satirizes the romantic concept of genius, the deification of the artist into "an oracle, a priest, indeed more than a priest a kind of mouthpiece of the 'in itself' of things, a telephone from the beyond . . . [a] ventriloquist of God" *(ein Orakel, ein Priester, ja mehr als ein Priester, eine Art Mundstück des 'An-sich' der Dinge, ein Telephon des Jenseits . . . dieser Bauchredner Gottes)*[13] *(KSA* V 346). This is not an attack on Schopenhauer and Wagner and romanticism alone, but also upon his own credo in his early years.

Nietzsche cautions that his true author or "will" does not operate from a moral point of view:

> For to our humiliation and exaltation, one thing above all must be clear to us. The entire comedy of art is neither performed for our betterment or education nor are we the true authors of this art world. On the contrary, we may assume that we are merely images and artistic projections for the true author and that we have our highest dignity in our significance as works of art—for it is only as an aesthetic phenomenon that existence and the world are eternally justified.
>
> *(Denn dies muss uns vor allem, zu unserer Erniedrigung und Erhöhung, deutlich sein, dass die ganze Kunstkomödie durchaus nicht für uns, etwa unserer Besserung und Bildung wegen, ausgeführt wird, ja dass wir ebensowenig die eigentlichen Schöpfer jener Kunstwelt sind: wohl aber dürfen wir von uns selbst annehmen, dass wir für den wahren Schöpfer derselben schon Bilder und Projectionen sind und in der Bedeutung von Kunstwerken unsere höchste Würde haben—denn nur als aesthetisches Phänomen ist das Dasein und die Welt ewig gerechtfertigt) (BT* 52, *KSA* I 47).*

It is precisely this view of art as metaphysical consolation for the basic horror underlying life—art as the absolute truth of being—which Nietzsche later will modify: no longer art as substitute for life, as "metaphysical supplement of the reality of nature," but life itself as an eternal justification for existence.

As Nietzsche reflects back on *The Birth of Tragedy* in *Ecce Homo*, he readily concedes that the book "smells offensively Hegelian" from the point of view of the "idea," namely, the all too systematic "antithesis of the Dionysian and the Apollonian—translated into the realm of metaphysics"—and furthermore conceiving of "history itself as the development of this

'idea.'" If, as Nietzsche continues, "in tragedy this antithesis is sublimated
into a unity" this union, however, appears itself as a fiction—a myth—in
which, already in *The Birth of Tragedy*, the importance of the Dionysian
predominates.

IV.   Decline of Vitality: Critique of Modernity with
Euripides and Socrates

The centrality of the Dionysian is clear from the fact that classical
Attic Tragedy as conceived by Aeschylus and Sophocles is born precisely
out of the vitality of Dionysian arch-power and condemned to die when this
power is suppressed and negated. The death of tragedy and thus the decline of Greek mythology coincides with the rise of a modern consciousness
embodied by the "artist-critic" Euripides, who himself is only the medium of
a more powerful and "newborn demon" called Socrates. Even before
Euripides, however, Greek myth followed a "natural" path towards death
which, in Nietzsche's eyes corresponds to a fatalistic meeting of myth with
reality, "for it is the fate of every myth to creep by degrees into the narrow
limits of some alleged historical reality . . . " Attic Tragedy is seen by
Nietzsche simultaneously as the greatest moment in art's history, and also
the shortest, since it the brief flicker of an heroic age—which, before its
inevitable decay, reached its peak when the Dionysian was not yet repressed:

> and in these hands it flourished once more with colors such as it had never dis-
> played, with a fragrance that awakened a longing anticipation of a metaphysical
> world. After this final effulgence it collapses, its leaves wither, and soon the
> mocking Lucians of antiquity catch at the discolored and faded flowers carried
> away by the four winds. Through tragedy the myth attains its most profound
> content (the Dionysian), its most expressive form (the Apollonian); it rises once
> more like a wounded hero, and its whole excess of strength, together with the
> philosophic calm of the dying, burns in its eyes with a last powerful gleam.
> *(und in seiner Hand blühte er noch einmal, mit Farben wir er sie noch nie gezeigt,
> mit einem Duft, der eine sehnsüchtige Ahnung einer metaphysischen Welt erregte.
> Nach diesem letzten Aufglänzen fällt er zusammen, seine Blätter werden welk, und
> bald haschen die spöttischen Luciane des Alterthums nach den von allen Winden
> fortgetragenen, entfärbten und verwüsteten Blumen. Durch die Tragödie kommt
> der Mythus zu seinem tiefsten Inhalt, seiner ausdrckvollsten Form; noch einmal
> erhebt er sich, wie ein verwundeter Held, und der ganze Ueberschuss von Kraft,
> samt der weisheitsvollen Ruhe des Sterbenden, brennt in seinem Auge mit letztem,
> mächtigen Leuchten) (BT 75, KSA I 74).*

With this impressive image of the giant heroine, the dying tragedy, Nietzsche prepares the terrain to highlight all the better the damages done by the critical modern countercurrent manifested in Socratism, and all philosophical thought built on a belief in reality over vision, or reason over speculation. Nietzsche presents the death of tragedy in the form of a conspiracy. The melancholy death of tragedy is consummated and stripped of its dignity by the death-blow of Socrates' eager agent, Euripides, who replaces the mythic Greek ideal with modern reality. Concretely this perversion of tragedy, and its subsequent vulgarization in the "New Attic Comedy" *(neuere attische Komödie)* happened because of what Nietzsche describes as the appearance of the spectator, this "faithful mask of reality" *(die treue Maske der Wirklichkeit)* on the stage. No longer does drama present heroes or idealized nature mirroring essential traits of human nature, but instead offers a "painful fidelity that conscientiously reproduces even the botched outlines of nature" *(zeigte jetzt jene peinliche Treue, die auch die misslungenen Linien der Natur gewissenhaft wiedergibt)*, chasing away the beneficial image of illusion *(BT 77, KSA I 76)*.

On stage Odysseus is superseded by the bourgeois, "the good-naturedly cunning house-slave" *(gutmüthig-verschmitzter Haussclave)*, who embodies "civic mediocrity" *(die bürgerliche Mittelmässigkeit)* by portraying everyday life stories of common mortals. In the wake of Euripidian drama, the aesthetic spectacle of the classical tragedy is perverted into "a game of chess—the New Comedy—with its perpetual triumphs of cunning and craftiness" *(schachspielartige Gattung des Schauspiels, die neuere Komödie mit ihrem fortwährenden Triumphe der Schlauheit und Verschlagenheit)*. Reason and critical thought rule over tragic wisdom and instinct. The "modern" Greek as educated by Euripides no longer needs art for metaphysical comfort but enjoys it for purely didactic purposes. The stage is no longer a place of Dionysian rapture shared by the "multitude" *(die Masse)*, but it becomes a classroom for the masses *(die Massen)*, who are taught "how to observe, debate, and draw conclusions according to the rules of art and with the cleverest sophistries" *(mit den schlausten Sophisticationen zu beobachten, zu verhandeln und Folgerungen zu ziehen)*. The New Attic Comedy ushered in the "enlightened masses" *(die aufgeklärte Masse)* versus the wise few. The consequence of such a change is loss of perspective and that "Greek cheerfulness," of which Nietzsche spoke all his life. This cheerfulness is willful, a consciously artificial superficiality born out of a profound wisdom about the fundamentally tragic nature of existence (*BT* 78, *KSA I* 78). It is in the preface to *The Gay Science* that Nietzsche speaks most enthusiastically of this life-affirming attitude:

> Oh those Greeks! They knew how to live. What is required for that is to stop courageously at the surface, the fold, the skin, to adore appearance, to believe in forms, tones, words, in the whole Olympus of appearance. Those Greeks were superficial—out of profundity.
> *(Oh diese Griechen! Sie verstanden sich darauf, zu leben: dazu thut Noth, tapfer bei der Oberfläche zu bleiben, den Schein anzubeten, an Formen, an Töne, an Worte, an den ganzen Olymp zudes Scheins zu glauben! Diese Griechen waren oberflächlich—aus Tiefe!)*[14] (*KSA* III 352).

With the rise of Socratic optimism reflected in the New Attic Comedy, "profundity," defined as knowledge and acceptance of the "tragic dissonance" on which human existence is based, is canceled out and the higher art of living turns into mere superficiality: "it is the cheerfulness of the slave who has nothing of consequence to be responsible for, nothing great to strive for, and who does not value anything in the past or future higher than the present" *(so ist es die Heiterkeit des Sclaven, der nichts Schweres zu verantworten, nichts Grosses zu erstreben, nichts Vergangenes oder Zukünftiges höher zu schätzen weiss als das Gegenwärtige)* (*BT* 78, *KSA* I 78).

Adrian del Caro sees in Nietzsche's denunciation of Socratic optimism, defined as a religion of truth through cognitive science, the romantic's pursuit of absolute primacy of creativity over cognitive values:

> For the romanticist, art serves to uncover truth, not to obscure it, because art is closest to the happening of truth. When the civilized person chooses to pursue truth by cognitive means, a wedge is driven between man and nature. It is the moment, in the language of many romanticists, when the mythology of a people is exploded in the process of attempting to ground religion historically. When the mythological core is sundered art and philosophy become sundered as well . . . such a division is highly artificial, according to the romanticist, and is one that forces the modern or civilized individual to lie at odds with himself. . . . (del Caro 193).

Paradoxically it is with Socratic optimism's vanquishing of Greek pessimism that the dissatisfaction of modern man is sealed. The optimistic spirit, which finds one of its most characteristic expressions in the philosopher Socrates, functions as an "enormous driving-wheel" not only "behind"

Socrates and through him, but as a force—or a drive—well ingrained in man, and thus present in many stages of history.

Nietzsche's critique of modern society from *The Birth of Tragedy* on is based on what he believes to be the devastating ascendance of a scientific world view with its delusion of limitless power over a tragic world view with its willingness to believe in beauty and illusion. Thus the optimistic spirit, blind to the darker truth of being, carries "the germ of destruction," which it injects into society. Praising the classical Greek world as a short lived but invaluable moment when the art of living reached perfection—an almost timeless moment when the form and content of existence fused—Nietzsche criticizes its opposite—the "naturalistic" *(naturalistische)* essentially "inartistic" *(unkünstlerische)* modern world. In order to arrive at the desirable image of "the music-making Socrates," i.e., again making a romantic fusion between two contrary principles, Nietzsche uses the very same method he condemns in what he calls "theoretical man." Highly interesting is the fact that Nietzsche, in his analysis and critique of the Euripidian drama picks out precisely those points which he later uses against Wagner, so that Euripides, in a way, becomes the forerunner, so to speak, of Wagnerian romantic opera.

One example can be seen in Nietzsche's concept of the actor. Having defined the "true" actor as "dispassionately cool" *(affectlos kühl)*, as he "who precisely in his highest activity is wholly mere appearance, and joy in mere appearance" *(der gerade in seiner höchsten Thätigkeit, ganz Schein und Lust am Scheine ist)*, Nietzsche condemns the new actor who mimics feelings where there are only "cool and paradoxical thoughts." This type of actor shows no comprehensive link to the work he is supposed to represent, but is merely searching for effect; he is public-oriented. The unity of form and content, as reached with the interplay of the Apollonian and Dionysian in classical Greek tragedy, is lost in Euripidian drama. It can either be "freezing" or "burning," but can never bring these two qualities together harmoniously:

Now, in order to be effective at all, it requires new stimulants, which can no longer lie within the sphere of the...Apollonian and the Dionysian. These stimulants are cool and paradoxical thoughts replacing Apollonian contemplation—and fiery affects, replacing Dionysian ecstasies; and, it may be added, thoughts and affects copied very realistically and in no sense dipped into the ether of art.
(und jetzt, um überhaupt zu wirken, neue Erregungsmittel braucht, die nun nicht mehr innerhalb der beiden einzigen Kunsttriebe, des apollinischen und dionysischen

liegen können. Diese Erregungsmittel sind kühle paradoxe Gedanken—an Stelle
der apollinischen Anschauungen—und feurige Affecte—an Stelle der dionysischen
Entzückungen—und zwar höchst realistisch nachgemachte, keineswegs in den
Aether der Kunst getauchte Gedanken und Affecte) (BT 83, KSA I 84).

Another example of artistic degeneration in Euripidian drama and by extension in modern opera, is the use of a certain type of music (the "new dithyramb") which is "tone painting" *(Tonmalerei)*, a musical "imitation by means of concepts" *(durch Begriffe vermittelte Nachahmung)* instead of the expression or symbol of "the inner essence, the will itself" *(das innere Wesen, den Willen selbst) (BT 106, KSA I 112).* Sarah Kofman points out that this is also one of the criticisms of which Nietzsche will accuse Wagner in his later texts:

> Making the sound a metaphor for the image, is to make bad music, like in opera: it is a downright abuse of power . . . The symbolism of music, then, is purely conventional; music becomes transformed into rhetoric . . . merely to stimulate deadened or slackened nerves. This musical rhetoric is no more than a caricature of Dionysianism, a counterfeit, a piece of play-acting.[15]

Yet another change brought about by "this un-Dionysian myth-opposing spirit" *(dieses undionysischen gegen den Mythus gerichteten Geistes)* is the loss of "eternal type" *(ewiger Typus)* in favor of psychologically explainable and thus understandable "character representation"—one more proof that scientific knowledge in the modern age is given a higher value than "artistic reflection of a universal law" *(künstlerische Wiederspiegelung einer Weltregel) (BT 108, KSA I 113).*

A last but no less important point in Nietzsche's critique of modern dramas is his criticism of their artificially constructed "denouements" *(Schlüssen).* Where there once was the sensation of metaphysical comfort at the end of a tragic play, now there is only "an earthly resolution of the tragic dissonance" *(eine irdische Lösung der tragischen Dissonanz),* a disappointingly happy ending in form of the "deus ex machina" *(BT 109, KSA I 114).*

V.   The Alexandrian Culture or the Illusion of Progress

Nietzsche's critique of the modern age is based on what one might now call his deconstructive method, and his psychological analysis of the Socratic paradox which continues to function through the ages.

Its contention is the modern belief in the (problematic) notion of truth—as opposed to myth—as the ultimate basis for value in life, a notion founded on the idea of infinite progress achieved through an ongoing process of uncovering. As it relates to contemporary literary theory, Peter Pütz has shown how Nietzsche, in his unmasking of the theoretical man's doomed optimism, has recognized the paradox or dialectics of Enlightenment, and thus anticipated critical theory by half a century:

> Enlightenment destroys the old myth, falling, however, into a new one. Enlightenment is reasonable (rational), but its relationship to reason is religious. Through reason and science it wishes to better the world progressively and to ennoble the individual.[16]

This task, according to Nietzsche is bound to fail.

For Nietzsche, the artist as he appears in the second half of *The Birth of Tragedy*, is always closer to the truth than the theorist, for he chooses instinctual wisdom over "positive" knowledge. While the artist wisely remains within the confines of appearance through covering veils, the theorist's task and pride consists "of an ever happy uncovering that succeeds through his own efforts" *(in dem Prozess einer immer glücklichen, durch eigene Kraft gelingenden Enthüllung) (BT 94, KSA I 98)*. Although small insights might be gained in the process of the scientific method, ultimate truth, despite one's efforts, keeps retreating. Truth eludes science, since it is itself built on a metaphysical "illusion" *(Wahnvorstellung)*, on "the unshakable faith that thought, using the thread of causality, can penetrate the deepest abyss of being, and that thought is capable not only of knowing being but even of correcting it" *(jener unerschütterliche Glaube, dass das Denken das Sein nicht nur zu erkennen, sondern sogar zu corrigieren im Stande sei) (BT 95, KSA I 99)*.

Aesthetic Socratism, which makes the idea of beauty dependent on intellectual clarity ("to be beautiful everything must be intelligible"), links aesthetics directly to the sphere of morality. Morality, and the corresponding Socratic maxims—"virtue is knowledge; man sins only from ignorance; he who is virtuous is happy"—try to negate the realm of tragedy. This delusion, which Nietzsche sees as a negative instinct accompanying science, has, however, an unexpectedly positive side to it. It pushes science "again and again to its limits at which it must turn into art" *(immer und immer wieder zu ihren Grenzen, an denen sie in Kunst umschlagen muss) (BT* 96, *KSA I* 99).

The true purpose of science, according to Nietzsche, is to turn into art. In excluding error as "the evil par excellence," the scientific man errs himself, since he fails to recognize that error, or what Nietzsche calls in aesthetic terms "dissonance," is at the bottom of all things and thus impossible to ignore, or as the scientist would have it, obliterate. In believing in the illusion of a linear progression towards absolute, ultimate, irrefutable truth, the logic of science bites its own tail, forced to recognize its futility in the darkness that defies "illumination" *(das Unaufhellbare)*. The recognition of blindness again constitutes—paradoxically—the Socratic optimist's "tragic insight," which to be endured, needs art as "protection and remedy" *(Schutz und Heilmittel) (BT* 98, *KSA* I 101).

Socratic culture (or Alexandrian, theoretical, or modern) is built on shaky ground, for it lives in fear of its own logical consequences. At some point it is forced to recognize that it no longer trusts the validity of its own foundations. Weakness, confusion, and disruption are the lot of the modern man, who appears to be so "pampered by his optimistic views" that he is forced to become his own censor, who above all suffers from incompleteness.

This existential dilemma is reflected in the modern genre of the opera, which is born not out of an aesthetic need but a nonaesthetic, i.e., moral and theoretical need. This is shown by opera's extra-artistic representational style, which subjects music to the text (the rediscovered language of [the] primitive man), and betrays by that a nostalgia for the idyllic life, the belief "in the primordial existence of the artistic and good man" *(an eine urvorzeitliche Existenz des künstlerischen und guten Menschen) (BT* 116, *KSA I* 122). The good and artistic primitive man, however, is an invention, a lie fabricated by the theoretician and "critical laymen," by "the man incapable of art" *(der kunstohnmächtige Mensch)*, incapable of aesthetic feeling, and unable to conceive of, much less to behold, an artistic vision. To achieve—at least—an effect, he turns for support from all manner of extra-artistic help—from the machinist to the decorator.

The tragic hero is replaced by "the eternally piping or singing shepherd" *(der ewig flötende oder singende Schäfer)*. From a lack of true feeling, he engages desperately in the imitation of passion, literally performing emotional excitement, a rather ridiculous endeavor, naively missing its mark "as if emotion had ever been able to create anything artistic" *(als ob je der Affect im Stande gewesen sei, etwas Künstlerisches zu schaffen)*

(*BT* 117, *KSA I* 124).

Nietzsche exposes opera as a pseudo-artistic phantom, the pitiful result of a pessimistic attitude towards life disguised under the cloak of optimism. The all too obvious show, however, provokes nausea in everyone who unmasks the artificiality of this idyllic reality as a mere "fantastically silly dawdling" *(ein phantastisch läppisches Getändel)*, a form of deception over "the terrible seriousness of true nature" *(den furchtbaren Ernst der wahren Natur)* (*BT* 119, *KSA* I 125). Operas in which the "ugly" and "disharmonic," (or in Socratic terms, "the unintelligible") are repressed; they can be nothing more than a form of mere entertainment whose only concern is either "a frivolous deification of the present or a dully dazed retreat" *(eine leichtsinnige Vergötterung der Gegenwart oder stumpf betäubte Abkehr)* (*BT* 138, *KSA* I 149).

For Nietzsche, however, the worth of an artwork, and thus of an entire people, who are the reflection of that artwork, resides precisely in its transcendental quality, in its ability "to press upon its experiences the stamp of the eternal" *(den Stempel des Ewigen zu drücken)*, to become time-less, to become classical (*BT* 137, *KSA I* 148). The modern age, in contrast, plagued by the hunger for knowledge, which it knows can never be satis-fied, treats art as a momentary remedy, stripping it of its universality, or its mythic, poetic power. Instead of the tragic myth, defined as a unifying and all inclusive principle, "a concentrated image of the world" *(das zusammengezogene Weltbild)* which lends creativity to a people, the present age with its "feverish and uncanny excitement" *(das fieberhafte und so unheimliche Sichregen)*, coming from its voluntary eviction from "the mythical home, the mythical maternal womb" *(der mythischen Heimat, des mythischen Mutterschoosses)*, has turned into a culture resembling an orphan grown into a starving beggar, whose "greedy seizing and snatching at food" can never be satisfied. Not only is "the most vigorous and whole-some food" *(die kräftigste, heilsamste Nahrung)*, i.e., art in its ideal form, lost on such a culture, but it becomes contaminated by this contact and turns into "history and criticism" *(Historie und Kritik)* (*BT* 135, *KSA* I 146).

Nietzsche's assessment of the modern and scientific age in *The Birth of Tragedy* comes from a romantic perspective. In the hope to re-vive and recover for a hungry present the spirit of a tragic and heroic past, he elevates art and artistic activity to metaphysical heights. Nietzsche's acute dissatisfaction with particularly Germany's state of the arts testifies to his romantic mistrust of scientificity. As has been suggested, however, parallel to his romantic vein runs another, which, in its extremely lucid, analytical, and relentlessly inquisitive or calmly reflective disposition represents another perspective, namely that of the classical skeptic.

This skeptical tendency in Nietzsche is already present in *The Birth of Tragedy* and continues to coexist with his romanticism, which even his greatest polemics do not succeed in canceling out. In fact, Nietzsche's polemic in the name of Dionysian classicism, against a romanticism related to all that is "modern," makes of Nietzsche, as Karl Heinz Bohrer attempts to show, the most eminent discoverer of romantic themes, and all the more emphatically subject to its effects. For he, like Baudelaire, was a romantic under modern conditions.[17]

Bohrer's concern is to show how Nietzsche, along with Baudelaire and Kierkegaard, prepared the way for a shift from a negative critique—historical, political, and philosophical—to a positive, creative, aesthetic rediscovery of romanticism from the early twentieth century on. This rediscovery stands under the sign of a modern aesthetics and analysis of consciousness *(Bewusstseinsanalyse)*. Its thesis states: romanticism is modernism. What distinguishes this modern aesthetics and analysis of consciousness is its apolitical and aphilosophical character, in opposition to the political and philosophical character of the criticism of romanticism of the nineteenth century. For a hundred years, says Bohrer, philosophers, historians, and sociologists, such as Hegel, Kierkegaard, Carl Schmitt, Lukàcs, and partially Max Weber, have condemned romanticism, preferring their own definitions for such concepts as reality and truth, excluding romanticism as unethical, apolitical, and above all irrational. And the cultural sciences of the twentieth century continue this line of reasoning in a Marxist or sociopolitical context, from Max Weber to Lukàcs to Habermas.

In opposition to this systematical discourse, based on the authority of such concepts as "the rational" or "reality," Bohrer presents the rediscovery and impact of "imagination" as the mark of modernism. The increasing calling into question of the concept "reality" occurs, according to Bohrer, already before the first World War, and is based on a new conception of experience, which showed its first signs in early psychoanalysis, phenomenology, and anthropology.

For Bohrer, this new "aesthetic" discourse is announced by two contradictory but complementary intellectual fields: the early works of Benjamin and the texts of French surrealism. From this Bohrer deducts that the rediscovery of romanticism under the sign and pathos of a romantic modernism rests on two pillars: a theoretical and an imaginative reevaluation. It is not certain, however, whether this dialectical differentiation is adequate in defining what Bohrer calls "the massive reorientation of the understanding of romanticism." Of course, this reorientation was not a *creatio ex nihilo* but was prepared by the seminal works of a few select thinkers of modernism. Kierkegaard's *The Concept of Irony* (1848), Baudelaire's essay "What is Romanticism" (1846), and finally some of Nietzsche's texts written between 1870 and 1878, in which his emphasis on aesthetics and his criticism of historical thinking all contributed. They first expressed the new positions on modernism—critically (or emphatically) searched for—and testify to the idea that romanticism is the true harbinger of modernism (Bohrer 23–24). Bohrer further extends this idea, asserting that in their process of reevaluating romanticism and its corollary modernity as ways of acting and behaving, modernity turns out to be the most radicalized expression of romanticism.

Some of Nietzsche's most complex and thought-provoking ideas about the modern existential and artistic condition are already found in an earlier text of the *Unfashionable Observations*, in which modernity is tied to history in such a way that both, as seen from the perspective of "life," become the cornerstones of a critique which concerns the predicament of our own present day modernity.

VI. Modern Life or the Unbearable Weight of Theoretical Knowledge

In the second of his *Unfashionable Observations*, published in 1873 under the title "On the Uses and Disadvantages of History for Life," Nietzsche investigates the impact of Socratic delusion (or the Enlightenment illusion) on the present age, which is marked by an (absence of) feeling most abhorred by Nietzsche: indifference. Already in *The Birth of Tragedy,* Nietzsche had differentiated between three historical stages of which the Alexandrian, suffering from an excessive love for knowledge, comes closest to modern times. In this essay, Nietzsche concentrates on his own century, which he diagnoses as sick because paralyzed by a "consuming fever of history" *(verzehrendem historischen Fieber)*, an obsessive drive to accumulate knowledge at any price, the price being ultimately its strength, dignity, and taste for life.[18] (*KSA* I 246).

This essay is crucial in order to assess Nietzsche's understanding of modernity as a misguided attitude toward life (and his simultaneous attempts to define a right one). It also presents the author's view of himself as a subject in opposition to though still a constitutive part of an age weaving and caught in a web of "ironic self-awareness" *(ironisches Selbstbewusstsein) (UD* 100, *KSA* I 302). Again, as with romanticism, Nietzsche does not condemn the modern condition as much as he condemns the lack of recognition of it. He strategically includes himself amongst those moderns—"a child of the present times" *(ein Kind dieser jetztigen Zeit)*—with the difference that he, in contrast to the mainstream—as a good "pupil of earlier times" *(Zögling älterer Zeiten)*—is disciplined, lucid, and honest enough to know and admit it. And most importantly, he acts upon it, physically, and intellectually, by writing about it. He sees his task as an enlightening challenge to traditional criticism, defining the profession of a classicist in an unusual way.

The term "unfashionable" is not to be taken in a metaphorical sense of "classical" or that which transcends one's own times, that which has absolute value, but literally, namely as that which is "acting counter to our time and thereby acting on our time and . . . for the benefit of a time to come" *(gegen die Zeit und dadurch auf die Zeit und hoffentlich zu Gunsten einer kommenden Zeit . . . wirken) (UD* 60, *KSA* I 247).

For Nietzsche, a society that thinks of itself only in terms of the last link in a historical chain, a society which is bogged down by a past which it reveres too much but also experiences as a burden, needs to learn again how to forget. In order to live with the knowledge that "existence fundamentally is—an imperfect tense that can never become a perfect one," or that "being is only an uninterrupted has-been, a thing that lives by negating, consuming itself" *(dass Dasein nur ein ununterbrochenes Gewesensein ist, ein Ding, das davon lebt sich selbst zu verneinen und zu verzehren, sich selbst zu widersprechen)*, one would have to be able to forget the past and seize the present moment, as if it were the one and only valid reality. An individual's or a people's physical vitality and cultural creativity depends on this faculty.

To illustrate his point most clearly, Nietzsche reverts to one of his favorite metaphors, the child which "having as yet nothing of the past to shake off, plays in blissful blindness between the hedges of past and future" *(das noch nichts Vergangenes zu verläugnen hat und zwischen den Zäunen der Vergangenheit und der Zukunft in überseeliger Blindheit spielt) (UD* 61, *KSA* I 249). For Nietzsche it is the ability of the child to block out whatever is not useful to its present concerns that allows it to catch a glimpse of happiness, and which eventually and fatally is extinguished when a greater awareness of life intrudes.

Paradoxically it is in this state of forgetting—the unhistorical state—that creative powers and regenerative forces for action reside and guarantee strength. Whereas the historical state, which Nietzsche defines as a hyper-lucid state in which one's consciousness is excessively aware of everything at once, brings with it a "degree of sleeplessness, of rumination" *(einen Grad von Schlaflosigkeit und Wiederkäuen)*, which is detrimental to one's spirit and vital forces. Both states are nevertheless equally important, and it depends on the "formative power" *(plastische Kraft)* of an individual, a people, or a culture, i.e., its power or will to fashion itself, whether a culture is living or dying.

Nietzsche considers a culture alive if it is aware of its potentials and its limits and knows when and how to use them. The unhistorical or instinctual strives for presentness, immediate self-realization, and self-gratification (one might call this the Dionysian), and ideally "constitutes the foundation upon which alone anything sound, healthy and great, anything truly human, can grow" *(das Fundament . . . auf dem überhaupt erst etwas Rechtes, Gesundes und Grosses wachsen kann)*. Since nothing is fixed in this universe, however, and the very idea of foundation is thus put into question, Nietzsche reformulates his thought by redefining the unhistorical as "an atmosphere within which alone life can germinate and with the destruction of which it must vanish" *(ist einer umhüllenden Atmosphäre ähnlich, in der sich Leben allein erzeugt, um mit der Vernichtung dieser Atmosphäre wieder zu verschwinden)*. People living unhistorically live unconsciously in a creative, human, and possibly blissful state, albeit without purpose, direction, or style. Nietzsche's critique of Rousseau is nowhere more pertinent.[19] Therefore the historical—consciousness, critical reason, and form—is for Nietzsche the crucial element in the formation of culture:

It is true that only by imposing limits on this unhistorical element by thinking, reflecting, comparing, distinguishing, drawing conclusions, only through the appearance within that encompassing cloud of a vivid flash of light—thus only through the power of employing the past for the purposes of life and of again introducing into history that which has been done and is gone—did man become man.

(Es ist wahr: erst dadurch, dass der Mensch denkend, überdenkend, vergleichend, trennend, zusammenschliessend jenes unhistorische Element einschränkt, erst dadurch dass innerhalb jener umschliessenden Dunstwolke ein heller blitzender Lichtschein entsteht, also erst durch die Kraft, das Vergangene zum Leben zu

gebrauchen und aus dem Geschehenen wieder Geschichte zu machen, wird der Mensch zum Menschen) (UD 64, KSA I 253).

This development, which is above all a reflection on Nietzsche's understanding of the art of living, begs to be translated into the realm of aesthetics. What Nietzsche does here, is to sketch out the contours of a theory of art which affirms the present, as well as recoils from an excessive emphasis on memory or uncritical respect for the authority of the past. Nietzsche's theory further implies not only the possibility but the necessity of an art (be it life or artwork in the literal sense), which reflects itself in and as the present, while being substantial enough to become history in turn.

The unhistorical is the unchanging, eternally willing, eternally creating element without moral, ethical, or formal concerns, and the historical is specific to one's time, establishing and representing rules, judging, choosing, ordering, and giving form. If these elements, taken as constitutive parts of a desired whole, which may be called life or art, unfold in such a way that the historical "captures" or "serves" the unhistorical, then life (and art) worthy of the name become possible.

The function of the historical (the form-giving or technical element) is above all to stay within its confines and not only to affirm but ideally to enhance the unhistorical—in short to yield to the will to power. From the point of view of art, this would mean that the expression of temperament and life is hierarchically superior to factual knowledge or technical skill. Despite the necessity of the historical setting of limits (the Apollonian), the unhistorical, "the womb not only of the unjust but of the just deed too" is the source of all creation:

> No painter will paint his picture, no general achieve his victory, no people attain its freedom without having first desired and striven for it in an unhistorical condition . . . As he who acts is . . always without a conscience, so is he also always without knowledge; he forgets most things so as to do one thing, he is unjust towards what lies behind him, and recognizes the rights only of that which is now to come into being and no other rights whatsoever.
> *(Kein Künstler wird sein Bild, kein Feldherr seinen Sieg, kein Volk seine Freiheit erreichen, ohne sie in einem derartig unhistorischen Zustande vorher begehrt und erstrebt zu haben. Wie der Handelnde immer gewissenlos ist, so ist er auch wissenlos, er vergisst das Meiste, um Eins zu thun, er ist ungerecht gegen das, was hinter ihm liegt und kennt nur Ein Recht dessen, was jetzt werden soll (UD 64, NN I 254).*

It is precisely in this radical impulse to erase the past and look single-mindedly to the future—the child's impulse—that Paul de Man locates Nietzsche's own modernity. According to de Man, Nietzsche's radical demand for an absolute forgetting as the only possible condition for action and, one must add, creation, places him in the company of Rimbaud, Artaud, and Baudelaire, whose modernity expressed itself in the same vehement and "unfashionable" fashion:

> Nietzsche's ruthless forgetting, the blindness with which he throws himself into an action lightened of all previous experience, captures the authentic spirit of modernity. It is the tone of Rimbaud when he declares that he has no antecedents whatever in the history of France, that all one has to expect from poets is *du nouveau* and Artaud when he asserts that 'written poetry has value for one single moment and should then be destroyed. Let the dead poets make room for the living . . . the time for masterpieces is past.'[20]

The question de Man attempts to elucidate is whether such a claim to modernity can ever be achieved or whether it is not the very condition of the impossibility of ever achieving a moment of true present that is the true subject of modernity. It is the assertion of the latter proposition, of course, which is inscribed in Nietzsche's text. De Man, however, fails to include in his discussion Nietzsche's attitude toward the paradox of modernity. The problem of modernity lies for de Man in the fact, that the moment of true presentness—modernity—is always defined by those who claim it, in terms of "point of origin that marks a new departure." From there, he argues that the idea of a new origin is futile and condemned in advance if one accepts, as de Man does, Nietzsche's "deeply pessimistic wisdom" which sees "existence" as an "uninterrupted pastness that lives from its own denial and destruction," as regression instead of development. For de Man, this description of life as regression cannot be ascribed to "cultural errors" liable to be corrected, but "lies much deeper in the nature of things." It is an existential truth, "a temporal experience of human mutability, historical in the deepest sense of the term." From there it follows, that the very moment of a new departure cannot be located or captured and much less retained or marked as an ontological point in time, for life implies "the necessary experience of any present as a passing experience that makes the past irrevocable and unforgettable, because it is inseparable from any present or future" (de Man 149). Paradoxically and ironically, modernity, defined as that which "invests its trust in the power of the present moment as an origin, but discovers that, in severing itself from the past, it has at the same time severed itself from the present," becomes not only homeless and timeless but empty. To experience the impossibility of being truly modern—completely emancipated from any previous moment of the past—is lived most radically in the act of writing. Or in de Man's words: "Modernity turns out to be indeed one of the concepts by means of which the distinctive nature of literature can be revealed in all its intricacy" (de Man 161).

The writer's drama, assuming he is as de Man is, always haunted by modernity's appeal and obsessed with the desire to be at the source of a new beginning, is that his very activity is bound by an inescapable law. Whereas the "historian" in the traditional sense has no claims to literary novelty and originality and therefore benefits from an "interpretative distance" and remains linguistically detached from the events he records (language and the events that the language denotes are clearly distinct entities), the writer in the modern sense is always already thwarted in his enterprise to write in and of things in their pure presentness. Since his language "is to some degree the product of his own action," and since "he is both the historian and the agent of his own language," he is also at one and the same time action and reflection, poet and critic, the embodiment of modernity itself. The self, subject, autobiographer, and biographer.

In his essay, Nietzsche claims a present which would be radically opposed to the very present his eyes are directed against, namely Germany shortly after the national reunification. However, a present which would be completely without any form of historical awareness, deprived of an instinct enabling it to choose what is right and good for its vital powers, is engaging in a fatal *laisser-aller*.

Nietzsche presents German culture as a pseudo-culture whose neglect of outer appearance reflects its poverty of inner substance. As a philologist, that is a historian of the past, and as a modern, a writer who likes to express himself in metaphors and parables, Nietzsche presents concrete examples in order to convey general ideas of "authentic cultures" past and present, which are so because of the recognition of and action upon their true needs. For Nietzsche, the Greeks are a worthy example because of their ability for self-creation, that is a will and capacity to organize the chaos which threatens people and individuals alike at any time in history. Nor has France become what Nietzsche sees as the highest seat of European culture without sacrifice, struggle, and the instinct to know what it needs. Its practice of convention is based on experience, a need for self-discipline, and a hatred for *laissez-aller*, a taste for aesthetics out of the will to self-fashion. These qualities lend a people character and a certain balance between form and content.

Nietzsche's own "ruthless forgetting" which de Man enlists as the sign of Nietzsche's affiliation with modernity has to be seen as a strategic move to counteract a paralyzing and deadly accumulation of memory and knowledge. Nietzsche's forgetting is not a canceling out or refusal of the past as much as it is in fact a selective screen necessary to prevent the continuous outpouring of knowledge streaming from "inexhaustible wells" *(unversieglichen Quellen)* over modern man, like a flood rushing him along and robbing him "of the foundation of all his rest and security, his belief in the enduring and the eternal" *(dem Menschen das Fundament aller seiner Sicherheit und Ruhe, den Glauben an das Beharrliche und Ewige, nimmt)* (*UD* 21, *KSA* I 330). Forgetting is the art "of enclosing oneself within a bounded horizon" *(sich in einen begrenzten Horizont einzuschliessen)*, the art of staking out one's own independent ground from which one is able to operate relatively unhindered by the influence of other phenomena or thoughts. Forgetting, in Nietzsche's sense, is a conscious act, a rebellious gesture towards the promise of one's originality.

Nietzsche stresses more than once and with biting irony that "we moderns have nothing whatever of our own" *(aus uns haben wir Modernen gar nichts)*, that "only by replenishing and cramming ourselves with the ages, customs, arts, philosophies, religions, discoveries of others, do we become anything worthy of notice, i.e., walking encyclopedias" *(nur dadurch, dass wir uns mit fremden Zeiten, Sitten, Künsten, Philosophien, Religionen, Erkenntnissen anfüllen und überfüllen, werden wir zu etwas Betrachtunswerthem, nämlich zu wandelnden Encyclopädien)* (*UD* 79, *KSA* I 273–74).

Set only on adding to the number of entries in the walking dictionary, accumulating with ever-increasing speed fact after fact, an appreciation for form vanishes, a disorientation results, brought about by a disconnection of form and content. Having defined the true culture of a people as the "unity of artistic style in all the expressions of the life of a people" *(als Einheit des künstlerischen Stiles in allen Lebensäusserungen eines Volkes)*, Nietzsche denounces modern man's indifference to the "real and existent" *(das Wirkliche, das Bestehende)*, his negligence of "outer appearance" to the profit of "a stream of new things worth knowing which can be stored tidily away in its coffers" *(ein wenn nur immer neue wissenswürdige Dinge hinzuströmen, die säuberlich in den Kästen jenes Gedächtnisses aufgestellt werden können).* This dislocation of content and form causes an increasing alienation from anything that is truly form-giving, life. With the loss of the idea of a "higher unity" *(höhere Einheit)*, which one may also define as a unity of style, decline begins its onslaught, and an existential need as negative and dark as a black hole takes shape.

Raising the concepts of stability and eternity as reassuring "horizons" against the depredations of modern scientific hubris, Nietzsche affects a meditative calm in contrast to the modern frenzy. Nietzsche's essay is an emancipatory text to the highest degree. The expression of hope and his belief in the possibility for a new and ground-breaking "first generation of fighters and dragon-slayers," testify to his will to the new.

At the same time, his awareness of the impossibility of a complete disengagement becomes clear through the insufficiency of language—the impossibility to define one's difference from the "material" that conditions our being—throwing the reality of this hope into question. The ambitious project which Nietzsche assigns to himself and to those few strong enough to take it on, depends on their ability to stay (self-)critically aloof thus avoiding the same mistake. The ideas of "health" and "culture" that the modern Germany of his time promoted are all seen as perverted concepts designating a perverse form of life which calls for a radical reevaluation by those who are not afraid and strong enough to bear the difficult task of self-creation (organizing one's chaos into a whole). It also requires self-knowledge (grasping one's real needs), which depends on specific virtues—honesty and strength of character:

> Its mission, however, is to undermine the concepts this present has of 'health' and 'culture' and to excite mockery and hatred against these hybrid monsters of concepts; and the sign that guarantees the superior robustness of its own health shall be that this youth can itself discover no concept or slogan in the contemporary currency of words and concepts to describe its own nature, but is only aware of the existence within it of an active power that fights, excludes, and divides, and of an ever more intense feeling of life.
>
> *(Ihre Mission aber ist es, die Begriffe, die jene Gegenwart von 'Gesundheit' und 'Bildung' hat, zu erschüttern und Hohn und Hass gegen so hybride Begriffs-Ungeheuer zu erzeugen; und das gewährleistende Anzeichen ihrer eigenen kräftigen Gesundheit soll gerade dies sein, dass sie, diese Jugend nämlich, selbst keinen Begriff, kein Parteiwort aus den umlaufenden Wort-und Begriffsmünzen der Gegenwart zur Bezeichnung ihres Wesens gebrauchen kann, sondern nur von einer in ihr thätigen kämpfenden, ausscheidenden, zertheilenden Macht und von*

einem immer erhöhten Lebensgefühle in jeder guten Stunde überzeugt wird) (*UD* 121, *KSA* I 331).

Nietzsche's invitation and challenge to live in an "unmodern way," in a heroically antithetical way, an active, creative, and thus essentially artistic way, is based on a highly selective, aristocratic world view. This becomes even clearer when he assigns to the genuine historian precisely the task of the modern artist as conceived of by none other than Baudelaire himself:

> Do not believe historiography that does not spring from the head of the rarest mind; and you will know the quality of a mind when it is obliged to express something universal or to repeat something universally known: the genuine historian must possess the power to remint the universally known into something never heard of before, and to express the universal so simply and profoundly that the simplicity is lost in the profundity and the profundity in the simplicity.
> *(Glaub teiner Geschichtsschreibung nicht, wenn sie nicht aus dem Haupte der seltensten Geister herausspringt; immer aber werdet ihr merken welcher Qualität ihr Geist ist, wenn sie genöthigt wird, etwas Allgemeines auszusprechen oder etwas Allbekanntes nocheinmal zu sagen: der ächte Historiker muss die Kraft haben, das Allbekannte zum Niegehörten umzuprägen und das Allgemeine so einfach und tief zu verkünden, dass man die Einfachheit über der Tiefe und die Tiefe über der Einfachheit übersieht)* (*UD* 94, *KSA* I 294).

The genuine historian is not a scientist but an artist, and his poetic activity promises to preserve the healthily instinctive, creative realm that a culture needs to thrive. Or as Peter Berkowitz puts it:

> the restoration of health depends upon the very task Nietzsche assigned to the genuine historian forming horizons and endowing existence with the character of eternity by means of edifying poems that take the shape of histories.[21]

Finally, Nietzsche's unconditional demand for the experience of life over the knowledge of culture and his vision of life as a form of art is to be seen in the larger context of his critique of decadence, which rests, like his critique of modernity, on the unresolved and unresolvable paradox of being part of that which one condemns. In light of this dilemma, one might choose exile, as Rimbaud and Nietzsche did, one might lose one's mind as Artaud and Nietzsche did, or one might push this paradox to its literary limits as Baudelaire, Nietzsche, and the symbolists did.

140

Notes

1 Friedrich Nietzsche, *Human, All Too Human,* trans. R. J. Hollingdale (Cambridge: Cambridge University Press, 1986), 210. References to this text are designated *HAH*. The German quotations are from Friedrich Nietzsche, *Sämtliche Werke, Kritische Studienausgabe,* 15 vols., eds. G. Colli and M. Montinari (Berlin: de Gruyter, 1988). References to the individual works are designated KSA, followed by volume and page number.

2 Adrian del Caro, *Nietzsche Contra Nietzsche* (Baton Rouge: Louisiana State University Press, 1989), 24. Further references to this text appear with the author's name.

3 Ernst Behler, *"Nietzsche und die Frühromantische Schule,"* *Nietzsche-Studien* 7 (1978): 65–66. Further references to this text are indicated with the author's name.

4 For a discussion on Nietzsche's criticism of German early-romanticism see Rudolf Reuber, *Aesthetische Lebensformen bei Nietzsche* (München: Wilhelm Fink, 1989), 53–57. Further references to this text are indicated with the author's name.

5 Friedrich Nietzsche, *Beyond Good and Evil*, trans. Walter Kaufmann (New York: Vintage, 1966), 193. References to this text are designated *BGE*.

6 Friedrich Nietzsche, *Daybreak,* trans. R. J. Hollingdale (Cambridge : Cambridge University Press, 1982), 117.

7 Friedrich Nietzsche, "Attempt at a Self-Criticism," *The Birth of Tragedy, Basic Writings of Friedrich Nietzsche,* trans. Walter Kaufmann (New York: Modern Library, 1968), 25. References to this text are designated *BT*.

8 Julian Young, *Nietzsche's Philosophy of Art* (Cambridge:Cambridge University Press, 1992), 25. References to this text appear with the author's name.

9 Walter Kaufmann, *Nietzsche, Philosopher, Psychologist, Antichrist* (Princeton: Princeton University Press, 1974), 131.

10 Camille Paglia, *Sexual Personae* (New York: Vintage Books, 1991), 96.

11 Friedrich Nietzsche, *Thus Spoke Zarathustra*, *The Portable Nietzsche,* trans. W. Kaufmann (New York: The Viking Press, 1954), 381.

[12] Friedrich Nietzsche, *Ecce Homo,* trans. W. Kaufmann (New York: Vintage Books, 1969), 331. References to this text are designated *EC.*

[13] Friedrich Nietzsche, *On the Genealogy of Morals,* trans. W. Kaufmann (New York: Vintage,1969), 103.

[14] Friedrich Nietzsche, *The Gay Science,* trans. W. Kaufmann (New York:Vintage, 1974), 38. References to this text are designated *GS.*

[15] Sarah Kofman, *Nietzsche and Metaphor*, trans. D. Large (Stanford: Stanford University Press, 1993), 10.

[16] Peter Pütz, *"Nietzsche im Lichte der kritischen Theorie,"* *Nietzsche Studien* 3 (Berlin: de Gruyter, 1974), 183. My translation.

[17] Karl Heinz Bohrer, *Die Kritik der Romantik* (Frankfurt a.M.:Suhrkamp, 1989), 84. Further references to this text appear with the author's name. Translation is mine.

[18] Friedrich Nietzsche, "On the Uses and Disadvantages of History for Life," *Untimely Meditations*, trans. R. J. Hollingdale (Cambridge: Cambridge University Press, 1983), 59. References to this text are designated in the text with *UD.*

[19] For Nietzsche's relation with Rousseau see Peter Heller, "Nietzsche in His Relation to Voltaire and Rousseau," James C. O'Flaherty, ed., *Studies in Nietzsche and the Classical Tradition* (Chapel Hill, NC, 1976).

[20] Paul de Man, *Blindness and Insight* (Minneapolis: University of Minnesota Press Press, 1971), 147. References to this text appear with the author's name.

[21] Peter Berkowitz, *Nietzsche, the Ethics of an Immoralist* (Cambridge, MA: Harvard University Press, 1995), 40.

Chapter 5

DECADENCE

I.   A Question of Perspectives

A discussion of Nietzsche's relationship to and critique of decadence as a physiological and cultural necessity and aesthetic concept calls for a look at his understanding of pessimism. The challenge in approaching the often discussed subject of Nietzsche and decadence lies in the fact that in Nietzsche's conceptual world and vocabulary, the terms romanticism, pessimism, modernity, and finally decadence are related in such an intricate fashion that an attempt to define each term in its own right seems an impossible or even useless enterprise. Therefore to heed Nietzsche's advice and stake out for oneself a certain horizon against limitless possibilities, to choose a perspective from which to direct one's focus and then to turn it around so as to find the way to one's task offers itself as the most inviting possibility for scanning the present field of investigation.[1]

To be sure, Nietzsche never places himself outside the subject of his interest. His "anti-romantic self-treatment" which he illustrates in the stunning preface of the second book of *Human, All Too Human*, arises from his capacity to think and act "as if." For Nietzsche it is above all a matter of good taste—especially for an "invalid" *(ein Kranker)*, as he diagnoses himself, to apply what he calls "the art of appearing cheerful, objective, inquisitive, above all healthy and malicious" *(die Kunst, mich heiter, objectiv, neugierig, vor allem gesund und boshaft zu geben)*, while at the same time embracing "everything painful and difficult precisely for [himself]" *(für alles, was gerade mir wehe that und hart fiel)*. He expresses the hope that at least a few people will not fail to notice that the "charm of his writing" *(der Reiz dieser Schriften)* lies precisely in the stoicism he affects in the face of what he sees as a rather grim reality, in the adoption of optimism "for the purpose of restoration" *(zum Zweck der Wiederherstellung)*, in brief in his perspectivism:

> . . . that here a sufferer and self-denier speaks as though he were not a sufferer and self-denier. Here there is a determination to preserve an equilibrium and compo-

sure in the face of life and even a sense of gratitude towards it, here there rules a vigorous, proud, constantly watchful and sensitive will that has set itself the task of defending life against pain and of striking down all those inferences that pain, disappointment, ill-humor, solitude and other swamp grounds usually cause to flourish like poisonous fungi.

(dass hier ein Leidender und Entbehrender redet, wie als ob er nicht ein Leidender und Entbehrender sei. Hier soll das Gleichgewicht, die Gelassenheit, sogar die Dankbarkeit gegen das Leben aufrecht erhalten werden, hier waltet ein strenger, stolzer, beständig wacher, beständig reizbarer Wille, der sich die Aufgabe gestellt hat, das Leben wider den Schmerz zu vertheidigen und alle Schlüsse abzuknicken, welche aus Schmerz, Enttäuschung, Ueberdruss, Vereinsamung und andrem Moorgrunde gleich giftigen Schwämmen aufzuwachsen pflegen) (HAH 212, KSA II 374).

Nietzsche's recommendations to others (and to himself) of certain "precepts of health" to counteract bouts of unhealthy romanticism, i.e., romantic pessimism, are thus accompanied by an acknowledgment of his own pessimism, which, however, Nietzsche never tires of defining and re-defining as "courageous," "strong," and finally "Dionysian." Nietzsche sees his own modernity in the way he gives a new direction to the idea of pessi-mism. Although he states that he adopts optimism only for the purpose of introducing an antithetical force of resistance, he does—as a rather strange pessimist—reveal an engaged optimism, apparent in the very idea that the dynamic resulting from the ongoing shift of perspective is ultimately fa-vorable to one's physical and mental health. He admits to a certain pride in the strangeness of his undertaking:

With this will in one's heart one has no fear of the fearful and questionable that characterizes all existence; one even seeks it out. Behind such a will there stands courage, pride, the longing for a great enemy. This has been my pessimistic perspective from the beginning—a novel perspective, is it not? a perspective that even today is still novel and strange?

(Man fürchtet, mit diesem Willen in der Brust, nicht das Furchtbare und Fragwürdige, das allem Dasein eignet; man sucht es selbst auf. Hinter einem solchen Willen steht der Muth, der Stolz, das Verlangen nach einem grossen Feinde.—Dies war meine pessimistische Perspective, wie mich dünkt? eine solche die auch heute noch neu und fremd ist?) (HAH 213, KSA II 376–77).

The one belief which underlies Nietzsche's critique of pessimism (including his critique of romanticism, modernism, and decadence) is that the value of life is the common denominator against which everything else is measured. It can be seen as the one and sole resting-pole in the ongoing tension provoked by his oscillation between one perspective and another. In other words, with Nietzsche, the notion, idea, or concept of life takes on the value of eternity, which Baudelaire sees as the indispensable element in the formation of the truly modern. True, life can be valued only from the perspective of death and death from the perspective of life, but Nietzsche's focus is and stays with the ideal of life, which, however, does not exclude his avowed taste for and adherence to aesthetic phenomena resulting from declining life. In *Ecce Homo*, Nietzsche places himself continuously on both sides, starting with a statement presented as a riddle: "already dead as my father, . . . as my mother I am still living and becoming old" *(als mein Vater bereits gestorben, als meine Mutter lebe ich noch und werde alt)*.[2]

And in a more summary way he affirms that "apart from the fact that I am a decadent, I am also the opposite" *(abgerechnet nämlich, dass ich ein décadent bin, bin ich auch dessen Gegenteil)*. Health and sickness are, nevertheless, not on equal footing with Nietzsche, for two lines later he specifies that "as *summa summarum*, I was healthy; as an angle, as a speciality, I was a *décadent*" *(als* summa summarum *war ich gesund, als Winkel und Specialität war ich* décadent*) (EC* 224, *KSA* VI 266).

In order to be able to shift perspectives, which aside from being a theoretical activity for Nietzsche, also constitutes the very realistic activity of turning one's sickness again into health—"one has to be healthy at bottom" *(dass man im Grunde gesund ist)*. Nietzsche in a way presents health as a decisive privilege in the process of overcoming one's handicaps—given that one really wants to overcome whatever nature one has been given—which reveals Nietzsche's realism, the selective and aristocratic tendencies underlying his train of thought. Ignoring modesty, a virtue respected by most, Nietzsche describes himself as a teacher par excellence, whose "subtler smell for the signs of ascent and decline" *(eine feinere Witterung für die Zeichen von Anfang und Niedergang)* surpass those of "any other being before" *(als je ein Mensch gehabt hat)*. He is the master of "that psychology of 'looking around the corner'" with "those fingers for nuances" that are, he implies, only given to those who get stronger from every blow they receive. His famous dictum "What does not kill him makes him stronger" only concerns those who are endowed with a minimum of strength. Nietzsche distinguishes between the two types, of which the latter—himself and few others—are representatives. For these few sickness becomes a positive factor, a source of health:

A typically morbid being cannot become healthy, much less make itself healthy. For a typically healthy person, conversely, being sick can even become an energetic *stimulus* for life, for living *more*.
(Ein typisch morbides Wesen kann nicht gesund werden, noch weniger sich selbst gesund machen; für einen typisch gesunden kann umgekehrt krank sein sogar ein energisches Stimulans *zum Leben, zum* Mehr-*leben sein*) (EC 224–25, KSA VI 266–67).

It is in the latter type that Nietzsche would like to find himself, always in the state of the grateful and serene convalescent who, emerging from the dark, sees everything in a new light, discovers life anew and tastes "all good and even little things, as others cannot easily taste them" *(alle guten und kleinen Dinge, wie sie Andere nicht leicht schmecken können)*, and turns his "will to health, to life, into a philosophy" *(aus [meinem] Willen zur Gesundheit, zum Leben, meine Philosophie)*.

The role of the convalescent who occupies a position in-between, who profits from the tension between two poles, from which he is equally close and removed at the same time, allows Nietzsche—who claims experience in both—to swing from one pole to the other in a manner of existential exercise:

Looking from the perspective of the sick toward *healthier* concepts and values and, conversely, looking again from the fullness and self-assurance of a *rich* life down into the secret work of the instinct of decadence—in this I have had the longest training, my truest experience. Now I know how, have the know-how, to *reverse perspectives*: the first reason why a 'revaluation of values' is perhaps possible for me alone.
(Von der Kranken-Optik aus nach gesünderen Begriffen und Werthen, und wiederum umgekeht aus der Fülle und Selbstgewissheit des reichen Lebens hinuntersehen in die heimliche Arbeit des Décadence-Instinkts—das war meine längste Uebung, meine eigentliche Erfahrung . . . ich habe es in der Hand, ich habe die Hand dafür, Perspektiven umzustellen: erster Grund, weshalb für mich allein vielleicht eine 'Umwerthung der Werthe' überhaupt möglich ist) (EC 223, KSA VI 266).

Valuing above all an ascending line of life taken from the perspective and experience of a declining tendency, prompts Nietzsche to engage in his project of the "transvaluation of all values," whose outline can be seen as early as *The Birth of Tragedy*, and within which the question of pessimism already stands at the center. There pessimism is not yet present in all its complexity, as it appears around 1886, the most prolific period of

Nietzsche's career. While finishing *Beyond Good and Evil*, he prefaced his new edition to *The Birth* with the essay "Attempt at Self-Criticism." He added a second book to *Human, All Too Human* with its important preface, and finally in 1887, he completed *The Gay Science* with an additional fifth book, another new preface, and "The Songs of Prince Vogelfrei."

II.   Two Kinds of Pessimism

In Nietzsche's vocabulary, the term pessimism precedes both the terms nihilism and decadence. All three terms pertain to a will to sickness and ultimately nothingness, to be distinguishing not from sheer optimism, which is under Nietzsche's attack as well, but from a will to health. It may be safe to say that the concepts pessimism and decadence have a closer affinity with each other and are practically interchangeable at certain moments, because very often their interest lies in their aesthetic implications. Nihilism, on the other hand, seems to address the philosophical question and the existential implications of the death of God.[3]

Although Albert Camus particularly examines Nietzsche's relationship to nihilism, his sharp-eyed assessment of Nietzsche's dealings with nihilism can also be applied to his views on pessimism and decadence. Of main interest for this study is Camus's short essay on Nietzsche in *The Rebel*, in which he compares Nietzsche's method to that of a surgeon, an incisiveness that can already be seen in the early essay "On the Uses and Disadvantages of History for Life."

> The provisional, methodical—in a word strategic—character of his thought cannot be doubted for a moment. With him nihilism becomes conscious for the first time. Surgeons have this in common with prophets: they think and operate in terms of the future. Nietzsche never thought except in terms of an apocalypse to come, not in order to extol it, for he guessed the sordid and calculating aspect that this apocalypse would finally assume, but in order to avoid it and to transform it into a renaissance. He recognized nihilism for what it was and examined it like a clinical fact . . . He wrote in his own manner, the *Discours de la Méthode* of his period, . . . with the mad lucidity of the twentieth century.[4]

Nietzsche's rational and scientific side is counterbalanced here by this last, striking twist. Whereas lucidity points towards cerebral and intuitive faculties, clear insight, and even logic, madness denotes the idea of a misused or misdirected overabundance, be it of knowledge, stimuli, or life. It sug-

gests a mind or being too overburdened to function within the confines of
this world. Ironically it is precisely this tipping of the scales, this lack of
balance, this misdirection of energies, which Nietzsche detects in the pessimism which he calls by turns "romantic,"[5] "modern" (*GS* 286, *FW* 3 58),
and "aesthetic."[6] One of the reasons Nietzsche makes the analysis and
reevaluation of pessimism his own cause is that he sees it (and respects it)
as the "last great event in the fate of our culture" *(das letzte grosse Ereignis
im Schicksal unserer Cultur)* (*GS* 330, *KSA* III 622).

Just how inseparable romanticism, pessimism, and modernity are
comes best to light in Aphorism 370 of *The Gay Science* in which, to answer the question in the title, "What is romanticism?", he reevaluates the
term.

Nietzsche begins with a summary of his state of mind as a young
and hopeful adept of Schopenhauer's philosophy and Wagner's music. His
hopes and belief in a German cultural renaissance were, he contends, the
result of a misunderstanding, which he proposes to correct here in the most
condensed fashion.[7]

Schopenhauer's philosophical pessimism seemed to represent "a
symptom of a superior force of thought . . . of more triumphant fullness of
life" (das Symptom von höherer Kraft des Gedankens . . . von siegreicher
Fülle des Lebens. . .), an attempt at overcoming eighteenth century ratio-
nalism. Wagner's music seemed the expression of "a Dionysian power of
the German soul" *(einer dionysischen Mächtigkeit der deutschen Seele).*
He proved blind to their true character and weakness, in short, their romanticism. It is important to point out that this "misunderstanding" includes
Nietzsche himself, who in one of his last and most polemical essays,
"Nietzsche Contra Wagner" admits readily to have been part of it: "It is
plain what I misunderstood in, equally what I read into, Wagner and
Schopenhauer—myself" *(Man sieht, was ich verkannte, man sieht
insgleichen, womit ich Wagnern und Schopenhauern beschenkte—mit
mir)*[8] (*KSA* VI 425).

Nietzsche does not deny what he had already said in *The Birth of
Tragedy*, namely that "every art, every philosophy may be viewed as a
remedy and an aid in the service of growing and struggling life" *(Jede
Kunst, jede Philosophie darf als Heil—und Hülfsmittel im Dienste des
wachsenden, kämpfenden Lebens angesehen werden)* (*GS* 328, *KSA*
III 620). Still adhering to his view that at bottom, existence is suffering,
which consequently demands sufferers, Nietzsche now changes his per-

spective from that of the early days, putting the emphasis on worldly, active coping with struggle, rather than on "metaphysical comfort" and promising fictions of redemption. He thus sets out to establish two categories of sufferers, of which the second is divided in two again.

> First those who suffer from the *over-fullness of life*—they want a Dionysian art and likewise a tragic view of life, a tragic insight—and then those who suffer from the *impoverishment of life* and seek rest, stillness, calm seas, redemption from themselves through art and knowledge, or intoxication, convulsions, anesthesia, and madness.
> *(einmal die an* der Fülle des Lebens *Leidenden, welche eine dionysische Kunst wollen und ebenso eine tragische Ansicht und Einsicht in das Leben,—und sodann die an* der Verarmung des Lebens *Leidenden, die Ruhe, Stille, glattes Meer, Erlösung von sich durch die Kunst und Erkenntniss suchen, oder aber den Rausch, den Krampf, die Betäubung, den Wahnsinn) (GS 328, KSA III 620).*

At the center of his critique of romantic pessimism lies the notion of creativity (the will to aesthetic expression) which for Nietzsche is the barometer of an individual's and people's health. The level of creativity is dependent on the amount of vitality with which they are imbued. Vitality is on the increase and prospering, if true needs are first of all recognized, and then met with the appropriate fuel and response. Vitality and creativity decline when those needs are ignored. For Nietzsche, those who think they suffer most, those "poorest in life" *(Lebensärmste)* have needs that are the wrong needs, e.g., Christianity and "a god who would be truly a god for the sick, a healer and saviour" *(einen Gott, der ganz eigentlich ein Gott für Kranke, ein Heiland wäre)*, as well as the calming comfort of theoretical reason, "logic, the conceptual understandability of existence" *(Logik, die begriffliche Verständlichkeit des Daseins).* Both are unmasked by Nietzsche as artificial, saving illusions, wrapping their practitioners in "a certain warm narrowness that keeps away fear and encloses one in optimistic horizons" *(eine gewisse warme furchtabwehrende Enge und Einschliessung in optimistische Horizonte).*

A seemingly simple question underlies Nietzsche's inquiry:

> Regarding all aesthetic values I now avail myself of this main distinction: I ask in every instance, 'is it hunger or super-abundance that has here become creative?' (In Hinsicht auf alle aesthetische Werthe bediene ich mich jetzt dieser Hauptunterscheidung: ich frage in jedem einzelnen Falle, 'ist hier der Hunger oder der Ueberfluss schöpferisch geworden?') *(GS* 329, *KSA* III 621).

Interestingly, but not surprisingly, Nietzsche's sharp, analytical eye seems to find more pleasure scrutinizing the creative force-fields of the two camps of romantic pessimists than in exploring the creative potential of his newly coined "Dionysian pessimism," which he offers as the only true alternative:

> That there still could be an altogether different kind of pessimism, a classical type—this premonition and vision belongs to me as inseparable from me, as my *proprium* and *ipsissimum*; only the word "classical" offends my ears, it is far too trite and has become round and indistinct. I call this pessimism of the future—for it comes! I see it coming!—*Dionysian* pessimism.
> *(Dass es noch einen ganz anderen Pessimismus geben könne, einen klassischen— diese Ahnung und Vision gehört zu mir, als unablöslich von mir, als mein* proprium *und* ipsissimum: *nur dass meinen Ohren das Wort "klassisch" widersteht, es ist bei weitem zu abgebraucht, zu rund und unkenntlich geworden. Ich nenne jenen Pessimismus der Zukunft—denn er kommt! Ich sehe ihn kommen!—den* dionysischen *Pessimismus) (GS* 330, *KSA* III 622).

A strange god-like figure, the "Dionysian god and man" meets the human condition with fearlessness and superiority. Since he "is richest in the fullness of life, . . . [he] can not only afford the sight of the terrible and questionable but even the terrible deed and any luxury of destruction, de-composition, and negation" *(Der Reichste an Lebensfülle . . . kann sich nicht nur den Anblick des Fürchterlichen und Fragwürdigen gönnen, sondern selbst die fürchterliche Tat und jeden Luxus von Zerstörung, Zersetzung, Verneinung) (GS* 328, *KSA* III 620).

Excess, infinitely preferable to the "warm narrowness," becomes a positive value, in the moral and aesthetic realms alike, a luxury indeed, because all energy is geared towards transformation and creation. "In his case, what is evil, absurd, ugly seems, as it were, permissible, owing to an excess of procreating, fertilizing energies that can still turn any desert into lush farmland" *(Bei ihm erscheint das Böse, Unsinnige und Hässliche gleichsam erlaubt, in Folge eines Ueberschusses von zeugenden, befruchtenden Kräften, welcher aus jeder Wüste noch ein üppiges Fruchtland zu schaffen im Stande ist) (GS* 328, *KSA* III 620).

Nietzsche's portrait of the strong Dionysian man as his own mas-ter, ever affirming and transforming at will all things into beautiful things— in brief, an artist of life—corresponds to an ideal he had set for himself on New Year's Day of 1882:

For the new year.—I still live, I still think: I still have to live for I still have to think
. . . Today everybody permits himself the expression of his wish and his dearest
thought; hence I, too, shall say . . . what thought shall be for me the reason,
warranty, and sweetness of my life henceforth. I want to learn more and more to
see as beautiful what is necessary in things; then I shall be one of those who make
things beautiful. *Amor fati*: let that be my love henceforth! I do not want to wage
war against what is ugly. I do not want to accuse; I do not even want to accuse
those who accuse. *Looking away* shall be my only negation. And all in all and on
the whole: some day I wish to be only a Yes-sayer.
*(Zum neuen Jahre.-Noch lebe ich, noch denke ich: ich muss noch leben, denn ich
muss noch denken. . .Heute erlaubt sich Jedermann seinen Wunsch und liebsten
Gedanken auszusprechen: nun, so will auch ich sagen . . . welcher Gedanke mir
Grund, Bürgschaft und Süssigkeit alles weiteren Lebens sein soll! Ich will immer
mehr lernen, das Nothwendige in den Dingen als das Schöne sehen:—so werde
ich Einer von denen sein, welche die Dinge schön machen. Amor fati: das sein
von nun an meine Liebe! Ich will keinen Krieg gegen das Hässliche führen. Ich
will nicht anklagen, ich will nicht einmal die Ankläger anklagen. Wegsehen sei
meine einzige Verneinung! Und, Alles in Allem und Grossen: ich will irgendwann
einmal nur noch ein Ja-sagender sein!) (GS 223, KSA III 521).*

This wish, which has to be seen as just that and maybe a superabundance of good-will in the face of deficient reality, comes close to that
inscribed in the idea of the conceptual "Ubermensch," defined by Francesca
Cauchi as "an ideal of the first rank, both in the sense of existing solely as
an idea and thus not real and actual, and as a thing conceived as perfect in
its kind—a perfect human being who will replace man who is a failure."[9]
Cauchi, whose main and arguable point is that Nietzsche's philosophy is
but a more extreme form of Schopenhauer's philosophy of world-denial, is
right nonetheless in stressing the irresolvable tension which inhabits all of
Nietzsche's work. As she justly points out, "the manifold contradictions in
Nietzsche's work reflect his violent inner battle between his self and his
anti-self, between what he was and what he wanted to be" (Cauchi 257).
This statement is valid particularly with regard to Nietzsche's relentless
activity not only to examine "clinically" but to overcome realistically his
most serious friend and enemy, romantic pessimism.

That the nature of a romantic pessimist is at least double makes
Nietzsche's analysis in Aphorism 370 of *The Gay Science* more complex
and tinges the black and white dichotomy of sickness and health with many
shades of gray. As an alternative to the question whether hunger or abundance is the source of creation, Nietzsche offers another dichotomy, "namely

the question whether the desire to fix, to immortalize, the desire for *being*, prompted creation, or the desire for destruction, for change, for future, for *becoming*" *(nämlich ob das Verlangen nach Starrmachen, Verewigen, nach Sein die Ursache des Schaffens ist, oder aber das Verlangen nach Zerstörung, nach Wechsel, nach Neuem, nach Zukunft, nach Werden)* (*GS* 329, *KSA III* 621). Considering what Nietzsche previously stated about the wrong needs of sufferers, and paying attention to the tone of his voice, it seems clear that he favors the impulse for change over the desire for stillness.

Nietzsche guards against giving definitive answers, and leaves room for a certain interpretative play, maintaining ambiguity while "closely" observing the different forms these opposing desires can take. Change and destruction or immortalization and fixity have no value in themselves. They are two equally strong drives which become interesting only insofar as they can appear as both manifestations of strength or weakness, and as the forceful expression of resentment. Therefore if the desire for destruction, change, and becoming springs from a "Dionysian" source, i.e., it becomes "an expression of an overflowing energy that is pregnant with future" *(der Ausdruck der übervollen, zukunftsschwangeren Kraft)*, it is considered by Nietzsche a constructive, beneficial drive. If, on the other hand, this desire is the expresssion of the blind hatred of the Christian shepherd's flock, all inveterate under-cover nihilists, "the ill-constituted, disinherited, and underprivileged who . . . must destroy because what exists, indeed all existence, all being outrages and provokes them" *(der Hass des Missrathenen, Entbehrenden, Schlechtweggekommenen . . . der zerstören muss, weil ihn das Bestehende, ja alles Bestehn, alles Sein selbst empört und aufreizt)*, then to reverse Nietzsche's image, all lush farmland, sooner or later, is bound to turn into barren desert.

The same distinction goes for the will to eternalize, which Nietzsche links more specifically to artistic activity. If this will to give lasting shape and form to phenomena stems from a natural generosity, combined with a deep sense of equilibrium, or is prompted "by gratitude and love" *(Dankbarkeit und Liebe)*—one thinks of *Amor fati*—then the result is great art. Nietzsche endows the idea of "classical" with an unusually colorful lightness, invoking as examples the "dithyrambic" quality of Rubens, the "blissfully mocking" *(selig-spöttisch)* poetry of the Persian Hafiz, or the "bright and gracious" *(hell und gütig)* style of Goethe. All of them are bathed in a glorious Homeric light. In contrast with romantic pessimism, which dwells in a morass of permanent dissatisfaction, this dionysian, life-affirming superabundance of energy, transformed into a quietly superior art (Nietzschean classicism), draws its power from a will to objectify, a will to turn away from the subjective towards something not only bigger and higher but, above all, other. Feeding on all the *negativa* imaginable and even cherishing them as a capital *raison d'être*, valuing their existence in proportion to the misery they contain or cause, the romantic pessimist finds a masochistic pleasure in his condition. He then exploits it fully by presenting it to others as an imperative. His is:

> the tyrannic will of one who suffers deeply, who struggles, is tormented, and would like to turn what is most personal, singular, and narrow, the real idiosyncrasy of his suffering, into a binding law and compulsion—one who, as it were, revenges himself on all things by forcing his own image, the image of his torture, on them, branding them with it.
> *(jener tyrannische Wille eines Schwerleidenden, Kämpfenden, Torturierten sein, welcher das Persönlichste, Einzelnste, Engste, die eigentliche Idiosynkrasie seines Leidens noch zum verbindlichen Gesetz und Zwang stempeln möchte und der in allen Dingen gleichsam Rache nimmt, dadurch, dass er ihnen sein Bild, das Bild seiner Tortur, aufdrückt, einzwängt, einbrennt) (GS 330, KSA III 622).*

In the realm of aesthetics, this attitude takes many interesting forms, and it is always its creative potential, variety, and virtuosity that leads Nietzsche further into his psychological investigations and analysis of the type of beings he calls romantic pessimists.

III.   From Romantic Pessimism to Decadence: France

The localization of the shift from the term romantic pessimism to that of decadence in Nietzsche is a complex question which has been addressed in many ways and from various angles. From a more general point of view, Erwin Koppen, in his extensive study of Wagner's crucial role in the development of European decadence, shows decadence as the term of choice to define a general *Verfallstimmung* (atmosphere of decline), and as a slogan for a literary style and aesthetic.

Decadence is intricately related to romanticism, if not born out of it—especially French romanticism—and Koppen pays close attention to the delaying of the term arriving in Germany via *fin de siècle* Vienna. Koppen argues that Nietzsche's term "romantic pessimism" can almost be equated with decadence, the question being mainly a terminological one.

He contends that since the term decadent was not available to Nietzsche until the time he focused on French literary criticism, Nietzsche made do with the term "romantic pessimism." As an example, Koppen cites Nietzsche's description of the romantic pessimists as they appear in the fifth book of *The Gay Science,* which he sees as a careful circumscription of the term decadent; Nietzsche enumerates qualities inherent in a decadent sensibility and its artistic expression, as they were already analyzed and named in France in the early 1830s by writers such as Désiré Nisard and Charles Nodier.[10]

From a more specific point of view, Mazzino Montinari establishes the beginning of Nietzsche's preoccupation with French literature and French literary criticism, and thus decadence, as early as 1883. While residing in Nice in the winter, Nietzsche becomes acquainted with the works of Théophile Gautier, Charles Baudelaire, Gustave Flaubert, Edmond and Jules de Goncourt, Guy de Maupassant, and Paul Bourget, to name only the most important ones. Careful to use the term in its widest sense, Montinari identifies these authors as representative of what he describes as a common tendency if not movement—"French Decadence." Montinari uses this arguable categorization mainly to highlight Nietzsche's curiosity and enthusiasm for French culture, especially for the traces of decadence he found in the works of nineteenth century French writers.[11]

Nietzsche's interest in the idea of decline is mainly an aesthetic one. Thus it is that France, in positive contrast to Germany, becomes Nietzsche's main source of inspiration after 1883. Whereas his many comments on Germany's political and cultural maladies at this time are often caustic, always tinged with regret, and hopeless about near-term recovery, Nietzsche's evaluation of French culture shows he feels a close affinity for the French *état d'esprit,* even in its decadent aspects. Above all, he respects the French decadents precisely because of their impressive productivity at the time, especially in the field of literature. In a note of the winter 1883–84, Nietzsche observes that "in regard to German culture, I have always had the premonition of decline" *(in Bezug auf die deutsche Cultur habe ich das Gefühl des Niedergangs immer gehabt),* and points to the fact that "the Germans are always latecomers dragging things into depth" *(die Deutschen kommen immer spät hinterdrein: sie tragen etwas in die Tiefe).*[12] France, on the other hand, appears already in the section "The Wanderer and his Shadow"(1880) of *Human, All Too Human* as the exclusive authority in questions of fashion and taste, and in general as "the nation which has up to now given modern mankind its finest books and its finest men" *(das Volk, welches der neueren Menschheit bisher die besten Bücher und die besten Menschen gegeben hat) (HAH 365, KSA II 651).*

During the winter of 1883–84, Nietzsche discovers the works of French writer Paul Bourget, whose essays on the relationship between contemporary French literature and society gave Nietzsche the opportunity to see further into the workings of what might be called the French *état d'âme.* The first mention of Nietzsche's reading of Bourget can be found in the same note of the winter of 1883–84 in which he connects Wagner with decadence as an artistic style: "Style of decadence in Wagner: the single phrase becomes sovereign, the subordination and arrangement become arbitrary. Bourget p. 25" *(Stil des Verfalls bei Wagner: die einzelne Wendung wird souverän, die Unterordnung und Einordnung wird zufällig. Bourget p. 25) (KSA* X 646).

Today Bourget's literary and critical contributions to nineteenth-century French cultural studies have fallen into relative obscurity. J. C. Fewster, in one of the rare articles on Bourget that are to be found today, suggests that the reason for this might reside in the fact that, due to his later writings and affiliation with the right-wing movement *action française,* he appears less as a progressive, open-minded thinker and more often as an incurable moralizer, a fervent Catholic, a radical spokesman for national renewal, and the maintenance of order, in a society threatened with social and cultural collapse.[13]

As Fewster points out, however, in his own time, Paul Bourget's combination of ideas and literary innovations made him eminent among the literary community, and won him a wide audience including Nietzsche.[14] His best known work—the one which inspired Nietzsche—is his *Essais de psychologie contemporaine,* the first volume of two, published in 1883. It is a collection of portraits of original authors, including Stendhal, Flaubert, Renan, Taine, and Baudelaire, whom Bourget considered representative of a specific historical climate, and through whom he attempted to explain a fundamental attitude of the modern spirit.[15] The main interest of these essays lies, as the title suggests, in Bourget's psychological approach to his analysis of culture, and in particular the phenomenon of decadence, which he opposed but by which he felt marked nevertheless.[16]

Mario Matucci, who considers Bourget one of the most important historians of morals of the second half of the nineteenth century, argues that what makes Bourget's texts interesting is his personal and intense involvement with literature. According to Matucci, the point of departure of Bourget's project was his *idée fixe* of "the book," his self avowed "literary intoxication," which fostered his belief in the determining role of literature as "initiator" of life. Matucci describes Bourget as thinking that since literature contains the truest image of the generation that produces it, it can express the *état d'âme* of a whole century, and reflect the feelings of the men of those times filtered through the soul of the author. With written word, authors become the most intelligible representative of an epoque, and their books, as significant testimony, assume a didactic function.[17]

Bourget, who sees his position as that of "an analyst without doctrine" (Bourget 11), perceives decadence, and its many styles of expression, as symptomatic of a pervasive pessimism. As Jean Pierrot points out, "his principal concern was to arrive at a diagnosis, from the viewpoint of social psychology, of the ills that afflict the soul of modern man."[18] And indeed the authors he profiles can be seen as seminal figures in the development of decadence (though to different degrees). They are "disquieting personalities who, because of their importance and their complexity can't submit to the discipline of the herd, they represent a danger for society as a whole while at the same time engendering an immensely rich and fascinating art. And it is to this art that Bourget's sympathies go" (Matucci 177).

Nietzsche might have recognized in Bourget a thinker not unlike himself, whose awareness of his own implication in and affinity with the subject of decadence made him original in the community of critics. Maybe Nietzsche discovered in Bourget an individual whose merit lies in his attempt to avoid a faulty reasoning which Nietzsche detected in others. In *Twilight of the Idols*, Nietzsche remarks:

> It is self-deception on the part of philosophers and moralists to imagine that by making war on decadence they therewith elude decadence themselves. This is beyond their powers: what they select as an expedient, as a deliverance, is itself only another expression of decadence—they alter its expression, they do not abolish the thing in itself.
> *(Es ist ein Selbstbetrug seitens der Philosophen und Moralisten, damit schon aus der* décadence *herauszutreten, dass sie gegen dieselbe Krieg machen. Das Heraustreten steht ausserhalb ihrer Kraft; was sie als Mittel, als Rettung wählen, ist selber nur wieder ein Ausdruck der* décadence—*sie verändern deren Ausdruck, sie schaffen sie selbst nicht weg).*[19]

Nietzsche's position is anticipated in Bourget's preface to the *Essais* wherein he defines pessimism as a logical continuation of the French romanticism of 1830, as an expression of *le mal du siècle,* and claims his right to study it as a sickness rather than condemn it or look away:

> Why not rather recognize and accept the fact that a great portion of today's youth goes through a crisis? It offers symptoms, visible to all who want to see without prejudice, of a sickness of moral life arrived at its most acute state. One exclaims: there goes the good old French gaiety. . . But if this gaiety has but almost entirely vanished, are there no reasons for this disappearance? Since when has a sickness been an absolute thing, incapable of degrees, irreconcilable with a certain portion of health? (Bourget 23).

It is Bourget's essay on Charles Baudelaire, in which he develops a theory of decadence, that is considered one of the main pieces of evidence of Nietzsche's encounter with Baudelaire and decadence. In this essay, Bourget's method of analysis and his major concerns come best to light, showing him moving back and forth between a desire to synthesize and a taste for meticulous analysis. He presents a survey of European civilization as a whole and then elaborates on his general conception of pessimism, which among the Germans is exemplified by the works of Schopenhauer, and among the French manifests itself as those "solitary and bizarre neuroses" (Bourget 13) expressed in particular in the works and personality of Baudelaire, who appears as the most complex of modern artists.

Exploring the infinite disharmony between himself and the world, marked by chronic unhappiness, and using any means available to escape reality, Baudelaire appears to exemplify both the general and particular. Baudelaire displays a systematic preference for the strange and the rare, the search for new sensations in a "mystical, licentious, and analytic attitude to love" (Bourget 5), he uses Catholicism for purely aesthetic purposes (faith will depart, but mysticism, even when expelled from the intelligence, will linger on in the sensations) (Bourget 8), and he hates nature and loves the artificial. All are traits common to a whole group of writers, but they find in the poet their most "rigorous" (Bourget 3) expression. Ironically, Baudelaire, as its archetypical representative, reveals in pessimism a positive dynamic quality, thanks to his ability to penetrate its inner logic, critically and creatively, and infuse it with novelty. Particularly in the third chapter of his essay "Theory of Decadence," Bourget attributes to Baudelaire essential qualities that set him apart from many others:

If a peculiar nuance in his conception of love, if a new way of interpreting pessimism make of Baudelaire's mind a psychological apparatus of a rare kind, which earns him a place apart in the literature of our epoch, it is because he has surprisingly well understood and exaggerated in extraordinary fashion this specialty and novelty. He was well aware that he arrived late in an aging civilization, and, instead of deploring this late arrival, as La Bruyère and Musset did, he took pleasure in it, he felt honored, I should say. He was a man of decadence and he made himself a theoretician of decadence. This might perhaps be the most disquieting aspect of this disquieting figure. It is perhaps he who exerted the most confusing seduction upon a contemporary soul (Bourget 19).

It is thus not only as the poet of *The Flowers of Evil* that Baudelaire established his predominant role in the development and expression of decadence. Bourget insists on Baudelaire's influential and educational powers, as a theoretician and artist, and as an individual who "had the courage to adopt at the youngest age this attitude and the temerity to stick to it" (Bourget 24). That Baudelaire was capable of fusing three separate personalities (the mystic, the libertine, and the analyst) to master analysis as well as synthesis is a major concern of the nineteenth-century critic:

Three men inhabit this man simultaneously . . . These three men are very modern, and the most modern is their reunion. The crisis of religious faith, life in Paris and the scientific spirit of the times have contributed to fashion and then to fuse these three kinds of sensitivities, formerly separated to the point of irreconcilability, in this creature without equivalent, . . . who was Baudelaire (Bourget 7).

IV.   Theory of Decadence

Bourget's analysis of decadence is interesting not only because of his precise diagnoses, but because of his attitude, which displays an untimely fairness with regard to its cultural enrichment. On the one hand, he recognizes that decadence constitutes a threat on the collective level of a nation. He defines it as the result of "an excess of critical thinking, excess of literature, and excess of science" (Bourget 29). On the other, he draws far more attention to its positive literary qualities. Indeed in one relevant passage of his essay on Baudelaire, he depicts decadence as the very essence of literary modernity, and it is to this passage that Nietzsche refers when defining Wagner's work.

Bourget begins by comparing society to a living organism constituted of smaller organisms, themselves composed of cells representing individuals. In order for this organism to function, all its constitutive parts would have to work energetically by themselves, and at the same time with what he calls "an energy of subordination" to the whole. If the single cell strives for independence, an imbalance, or "anarchy" results, which brings "decadence" or the disintegration of the whole to the profit of its rebellious parts. It is Bourget's merit to have translated this process, defined here in the term of "law," into the realm of language and literature, where, most interestingly, it results in a "style," that is something which can again be defined, through common properties, as a unifying principle:

> A style of decadence is the one where the unity of the book disintegrates to make room for the independence of the page, where the page disintegrates to make room for the independence of the sentence, and the sentence to make room for the independence of the word. Examples abound in present literature, which corroborate this hypothesis and justify this analogy (Bourget 20).

Distinguishing between two perspectives in the perception and judgment of decadence, Bourget clearly favors the method and perspective of the *psychologue pur* (pure psychologist) over the reasoning of politicians and moralists, who are exclusively concerned with the quantity of work produced by this social mechanism. Whereas the latter see everything in the light of collective effort and action, the psychologist studies precisely the independent parts of this mechanism, which, taken as singular "cases," reveal themselves to be striking material for the cultural enrichment of a nation. For every failure as collective beings (not active in the public or private sector, not future-oriented, not devoted to religious faith), "the citizen" of a decadent period has to offer other qualities, which largely make up for these shortcomings, and especially when these values are translated into the realm of literature.

According to Bourget, the general argument against decadence, which is that it has no concern for the morrow, becomes irrelevant in literature, where "alterations of vocabulary" and the "subtleties of words," bring about a new style which might prove unintelligible to later generations but expresses most truthfully a spirit of refinement characterizing all periods of decadent sensibility. Putting himself in the mind of the psychologist who argues in favor of decadence, Bourget aligns himself with all those, who, like Baudelaire, claim their right to be modern at all costs:

What does it matter? Is it the the goal of the writer to pose as a perpetual candidate for popular vote in all centuries? We find pleasure in what you might call our corruption of style, and we please at the same time those refined ones of our race and present hour. The question remains open as to whether our exception is not an aristocracy, and if, in the realm of aesthetics, the plurality of popular vote represents something other than the plurality of ignorance. Apart from the fact that it is childish to believe in immortality, since times are near when men's memory, overburdened by the prodigious amount of books, suffers bankruptcy, it is deception not to have the courage to one's intellectual pleasure. Let us therefore delight in the singularities of our ideals and form, and pay the price of imprisonment in a solitude without visitors (Bourget 23).

That Nietzsche agreed to a large degree with Bourget's assessment and maybe even recognized himself as yet another, if stronger, exceptional artist within this small group of singulars, comes as no surprise when considering the following passage from a letter to his friend Peter Gast. Referring to his reading of the *Journal* of the Goncourt brothers, "the most interesting novelty," and the famous dinners "Chez Magny" where "the most spiritual and skeptical bunch of Parisian intelligentsia" convened, namely Sainte Beuve, Flaubert, Théophile Gautier, Taine, Renan, the Goncourts, Schérer, Gavarni, and sometimes Turgenev, Nietzsche comments:

Exasperated pessimism, cynicism, nihilism, alternating between exuberance and good humor; I myself did not fit in badly within this group—I know these gentlemen by heart, so much so, that I am actually already fed up with them. One has to be more radical: at bottom, all lack the main thing—'la force.'
(Exasperierter Pessimismus, Zynismus, Nihilismus, mit viel Ausgelassenheit und gutem Humor abwechselnd; ich selbst gehörte gar nicht übel hinein—ich kenne diese Herrn auswendig, so sehr dass ich sie eigentlich bereits satt habe. Man muss radikaler sein: im Grunde fehlt es bei allen an der Hauptsache—'la force').[20]

This letter, written on November 10, 1887, already suggests Nietzsche's growing effort to achieve some distance from what he had diagnosed as part of his entire being. Even while shifting the emphasis onto overcoming decadence rather than participating in it, however, Nietzsche bounces back and forth between the two poles—decadence and its contrary—preventing any definitive "solution" to the problem.

Therein lies another parallel between Bourget and Nietzsche. Bourget had avowed in his preface to the *Essais* that a positive conclusion to the *mal du siècle* was voluntarily lacking. It was his belief that by taking seriously, almost tragically, the drama which plays itself out in the mind and hearts of one's generation, one affirms, by writing about it, a certain belief in "the obscure and painful, adorable and inexplicable, which is the human soul" (Bourget 27). Thus the very act of writing, as a creative process, becomes in itself an act of faith, which may relieve the writer from the necessity of drawing final conclusions to questions regarding the complexity of man's inner life. Nevertheless, the effort to find a definition of the common traits of the decadent sensibility and its expressions testifies to a strong concern for the reconstruction of something which by its nature eludes this process. The idea of synthesis never leaves the mind of the nineteenth-century thinker. It is very much on Nietzsche's mind in *Beyond Good and Evil* (1885) when he discusses the state of affairs in Europe. Nietzsche's reasoning goes as follows: a pessimistic skepticism reigns in Europe, which brings about a weakening of the will in its worst but at the same time most alluring forms:

> Paralysis of the will: where today does one not find this cripple sitting? And often in such finery! How seductive this finery looks! This disease enjoys the most beautiful pomp-and-lie costumes; and most of what today displays itself in the showcases, for example, as 'objectivity,' 'being scientific,' 'l'art pour l'art,' 'pure knowledge, free of will,' is merely dressed-up skepticism and paralysis of the will: for this diagnosis of the European sickness I vouch.
> *(Willenslähmung: wo findet man nicht heute diesen Krüppel sitzten! Und oft noch wie geputzt! Wie verführerisch herausgeputzt! Es gibt die schönsten Prunk— und Lügenkleider für diese Krankheit; und dass zum Beispiel das Meiste von dem, was sich heute als 'Objektivität,' 'Wissenschaftlichkeit,' 'l'art pour l'art,' 'reines willensfreies Erkennen' in die Schauläden stellt, nur aufgeputzte Skepsis uns Willenslähmung ist,—für diese Diagnose der europäischen Krankheit will ich einstehen) (BGE 130, KSA V 138).*

Nietzsche's uncovering of the reality which underlies the spirit of decadence, clearly defined as such in this passage, namely an incapacity to overcome this sickness, reveals above all Nietzsche's own sensitivity to the seductive powers of this masquerade. Keeping in mind that Nietzsche only recently encountered French decadence, it is not surprising that he turns his attention to France, where an extraordinary proliferation of this sickness is taking place, a phenomenon Nietzsche never tires of investigating and exploiting.

Contending that sickness of the will is most advanced where culture has flourished the longest, Nietzsche regards France as the most afflicted country. This illness, however, bears in itself an undeniable fortitude for France,

having always possessed a masterly skill at converting even the most calamitous
turns of its spirit into something attractive and seductive, now really shows its
cultural superiority over Europe by being the school and display of all the charms
of skepticism.
*(welches immer eine meisterhafte Geschicklichkeit gehabt hat, auch die
verhängnisvollen Wendungen seines Geistes in's Reizende und Verführerische
umzukehren, zeigt heute recht eigentlich als Schule und Schaustellung aller Zauber
der Skepsis sein Cultur-Uebergewicht über Europa) (BGE 131, KSA V 139).*

Nietzsche's connection between sickness and cultural wealth, or
in the words of Kaufmann, between "artistic genius and physical and mental disease" (Kaufmann 132), and his nuanced appreciation of the negative
as capable of bringing about positive phenomena, is perhaps one of the
most intriguing aspects of his evaluation of decadence. Paradoxically it is
precisely late French romanticism as the hearth of decadence, which in-
spires Nietzsche to visualize, in the famous Aphorism 256 in *Beyond Good
and Evil*, a unified Europe formed by "all the more profound and comprehensive men of this century" *(allen tieferen und umfänglicheren Menschen
dieses Jahrhunderts)*, whose "over-all direction of the mysterious workings of their soul was to prepare the way for this new synthesis and to
anticipate experimentally the European of the future" *(war es die eigentliche
Gesamtrichtung in der geheimnisvollen Arbeit ihrer Seele, den Weg zu jener
neuen Synthesis vorzubereiten und versuchsweise den Europäer der Zukunft
vorwegzunehmen) (BGE 196, KSA V 202).*

It seems puzzling at first to see the names of Napoleon, Goethe,
Beethoven, Stendhal, and Heinrich Heine mentioned together as representatives of this synthesis in one sentence. And when Nietzsche adds to this
heterogeneous collection Schopenhauer and Richard Wagner, one is left to
wonder what these men might have in common and what kind of synthesis
Nietzsche has in mind. To name all in one breath a French dictator, a
German classicist, two German musicians as different as Beethoven and
Wagner, a German expatriate author, a French writer as resistant to classi-
fication as Stendhal, and Schopenhauer, the ultimate promoter of philosophical pessimism point to Nietzsche's particular method of analysis.

Under Nietzsche's pen, certain unique individuals, such as the
above-mentioned ones, become specific types representative of a certain
idea Nietzsche is seeking to develop. This technique serves Nietzsche in
two ways: he is able to leave intact the uniqueness of each individual while
making a connection and shedding some light on their common qualities.

In the case above, Nietzsche highlights the type of strength and health gained in overcoming adversity—be it on the political or social level, or constituted by sickness and suffering.

What is at stake for Nietzsche is to show how these artists responded to permanent obstacles and expressed themselves through a restless and defiant creativity, which, at its best, transcends national identity. The nexus of the arts taken together—music, painting, and literature—is of prime importance in Nietzsche's vision of Europe's future. Schopenhauer, and especially Wagner, who increasingly gains in importance in Nietzsche's evaluation of decadence, serve as a link between the first and the second half of the century. Nietzsche's portrayal of artists as types, and as individuals possessed by an inner drive to create in spite of themselves and in spite of unfavorable conditions, deserves to be quoted in its entirety, since it represents one of the most poignant examples of Nietzsche's own participation in the frenzied search for expression, which characterizes these "last great seekers" and "masters of new means of language" *(diese letzten grossen Suchenden . . .diese Meister neuer Sprachmittel)* of the nineteenth century (as well as our own):

Literature dominated all of them up to their eyes and ears—they were the first artists steeped in world literature—and most of them were themselves writers, poets, mediators and mixers of the arts and senses [as a musician, Wagner belongs among painters; as a poet, among musicians; as an artist among actors]; all of them were fanatics of expression 'at any price'—I should stress Delacroix, who was most closely related to Wagner—all of them great discoverers in the realm of the sublime, also of the ugly and gruesome, and still greater discoverers concerning effects, display, and the art of display windows—all of them talents far beyond their genius—virtuosos through and through, with uncanny access to everything that seduces, allures, compels, overthrows; born enemies of logic and straight lines, lusting after the foreign, the exotic, the tremendous, the crooked, the self-contradictory;

(Allesamt beherrscht von der Literatur bis in ihre Augen und Ohren—die ersten Künstler von weltliterarischer Bildung—meistens sogar selber Schreibende, Dichtende, Vermittler und Vermischer der Künste und Sinne [Wagner gehört als Musiker unter die Maler, als Dichter unter die Musiker, als Künstler überhaupt unter die Schauspieler]; allesamt Fanatiker des Ausdrucks 'um jeden Preis'— ich hebe Delacroix hervor, den Nächstverwandten Wagner's— allesamt grosse Entdecker im Reiche des Erhabenen, auch des Hässlichen und Grässlichen, noch grössere Entdecker im Effekte, in der Schaustellung, in der Kunst der Schauläden, allesammt Talente weit über ihr Genie hinaus—,Virtuosen durch und durch, mit unheimlichen Zugängen zu Allem, was verführt, lockt, zwingt, umwirft, geborene Feinde der Logik und der geraden Linien, begehrlich nach dem Fremden, dem

Exotischen, dem Ungeuren, dem Krummen, dem sich Widersprechendem) (BGE 197, KSA 202).

   Considering Nietzsche's previous analysis of sickness of the will as one of the factors linking these people together, it is all the more intriguing that he continues in self-contradictory fashion to contribute to a myth whose underlying reality he now dismisses for the sake of the pleasure he obviously has in painting a compelling picture. In this passage, the critic fuses with the artists who are:

> as human beings, Tantaluses of the will, . . . who knew themselves incapable, both in their lives and works, of a noble tempo, a *lento*—take Balzac, for example—unbridled workers, almost self-destroyers through work; antinomians and rebels against custom, ambitious and insatiable without balance and enjoyment . . . on the whole, an audaciously daring, magnificently violent type of higher human beings who soared, and tore others along to the heights—it fell to them first to teach their century—and it is the century of the *crowd*!—the concept 'higher man'—
> *(als Menschen Tantalusse des Willens, . . . welche sich im Leben und Schaffen eines vornehmen tempo, eines* lento *unfähig wussten,—man denke zum Beispiel an Balzac—zügellose Arbeiter, beinahe Selbstzerstörer durch Arbeit; Antinomisten und Aufrührer in den Sitten, Ehrgeizige und Unersättliche ohne Gleichgewicht und Genuss; . . . im Ganzen eine verwegen-wagende, prachtvoll gewaltsame, hochfliegende und hoch emporreissende Art höherer Menschen, welche ihrem Jahrhundert—und es ist das Jahrhundert der* Menge!—*den Begriff "höherer Mensch" erst zu lehren hatte) (BGE 197, KSA V 202–203).*

   This picture would be a perfect example of an endorsement of such frantic productivity were it not for Nietzsche's brief and sudden objection to and distancing from these types who were not like Nietzsche, "profound and original enough for a philosophy of the Antichrist" *(tief und ursprünglich genug zu einer Philosophie des Antichrist)*, but instead, showing their weakness, "all of them broke and collapsed in the end before the Christian cross" *(allesamt zuletzt an dem christlichen Kreuze zerbrechend und niedersinkend) (BGE 197, KSA V 203).*
   This objection is linked to Nietzsche's critique of Christianity as the ultimate inventor and promoter of moral standards which keep their followers in check and stifle the necessary life-drive for self-realization. Thus art, as conceived here from an extra-moral point of view, as *l'art pour l'art* becomes a positive outlet for self-expression. What it lacks, what its producers lack, is a more radical affirmation of art's true goal, which is not

to be purposeless but rather to be "the great stimulus for life" *(die grosse Stimulans fürs Leben)* (*TI* 81, *KSA* VI 127).

Where Nietzsche seems to differ from artists such as Flaubert and Baudelaire, whose names are absent in the passage above, but who are recognizable as parts of the picture, is when he chooses to emphasize life over art, dividing the question of the artist's inner motivation into two perspectives: "Is his basic instinct directed towards art, or is it not rather directed towards the meaning of art, which is life? towards a desideratum of life—?" *(Geht dessen unterster Instinkt auf die Kunst oder nicht vielmehr auf den Sinn der Kunst, das Leben? auf eine Wünschbarkeit von Leben?)* (*TI* 81, *KSA* VI 127).

As Ernst Behler points out, it is here that one touches on Nietzsche's deeply ambivalent attitude towards art, which in one way he sees as a completely autonomous sphere of activity, and then again as an essentially useful, life-preserving and life-promoting task. This equivocalness in Nietzsche's conception of art shows itself not only in the various texts from particular phases of his life, but is often condensed in a single concept, a term such as decadence, about which he expresses in one breath the most contradictory thoughts.[21] Indeed just as decadence appears as a collective noun for a multitude of different physiological, psychological, and aesthetic phenomena, the "decadents" themselves, especially Wagner and those associated with him in Nietzsche's notes, e.g., Delacroix, Baudelaire, and even Poe, become indispensable contributors to Nietzsche's own work on decadence. Their complexity fueled his understanding of decadence, and kept alive the tension which continued to exist for Nietzsche between life and art.

Of all the "types" of artists Nietzsche encountered through literature and life, Wagner is the one who stands in the foreground, and serves Nietzsche to comprehend and perform—literally and literarily—this tension which tends to elude any final conclusion.

In Wagner, all the formative elements of decadence come together for Nietzsche, but in spite of his unrelenting effort to come to terms with his personal Wagnerian experience, and the growing phenomenon of *Wagnérisme* in France and Germany, his experience and analysis never go beyond the form of an open-ended sketch.

Notes

1 In the essay "On the Uses and Disadvantage of History for Life," Nietzsche underlines the productiveness of imposing a horizon, (63).

In Aphorism 4 of the preface of the second book of *Human, All Too Human,* Nietzsche states that turning against himself leads him back to his task (*HAH* 211).

2 Friedrich Nietzsche, *Ecce Homo,* trans. W. Kaufmann (New York: Vintage, 1969), 222. References to this text are designated *EC.*

3 A detailed account of Nietzsche's usage of nihilism as the overall heading for pessimism and decadence can be found in Elizabeth Kuhn, "Nietzsches Quelle des Nihilismusbegriffs," *Nietzsche-Studien* 21 (Berlin: de Gruyter, 1984), 253–78.

4 Albert Camus, *The Rebel,* trans. Anthony Bower (New York: Vintage Books, 1960), 65–66.

5 Friedrich Nietzsche, *The Gay Science,* trans. W. Kaufmann (New York: Vintage,1974), 327. This text is designated *GS.*

6 Friedrich Nietzsche, *Nachgelassene Fragmente*, *Kritische Studienausgabe,* 15 vols., eds. G.Colli and M. Montinari (Berlin: de Gruyter, 1988), XII 409. References to these posthumous fragments are designated *KSA*, followed by volume and page number. Translation is mine.

7 A later version of this aphorism appears in "Nietzsche Contra Wagner" under the title "We Antipodes." Although Kaufmann helpfully points out the various modifications Nietzsche operated (Nietzsche adds mainly relevant examples), it seems that both texts agree on the question of romantic pessimism.

8 Friedrich Nietzsche, "Nietzsche Contra Wagner" *The Portable Nietzsche,* trans. W. Kaufmann (New York: The Viking Press, 1954), 669. References to this text are indicated by *PN.*

9 Francesca Cauchi, "Nietzsche and Pessimism: The Metaphysics Hypostatized" *The History of European Ideas,* vol. 13 (3) (Tarrytown, NY, 1991): 257.

10 Erwin Koppen, *Dekadenter Wagnerismus* (Berlin: De Gruyter, 1973), 165.

11 Mazzino Montinari, "Aufgaben der Nietzsche-Forschung heute: Nietzsches

Auseinandersetzung mit der französischen Literatur des 19. Jahrhundersts," *Nietzsche Heute,* pub. Sigrid Bauschinger, Susan l. Cocalis and Sara Lennox (Bern: Francke Verlag, 1988).

[12] Friedrich Nietzsche, *Nachgelassene Fragmente Kritische Studienausgabe* vol. 10, eds. Colli and Montinari (Berlin: de Gruyter,1988), 645. Further references appear in the text as *KSA*. Translation is mine.

[13] J. C. Fewster, "Au Service de l'ordre: 'Paul Bourget and the Critical Response to Decadence in Austria and Germany,'" *Comparative Literature Studies* 29.3 (Summer 1992): 259–73.

[14] For a discussion of Bourget's biography and works of fiction, see Armand E. Singer, *Paul Bourget* (Boston: Twayne, 1976).

[15] Paul Bourget, *Essais de Psychologie contemporaine,* 2 vols. (Paris: Plon, 1931–33). References to this text appear with the author's name. Translation is mine.

[16] The most extensive study of Bourget's "inner duality" is found in Michel Mansuy, *Un Moderne, Paul Bourget, Annales Littéraires de l'Université de Besançon* 38 (Paris: Les Belles Lettres, 1960).

[17] Mario Matucci, "Les Essais de Paul Bourget, entre pessimisme et décadence," *Lettres et Réalités* (Aix en Provence: Université de Provence, 1988), 166.

[18] Jean Pierrot, *The Decadent Imagination*, trans. Derek Coltman (Chicago: The University of Chicago Press, 1981), 13.

[19] Friedrich Nietzsche, *The Twilight of the Idols*, trans. R. J. Hollingdale (London: Penguin Classics, 1968), 34. References to this text are designated *TW*.

[20] Friedrich Nietzsche, *Sämtliche Briefe Kritische Studienausgabe*, vol. 8, eds. Colli and Montinari (Berlin: de Gruyter, 1986), 191–92. References to Nietzsche's correspondence are indicated with *KGB,* followed by volume and page number. Translation is mine.

[21] Ernst Behler, *Derrida-Nietzsche Nietzsche-Derrida* (Paderborn: F. Schoeningh, 1988), 103.

Chapter 6

RICHARD WAGNER

I.   *A Collision of "Stars"*

Although it seems that discussions of the relationship between Nietzsche and Wagner might at some point reach the level of exhaustion, recent scholarship shows a continuing interest and fascination with the topic. Indeed, any discussion of Nietzsche has to take into consideration Richard Wagner, whose personality and artwork become paradigmatic for Nietzsche's critique of modernity and the spirit of decadence. It is not surprising that as the twentieth century comes to a close, a renewed concern with the evaluation of the present cultural state of affairs takes place, and that parallels are drawn—or destroyed—between the end of the nineteenth century and ours.[1] It is Nietzsche's program from the very beginning to understand and describe the specificity of his own times, which for him were marked by a declining tendency in relation to his own specific and individual vision toward a future in which ascending virtues would again gain ground. In *The Birth of Tragedy*, he had already located the germ of decadence in the collective noun of Socrates whose promotion of faith in the power of reason led to the decay of Greek culture. Ever since their so-called break, officially dated 1878, it is Wagner who steps into the foreground as the most accomplished specimen in which all modern "virtues" come together and are expressed in the form of his *Gesamtkunstwerk*. First progressively, then exclusively in 1888, Wagner represents all that is wrong with modernity, while at the same time—and this explains why the debate continues—offering Nietzsche (and later cultural critics such as Adorno and Foucault) a large terrain to exercise and sharpen his analysis of the inner workings of culture formation and disintegration.

One of the points Nietzsche keeps stressing throughout his battle with Wagner, is that Wagner's popularity could only gain such wide scope because he invented and filled a market gap at the right time. It is as a "clever rattlesnake" *(kluge Klapperschlange)*, as the "master of hypnotic tricks" *(der Meister hypnotischer Griffe)*, as "a first rate actor" *(ein ganz grosser Schauspieler)* that Wagner conquered the market which seemed to be waiting only for him, and which he saw fit to exploit at all costs. For, as Nietzsche remarked more than once, his was the century of the masses, and Wagner not only recognized this but contributed to it by erecting Bayreuth as its temple in 1873.[2] Bayreuth was thought to have been the cornerstone of Nietzsche's break with Wagner. As Dieter Borchmeyer points out, however, Nietzsche's critical distancing from Wagner can already be traced back to his posthumous fragments of the year 1874–75, most of them preparatory notes to what was to become his last official tribute to the musician, the laudatory speech of 1876, "Wagner in Bayreuth."[3]

In the beginning Nietzsche was not against the project and had prepared a promotional text for it. The text, "An Appeal to the German Nation," however, was never printed. As it turned out, Bayreuth not only was a disappointment but also gave Nietzsche the emancipatory incentive to follow his own path upon which Wagner's shadow accompanied him all along. In these notes almost all the arguments of the later polemical essays are already present. These fragments show Nietzsche's concern with "absolute music" and an attempt to comprehend and describe the complexity of the character of Wagner's artist. There he already appears as a "musical rhetorician," a "misplaced actor," a "dilettante," and an "organizer of the masses." The critique of histrionic art—the stigmata of modern art par excellence—slowly takes shape. Wagner's character flaws are also mentioned: his intolerance for other musicians around him (e.g., Brahms), his taste for luxury, his tyrannical sense for the colossal, his lack of moderation and his anti-Semitism (*KSA* VIII 191–92). Consequently, in "Wagner in Bayreuth," Nietzsche already speaks with "a foreign tongue" as Borchmeyer puts it and in *Ecce Homo,* Nietzsche remembers his experience of Bayreuth as a shock-like awakening from a dream turning into a nightmare:

> Wherever was I? There was nothing that I recognized; I scarcely recognized Wagner. In vain did I leaf through my memories. . . The incomparable days when the foundation stone was laid, the small group of people that had belonged, had celebrated, and did not need first to acquire fingers for delicate matters—not a trace of any similarity. *What had happened?*—Wagner had been translated into German! The Wagnerian had become master over Wagner.—*German* art. The *German* master. *German* beer.
> *(Wo war ich doch? Ich erkannte nichts wieder, ich erkannte kaum Wagner wieder.*

*Umsonst blätterte ich in meinen Erinnerungen. . . Die unvergleichlichen Tage
der Grundsteinlegung, die kleine zugehörige Gesellschaft, die sie feierte und der
man nicht erst Finger für zarte Dinge zu wünschen hatte: kein Schatten von
Aehnlichkeit. Was war geschehen?—Man hatte Wagner ins Deutsche übersetzt!
Der Wagnerianer war Herr über Wagner geworden!—Die deutsche Kunst! der
deutsche Meister! das deutsche Bier!) (EC 284, KSA VI 323).*

Borchmeyer invites the reader to a cautionary reading of this passage, for he states that Nietzsche's sudden leaving of Bayreuth was mainly
prompted by his poor health which no longer allowed the philosopher to
attend the long performances. This does not, however, exclude the fact
that Nietzsche was also appalled by the scene in general. Contrary to his
earlier establishment of Nietzsche distancing himself from Wagner in 1874,
Borchmeyer now asserts that Bayreuth itself did not contribute to a final
rupture between the two. In spite of the fact that Nietzsche followed the
performances until 1882 from afar, his notes and letters around the time
attest to an increasing alienation from Wagner and especially from
"Wagnerism."[4]

It is indeed questionable whether a single event was the cause of
the rift. It seems more likely that the confluence of character traits and
ideological tendencies in Wagner himself and above all their effects on his
art contributed to a progressive drifting away on the part of Nietzsche.
Apart from Bayreuth, however, there is the incident of the "mortal insult"
of which Martin Gregor-Dellin speaks in his biography on Wagner whereby
Wagner revealed to his inner circle that Nietzsche's sexual practices and
possible homosexuality were likely explanations for his poor health.[5] Both
Gregor-Dellin and Nietzsche's most recent biographer Curt Paul Janz, identify "the mortal insult" with the hypothesis that Wagner's indiscretion,
reaching Nietzsche's ears shortly thereafter, must have contributed to
Nietzsche's retreat.[6] Indeed Mazzino Montinari finds in the posthumous
fragments of the summer of 1878 two notes which can be interpreted as a
reaction to this insult, and he cites the letter from February 23, 1883, to
Overbeck in which Nietzsche makes mention of a "mortal insult" standing
between him and Wagner. Montinari rightfully puts this incident into perspective when he brings to our attention another letter, which Montinari
published for the first time in 1980 after the publication of Gregor-Dellin's
book. Nietzsche wrote this letter to his friend and confidante Malwida von
Meysenbug on February 21, 1883, shortly after Wagner's death:

Wagner has insulted me in a mortal way— . . . I have felt his slow retreat and
sneaking back toward Christianity and the church as a personal affront: my entire
youth and its course seem sullied, insofar as I had believed in the genius of a man
who was capable of taking such a step.
*(Wagner hat mich auf eine tödliche Weise beleidigt . . . sein langsames
Zurückgehen und—Schleichen zum Christenthum und der Kirche habe ich als
persönlichen Schimpf für mich empfunden: meine ganze Jugend und ihre Richtung
schien mir befleckt, insofern ich einem Geiste, der dieses Schrittes fähig war,
gehuldigt hatte) (KSA VI 335).*[7]

Indeed, that Nietzsche felt betrayed by Wagner's return to the Christian faith is illustrated by Nietzsche's vehement criticism of *Parsifal*,
Wagner's last work which took the composer almost twenty years to accomplish. Borchmeyer points out that Nietzsche knew about the project
and its content by 1869 and cites a letter of 1877 to Cosima Wagner, where
Nietzsche, according to Borchmeyer, still approves of the work: "The wonderful promise of *Parcival* may console us in all things where consolation
is needed" (*Die herrliche Verheißung des* Parcival *mag uns in allen Dingen
trösten, wo wir Trost bedürfen) (KSA* V 288). The last part of this sentence
has a restrictive undertone, however, foreshadowing Nietzsche's increasing opposition to the idea of art as remedy, art as "metaphysical comfort"
from *Human, All Too Human* on. It is expressed clearly in his "crusade"
against romantic pessimism, which appears in its most concentrated form
in "An Attempt at Self-Criticism." For Nietzsche, *Parsifal* becomes anything but consolation, and he might already have had a premonition of it
when he wrote the letter to Cosima Wagner.

On the other hand, the example of the *Parsifal* controversy shows
clearly that readers must meet Nietzsche's negative remarks with extreme
caution, since his positions forever oscillate between two extremes.[8] The
essay "The Case of Wagner"(1888) brings this to light. After having employed, in Wagnerian fashion himself, all rhetorical and stylistic means to
convince the reader of the dangers of Wagner's music, he adds in all fairness: "*Parsifal* will always retain its rank—as the stroke of genius in seduction.—I admire this work; I wish I had written it myself; failing that, I
understand it" *(Der* Parsifal *wird in der Kunst der Verführung ewig seinen
Rang behalten, als der Geniestreich der Verführung. . . Ich bewundere
dies Werk, ich möchte es selbst gemacht haben; in Ermangelung davon
verstehe ich es. . .)*[9] *(CW* 641, *KSA* VI 43). It is perhaps the very notion of
understanding rather than a sympathetic fellow-feeling which character-

izes Nietzsche's relation to Wagner in the later years, although there again, textual evidence regarding this statement is not conclusive.

According to Fischer-Dieskau, Wagner was met with Nietzsche's silence when he talked about *Parsifal* during their last encounter in the summer of 1877. Dwelling on the wonders of his religious experience rather than on the purely artistic vision of the project, the "reformed" atheist did not seem credible to Nietzsche who suspected Wagner's conversion to be motivated by the will to fame and success. Wagner's alleged remark "the Germans do not want to hear anything about pagan gods and heroes, what they want is something Christian" must have confirmed Nietzsche's suspicions (Fischer-Dieskau 208).[10]

Shortly thereafter, Nietzsche received from Wagner the written version of *Parsifal* to which he responded by sending to Wagner, in the spring of 1878, a copy of his new book *Human, All Too Human*. This last exchange marks the end of the official friendship between the two, as *Human, All Too Human* provoked in Wagner the same feeling of alienation Nietzsche had experienced with *Parsifal*. In spite of all these events and facts, the idea of a definitive break between Wagner and Nietzsche remains questionable not only because of the unresolvable ambivalence pervading their relationship but also because Nietzsche himself may have considered it, as the title of the aphorism says, a "star friendship" in the symbolic as well as modern sense:

> We were friends and have become estranged. But this was right, and we do not want to conceal and obscure it from ourselves... There is probably a tremendous but invisible stellar orbit in which our very different ways and goals may be included as small parts of the path... But our life is too short and our power of vision too small for us to be more than friends in the sense of this sublime possibility.—Let us then believe in our star-friendship even if we should be compelled to be earth enemies.
>
> *(Wir waren Freunde und sind uns fremd geworden. Aber das ist recht so und wir wollen's uns nicht verhehlen und verdunkeln, als ob wir uns dessen zu schämen hätten... Es gibt wahrscheinlich eine ungeheure unsichtbare Curve und Sternenbahn, in der unsere so verschiedenen Strassen und Ziele als kleine Wegstrecken einbegriffen sein mögen... Aber unser Leben ist zu kurz und unsere Sehkraft zu gering, als dass wir mehr als Freunde im Sinne jener erhabenen Möglichkeit sein könnten.—Und so wollen wir unsere Sternen-Freundschaft glauben, selbst wenn wir einander Erden-Feinde sein müssten) (GS 225, KSA III 523).*

Of course, Nietzsche and Wagner's "disaccord" cannot be reduced and settled as a private affair, nor can the star friendship be seen as a happy ending.

Massimo Zumbini justly argues that Nietzsche's critique of Wagner situates itself on a "meta-personal" *(überpersönliches)* level. For present times and later, this critique has significance only insofar as it contains the critique of an entire epoch as well. Not without reason does Wagner become the sign of modernity. Nietzsche's "Wagner-critique" has to be recognized in its truest sense, namely as a critique of the times *(Zeitkritik)*.[11] Significantly, however, it is not until Wagner's death, when utter silence falls between them, that Nietzsche's main discussion of Wagner, and all that he represents, truly begins.

II.   A Question of Modern Optics

In his Turinese letter of 1888, entitled "The Case Of Wagner," Nietzsche's discussion moves on two planes: ideological and artistic. Although these planes are intrinsically interwoven, it is important to distinguish them in light of Nietzsche's own complex views on the question of art. On the one hand, there is Nietzsche's critique of the political and moral underpinnings of Bayreuth, namely, Christian dogma, patriotism, and the question of race, which are reflected in and thus pervert Wagner's art. At the same time, Nietzsche concentrates on European decadence, especially its manifestation in late French romanticism, as the most important point of reference for his evaluation of Wagner's work. Wagner "belongs" to European decadence, he is its "protagonist, its greatest name"*(ihr Protagonist, ihr grösster Name)* (*CW* 621, *KSA* VI 22). It is from this perspective that Wagner's case becomes Nietzsche's own.

"The Case of Wagner" represents to this day Nietzsche's most stunning portrait of Wagner and all he represents, a complex and mobile mosaic, a physiological and psychological study of the quintessential modern artist by an artist who was modern in spite of himself. In her article on Wagner and Nietzsche, Sarah Kofman addresses this point in the following way:

> The example of Wagner as a "case" with which Nietzsche, doctor par excellence of famous diagnostic skills, has been very familiar for quite some time. He has often been consulted regarding the patient, who himself professes to be the right physician for cases of hysteria. Doctor Nietzsche, however, for his part, defends an opposing view: to wit, that this patient is a most nefarious danger to the health

of women and young people. Has the doctor "been" consulted? Well, rather, he consulted himself; for behind the case of Wagner . . . lies the case of Nietzsche.[12]

Interestingly, Nietzsche not only agrees with this analysis but even posits it as the precondition for his entire undertaking which is based on the recognition that "perhaps nobody was more dangerously attached to—grown together with—Wagnerizing" *(niemand war vielleicht gefährlicher mit der Wagnerei verwachsen. . .)* than himself. By the same token, however, he also claims that nobody resisted Wagner harder, that nobody was happier to be rid of "Wagnerizing" than he. Nietzsche's choice of the term "Wagnerizing," over Wagner the man, is an important indication of the target of his investigation, which includes the modern "public" in the largest sense as well as all "modern" artists of whom Wagner appears only as the most perfected one.

Since from Nietzsche's point of view, all subjects under investigation need to be approached from a distance, he takes the perspective of the philosopher whose task is no less ambitious than to "overcome his time in himself, to become 'timeless.'" *(seine Zeit in sich zu überwinden, 'zeitlos' zu werden).* Experience is the precondition for any worthy analysis. To accomplish the philosopher's task, which is to become "the bad conscience of his time" *(das schlechte Gewissen seiner Zeit zu sein)*, a keen eye "that beholds the whole fate of man at tremendous distance" *(das die ganze Thatsache Mensch aus ungeheurer Ferne übersieht)*, special self-discipline, "a profound estrangement, cold sobering up—against everything that is of his time, everything timely *(eine tiefe Entfremdung, Erkältung, Ernüchterung gegen alles Zeitliche, Zeitgemässe)* is necessary and gained only through the exercise of "self-overcoming" *(Selbstüberwindung)* and "self-denial" *(Selbst-Verläugnung)*.

Is it not, however, also an exercise in self-persuasion when Nietzsche adopts the perspective of the philosopher so insistently? Indeed, before beginning his discussion, Nietzsche opposes the artist's perspective to that of the philosopher. Whereas the artist seems to remain locked within the desire to experience art at all costs, the philosopher's pleasure lies precisely in the difficult process of distanciation after experience; when successful, it provides him with the crucial insight that the artist lacks for want of rigor and self-discipline. Thus Nietzsche *understands* the artist, but feels more affinity with the philosopher himself, whose concerns are the underlying principles and conditions beneath art's "surface":

I understand perfectly when a musician says today: 'I hate Wagner, but I can no longer endure any other music.' But I'd also understand a philosopher who would declare: 'Wagner sums up modernity. There is no way out, one must first become a Wagnerian.'
(Ich verstehe es vollkommen, wenn heute ein Musiker sagt 'ich hasse Wagner, aber ich halte keine andere Musik mehr aus'. Ich würde aber auch einen Philosophen verstehen, der erklärte: 'Wagner resümiert die Modernität. Es hilft nichts, man muss erst Wagnerianer sein. . . ') (*CW* 612, *KSA* VI 12).

That Wagner sums up modernity is, as Zumbini states, "beginning and end, the prerequisite and conclusion of Nietzsche's criticism" (Zumbini 256). The structure of the entire essay is symmetrically framed by the following two remarks. In the preface, Nietzsche writes: "But confronted with the labyrinth of the modern soul, where could he [the philosopher] find a guide more initiated, a more eloquent prophet of the soul, than Wagner? Through Wagner, modernity speaks most intimately." *(Aber wo fände er für das Labyrinth der modernen Seele einen eingeweihteren Führer, einen beredteren Seelenkündiger als Wagner? Durch Wagner redet die Modernität ihre intimste Sprache)*. And in the "Epilogue," Nietzsche resumes:

A diagnosis of the modern soul—where would it begin? With a resolute incision into this instinctive contradiction, with the vivisection of the most instructive case.—The case of Wagner is for the philosopher a windfall—this essay is inspired, as you hear, by gratitude.
(Eine Diagnostik der modernen Seele—womit begönne sie? Mit einem resoluten Einschnitt in diese Instinktwidersprüchlichkeit, mit der Herauslösung ihrer Gegensatz-Werthe, mit der Vivisektion vollzogen an ihrem lehrreichsten Fall.— Der Fall Wagner ist für den Philosophen ein Glücksfall,—diese Schrift ist, man hört es, von der Dankbarkeit inspiriert) (*CW* 648, *KSA* VI 53).

Interestingly, it is not with Wagner that Nietzsche begins his essay, but he starts out with the praise of Bizet in whose music Nietzsche affirms—all too enthusiastically, it seems—the qualities and values which he sees negated in Wagner and modern society at large. By contrasting Bizet and Wagner, Nietzsche makes a strategic move. In order to highlight the negative, he is in need of a vivid example of its opposite. Whereas Wagner epitomizes modern man who always stands between two chairs, saying yes and no at the same time, Bizet stands here as the example of courage to one's character and fate. Wagner's orchestral tone is "brutal, artificial and innocent," Bizet's is light, subtle and polite. Whereas Wagner's "infinite melody" shatters unity, Bizet's approach is "classically" whole-some and unpretentious for it "builds," "organizes," and above all "finishes." Wagner's attitude of superiority toward the public, always treated "as if," makes him "the most impolite genius in the world" *(das unhöflichste Genie der Welt)*, whereas Bizet respects and appeals to his public's intelligence. Nietzsche insists on this point for he notably was the first to be deceived by what he calls now Wagner's "counterfeit" *(Falschmünzerei)* music and the "lie of the great style" *(die Lüge des grossen Stils) (CW 613, KSA VI 13–14).* Bizet's example contrasted to Wagner's serves Nietzsche mainly in his attempt at illustrating concretely that which he defines theoretically in the "Epilogue":

> I offer my conception of what is modern.—In its measure of strength every age also possesses a measure for what virtues are permitted and forbidden to it. Either it has the virtues of ascending life: then it will resist from the profoundest depth the virtues of declining life. Or the age itself represents declining life: then it requires the virtues of decline, then it hates everything that justifies itself solely out of abundance, out of the overflowing riches of strength. Aesthetics is tied indissolubly to these biological presuppositions: there is an aesthetics of decadence, and there is a classical aesthetics—'the beautiful in itself' is a figment of the imagination, like all of idealism.
> *(Ich gebe meinen Begriff des Modernen.—Jede Zeit hat in ihrem Maass von Kraft ein Maass auch dafür, welche Tugenden ihr erlaubt, welche ihr verboten sind. Entweder hat sie die Tugenden des aufsteigenden Lebens: dann widerstrebt sie aus unterstem Grunde den Tugenden des niedergehenden Lebens. Oder sie ist selbst ein niedergehendes Leben,—dann bedarf sie auch der Niedergangs-Tugenden, dann hasst sie Alles, was aus der Fülle, was aus dem Ueberreichthum an Kräften sie alleine rechtfertigt. Die Aesthetik ist unablöslich an diese biologischen Vorraussetzungen gebunden: es gibt eine décadence-Aesthetik, es gibt eine klassische Aesthetik,—ein 'Schönes an sich' ist ein Hirngespenst, wie der ganze Idealismus) (CW 646, KSA VI 50).*

The opposition of decadent and classical is foremost a distinction between two tendencies. Decadent and classical are not two absolute terms to be affirmed or negated in themselves, but both have their place in space and time. They are linked to a certain interpretation of moral values, namely life-affirming ones and life-negating ones. Nietzsche distinguishes between two sets of moralities in thus continuing the above passage:

> In the narrower sphere of so-called moral values one cannot find a greater contrast than that between a master morality and the morality of Christian value concepts:

the latter developed on soil that was morbid through and through . . . master morality. ('Roman,' 'pagan,' 'classical,' 'Renaissance') is conversely, the sign language of what has turned out well, of ascending life, of the will to power as the principle of life. The former gives to things out of its own abundance—it transfigures, it beautifies the world and makes it more rational—the latter impoverishes, pales, and makes uglier the value of things, it negates the world.

(In der engeren Sphäre der sogenannten moralischen Werthe ist kein grösserer Gegensatz aufzufinden, als der einer Herren-Moral und der Moral der christlichen Werthbegriffe: letztere, auf einem durch und durch morbiden Boden gewachsen . . . die Herren-Moral. ['Römisch,' 'heidnisch,' 'klassisch,' 'Renaissance'] umgekehrt als die Zeichensprache der Wohlgeratenheit, des aufsteigenden Lebens, des Willens zur Macht als Princips des Lebens) (CW 646, KSA VI 50).

This distinction seems to suggest that Nietzsche speaks up unmistakably for the classical against the decadent. This contrast however, does not mean an absolute judgment of these two value systems. It stresses their difference, which has to be recognized and kept intact:

These opposite forms in the optics of value are both necessary: they are ways of seeing, immune to reasons and refutations. One cannot refute Christianity; one cannot refute a disease of the eye. . . The concepts of 'true' and 'untrue' have, as it seems to me, no meaning in optics. What alone should be resisted is that falseness, that deceitfulness of instinct which refuses to experience these opposites as opposites—as Wagner, for example, refused, being no mean master of such falsehood. To make eyes at master morality . . . while mouthing the counter doctrine!

(Diese Gegensatzformen in der Optik der Werthe sind beide notwendig: es sind Arten zu sehen, denen man mit Gründen und Widerlegungen nicht beikommt. Man widerlegt das Christenthum nicht, man widerlegt eine Krankheit des Auges nicht. Die Begriffe "wahr" und "unwahr" haben, wie mir scheint, in der Optik keinen Sinn. Wogegen man allein sich zu wehren hat, das ist die Instinktdoppelzüngigkeit, welche diese Gegensätzte nicht als Gegensätze empfinden will: wie es zum Beispiel Wagner's Wille war, der in solchen Falschheiten keine kleine Meisterschaft hatte. Nach der Herren-Moral hinschielen . . . und dabei die Gegenlehre im Munde führen!) (CW 647, KSA VI 51).

To embrace a decadent or a classical world view, that is to negate life or affirm it, is a matter of choice. Once the choice has been made, it is important to stand behind the values which accompany this choice. Modern man is characterized by his inability to make this choice and Nietzsche sees Wagner and his music reflecting this duplicity in the most cunning way.

III.   Nietzsche's Paradox

According to Nietzsche, Wagner's music is the seductive masquerade of a person who has abdicated to a nihilistic world view. He presents Wagner's drama as the story of a disastrous clash between two world views, and the subsequent and even more disastrous will to reconcile these world views, which are by Nietzsche's definition irreconcilable. Figuratively speaking, Wagner started out as a radical, a revolutionary whose art reflected the healthy instinct to "overthrow everything traditional, all reverence, all fear." As such, Wagner was the captain of a ship which gaily followed its course, when suddenly, this ship hit a reef named Schopenhauer. The problem, however, in Nietzsche's eyes is not so much the suffering of shipwreck as the subsequent dealing with it. To leave the ship and swim to shore would have been one solution. To join the reef and remain on it, another. But what does Wagner do? asks Nietzsche. He turns his accident into the goal of his voyage, remaining shipwrecked on his ship, stuck to the reef. In other words, Wagner becomes untrue to himself, allowing his instincts to be corrupted by his adoption of nihilistic values which he then turns into a necessity. Wagner gave up on himself and his art became the medium through which he masked his despair. This perversion of instinct— to turn failure into the necessary goal of one's enterprise and glorifying it through one's art—testifies of Wagner's sickness. In its artistic expression and influence, this perversion is also his great achievement. He turns his own calamity to his advantage therefore becoming "a typical decadent who has a sense of necessity in his corrupted taste, who claims it as a higher taste, who knows how to get his corruption accepted as law, as progress, as fulfillment" *(ein typischer décadent, der sich nothwendig in seinem verdorbenen Geschmack fühlt, der mit ihm einen höheren Geschmack in Anspruch nimmt, der seine Verderbnis als Gesetz, als Fortschritt, als Erfüllung in Geltung zu bringen weiss) (CW* 620, *KSA* VI 21). This particular talent of Wagner, namely to translate his own dilemma onto the stage, reflects itself in the theme of redemption, which Nietzsche exposes as a modern *deus ex machina*, an artificial and all too easy way out of conflicting situations. Again, Nietzsche does not question the need for redemption as such, for this need is the "quintessence of all Christian needs" but he points at Wagner's hubris which is to appear more Christian than the Christians for the sake of redemption through art. Whereas the Christian is too modest for Nietzsche's taste, wanting nothing more than "to be rid of himself," Wagner is not modest enough. To the contrary, he preaches Christian morality while his underlying motivation is driven by a dubious will to power. Wagner's personality was precisely only whole in its duplicity and this is what Wagner did not acknowledge. It is in this aspect that Wagner, in spite of himself, was "the whole corruption" *(die ganze Verderbnis)* and the embodiment of "the courage, the will, the conviction in corruption" *(der Muth, der Wille, die Ueberzeugung in der Verderbnis)* (*CW* 643, *KSA* VI 47).

Wagner's corruption is sealed by his espousal of the "ascetic ideal" which Nietzsche analyzes in *On the Genealogy of Morals*. In the first essay of this book, Nietzsche examines the psychology of Christianity and uncovers the mystification inherent in morality and religion. The former presents itself as a collection of facts, although it is merely an interpretation of certain phenomena; while the latter promotes the view that Christianity is born of the holy "Spirit" although it is merely born of the spirit of "ressentiment"—a reactionary movement against the domination of aristocratic values.

In the second essay, Nietzsche examines the psychology of moral conscience which while pretending to be the voice of God in man, is in fact a covering up of man's inherent cruelty, a "bad conscience."

In the third essay, Nietzsche discusses the meaning of the ascetic ideal. This ideal, erected by the agents of Christianity to control and turn man's natural instincts against himself, is the very ideal of decadence. It comprises "all the unnatural inclinations, all those aspirations to the beyond, to that which runs counter to sense, instinct, nature, animal, in short all ideals hitherto, which are one and all hostile to life and ideals that slander the world" *(nämlich die unnatürlichen Hänge, alle jene Aspirationen zum Jenseitigen, Sinnwidrigen, Instinktwidrigen, Naturwidrigen, Thierwidrigen, kurz die bisherigen Ideale, die allesamt lebensfeindlichen Ideale, Weltverleumder-Ideale)* (*KSA* V 335).[13]

Sarah Kofman, who ties Nietzsche's critique of Wagner to his critique of the ascetic ideal points to the fact that the unrestricted power of the ascetic ideal lies in its infiltration into all domains of life and its appropriation by everybody: artists, woman, philosophers, scholars, invalids, and not only by priests or saints. There is no single essence of the ascetic ideal, but a plurality of meanings, which, however, does not preclude a common thread, namely:

a will to nothingness that is always a mask—the necessary response of a distinctive kind of life to specific conditions of existence, a subtle and indirect manner
that life still has of affirming itself. This is the paradox: the will to nothingness is
a strategy of life to maintain itself as life. It is the still-alive part of a living being
in the process of degenerating and dying, which remains able either to invent this
ideal or to appropriate it for its own use in order to continue to exercise its will to
power... The Nietzschean suspicion reveals that, far from exhibiting a nihilation
of the will, the ascetic is an extraordinary case of willing (Kofman 195).

This paradox takes its most interesting form when it is appropri-
ated by artists. Wagner becomes the most refined case in willing that which
runs counter to his true nature. Elsewhere Nietzsche recognizes this nature
as one marked by suffering, solitude, and melancholy. In his polemic
Nietzsche Contra Wagner, Nietzsche refers to the true and thus creative
side of Wagner, which to his detriment the musician fails to see as such:

It escapes him that his spirit has a different taste and inclination—the opposite
perspective—and prefers to sit quietly in the nooks of collapsed houses: there,
hidden, hidden from himself, he paints his real masterpieces, . . . only there does
he become wholly good, great and perfect, perhaps there alone Wagner is one
who suffered deeply—that is his distinction above other musicians. I admire
Wagner wherever he puts himself into music.
*(Es entgeht ihm, dass sein Geist einen anderen Geschmack und Hang—eine
entgegengesetzte Optik—hat und am liebsten still in den Winkeln
zusammengestürzter Häuser sitzt: da, verborgen, sich selber verborgen, malt er
seine eigentlichen Meisterstücke...da erst wird er ganz gut, gross und vollkommen,
da vielleicht allein.—Wagner ist Einer, der tief gelitten hat—sein Vorrang von
den übrigen Musikern,—Ich bewundere Wagner in Allem, worin er sich in Musik
setzt)*[14] (*KSA* VI 418).

Abandoning this other side in favor of success, shifting his power
into what Nietzsche perceives as the wrong direction, calculating effects in
order to "throw" his audience at any price, Wagner not only corrupts himself and his music but also everybody who is lured into his seductive web:

Wagner represents a great corruption of music. He has guessed that it is a means
to excite weary nerves—and with that he has made music sick. His inventiveness
is not inconsiderable in the art of goading again those who are weariest, calling
back into life those who are half dead. He is a master of hypnotic tricks, he man-
ages to throw down the strongest bulls. Wagner's success—his success with
nerves and consequently woman—has turned the whole world of ambitious musicians into disciples of his secret art. And not only the ambitious, the clever,too.—
Only sick music makes money today.

(Wagner ist ein grosser Verderb für die Musik. Er hat in ihr die Mittel errathen, müde Nerven zu reizen,—er hat die Musik damit krank gemacht. Seine Erfindungsgabe ist keine kleine in der Kunst, die Erschöpftesten wieder aufzustacheln, die Halbtoten ins Leben zu rufen. Er ist der Meister hypnotischer Griffe, er wirft die Stärksten noch wie Stiere um. Der Erfolg Wagner's—sein Erfolg bei den Nerven und folglich bei den Frauen—hat die ganze ehrgeizige Musiker-Welt zu Jüngern seiner Geheimkunst gemacht. Und nicht nur die ehrgeizige, auch die kluge. . . Man macht heute Geld mit kranker Musik) (CW 622, *KSA* VI 23).*

Two words stand out in this passage: inventiveness and success. Wagner's intelligent appropriation of all the means that music provides to convey "meaning" and ideas, things that have nothing to do with music as such, his exclusive use of overwhelming effects, his histrionics, his imitation of the great style which Nietzsche exposes as incapacity in disguise, all contribute to Wagner's success. This success of an art which has become a mass commodity for "German youths, horned Sigfrieds and other Wagnerians" for "the culture crétins, the petty snobs, the eternally feminine, those with a happy digestion, in sum the people" is what Nietzsche accuses most strongly.[15]

That nobody resists him is only further proof of the era's overall decadence. Wagner has recognized what the public wants and delivers in the most shameless way. Success corrupts and corruption brings success. Wagner exploits the vicious circle and thrives in it, which prompts Nietzsche, angrily, to dispossess Wagner of any claim to authenticity, for "great success, success with the masses no longer sides with those who are authentic—one has to be an actor to achieve that" *(der grosse Erfolg, der Massenerfolg ist nicht mehr auf Seiten der Echten, man muss Schauspieler sein, ihn zu haben).* Wagner as the seducer and spokesman for the masses betrays especially in this respect the idea of art such as Nietzsche envisions it in *The Gay Science*, namely "a mocking, light, fleeting, divinely untroubled, divinely artificial art that, like a pure flame, licks into unclouded skies. Above all, an art for artists, for artists only!" *(eine spöttische, leichte, flüchtige, göttlich unbehelligte, göttlich künstliche Kunst, welche wie eine helle Flamme in einen unbewölkten Himmel hineinlodert! Vor allem eine Kunst für Künstler, nur für Künstler!) (GS* 37, *KSA* III 351).

Nietzsche's critique reaches the summit when he arrives at the conclusion that Wagner is not a musician at all, but a calculating "tyrant" whose actor genius made him become a musician. He was no musician by instinct but by sheer willpower. Wagner's greatest inventiveness and consequently success lies precisely in his subordination of music to rhetoric, acting, and stage production. With Wagner, music is nothing more than a tool, a language of persuasion to be understood by the lowest common denominator. As such Wagner joins the rank of Victor Hugo, who for Nietzsche represents yet another example of such tyrannical mentality. For Nietzsche, both "signify the same thing: in declining cultures, when the decision comes to rest with the masses, authenticity becomes superfluous, disadvantageous, a liability. Only the actor still arouses great enthusiasm" *(sie bedeuten ein und dasselbe: dass in Niedergangs-Culturen, dass überall, wo den Massen die Entscheidung in die Hände fällt, die Echtheit überflüssig, nachtheilig, zurücksetzend wird. Nur der Schauspieler weckt noch die grosse Begeisterung) (CW 635, KSA VI 37).*

Although Nietzsche denounces and rejects the underlying motivation and principles of Wagner's art production, he nevertheless acknowledges Wagner's necessity in the perfection and inexorable development of decadence. Even if Wagner has no place in the history of music, as Nietzsche seems to affirm, he certainly cannot be ignored as the accomplished picture of the decay in art, the inventor and perfecter of the "style" of decadence as Bourget had defined it. Wagner put an end to the idea of an artwork as an organic unity. He had shattered the "whole" into pieces, and as the "greatest miniaturist in music" *(als unseren grössten Miniaturisten in der Musik)*, in which he is the master of the first rank, had given life to the detail at the expense of the entirety, recreating, in the form of the *Gesamtkunstwerk*, an illusory totality which reveals itself to be "composite, calculated, artificial, and artifact" *(zusammengesetzt, gerechnet, künstlich, ein Artefakt) (CW 626, KSA VI 28).*

The seductive effect does not leave Nietzsche's own nerves untouched for he states that Wagner's "wealth of colors, of half shadows, of the secrecies of dying light spoils one to such an extent that afterward almost all other musicians seem too robust" *(sein Reichthum an Farben, an Halbschatten, an Heimlichkeiten absterbenden Lichts verwöhnt dergestalt, dass einem hinterdrein fast alle anderen Musiker zu robust vorkommen).* Apart from the fact that here Wagner—almost imperceptibly—regains the status of musician, Nietzsche also confers to Wagner a certain authenticity precisely in his quality as painter of the decadent mood, which after all is a reality one cannot feign to ignore or eliminate. Nietzsche states:

One does not understand a thing about Wagner as long as one finds in him merely an arbitrary play of nature, a whim, an accident. He was no 'fragmentary,' 'hapless,' or 'contradictory' genius. . . Wagner was something perfect, a typical decadent in whom there is no trace of 'free will' and in whom every feature is necessary.

(Man versteht Nichts von Wagner, so lange man in ihm nur ein Naturspiel, eine Willkür und Laune, eine Zufälligkeit sieht. Er war kein 'lückenhaftes,' kein 'verunglücktes,' kein 'contradiktorisches' Genie. . . Wagner war etwas vollkommenes, ein typischer Decadent, bei dem jeder 'freie Wille' fehlt, jeder Zug Nothwendigkeit hat) (CW 625, KSA VI 27).

It is perhaps from this perspective that Nietzsche's critique of Wagner reveals its most interesting angle. Paradoxically it is as a decadent that Wagner is the most progressive of all artists. The very artificiality which Nietzsche seems to condemn in favor of an authenticity defined as a quality pertaining to truthful and honest commitment—if only of a few—to art alone, becomes the mark of authenticity for decadence. It is to Wagner's credit to have committed himself, even if unbeknownst to himself—to decadence. Nietzsche suddenly turns the table around. Bizet is forgotten and Wagner's position is as if restored.

When in this essay I declare war upon Wagner . . . the last thing I want to do is start a celebration for any other musicians. Other musicians don't count compared to Wagner. Things are bad in general. Decay is universal. The sickness goes deep. If Wagner nevertheless gives his name to the ruin of music . . he is certainly not its cause. He merely accelerated its tempo. . . He had the naïveté of décadence: this was his superiority.

(Wenn ich in dieser Schrift Wagnern den Krieg . . so möchte ich am allerwenigsten irgend welchen anderen Musikern damit ein Fest machen. Andere Musiker kommen gegen Wagner gar nicht in Betracht. Es steht schlimm überhaupt. Der Verfall ist allgemein. Die Krankheit liegt in der Tiefe. Wenn Wagner der Name bleibt für den Ruin der Musik . . . so ist er doch nicht dessen Ursache. Er hat nur dessen tempo beschleunigt. . . Er hat die Naivität der décadence: dies war seine Ueberlegenheit) (CW 642, KSA VI 46).

Nietzsche's quasi-redemption of Wagner after the heavy blows he dealt throughout the entire essay may come as a surprise. As has been suggested earlier, however, the logic behind this essay lies precisely in the irreconcilability between oppositional statements. Nowhere has Nietzsche expressed in clearer fashion his own entangled "drama" from which there is no way out. Certainly the Wagner of Bayreuth remains a stranger to

Nietzsche. But his resistance to Wagner as the artist of decadence in its purely aesthetic sense is always counterbalanced by an almost desperate affirmation of it, first of all because of its necessity. That Nietzsche's critique is not a call for a turning back to the past is best expressed in the words he sinks into the ears of the Conservatives in *The Twilight of the Idols*.

     There he states that the belief, still strong in modern times, in the possibility of a bringing back of mankind toward earlier and better standards of morals and virtues is erroneous. Even though people still "dream of the crabwise retrogression of all things . . . no one is free to be a crab" *(die als Ziel den Krebsgang aller Dinge träumen. Aber es steht niemandem frei, Krebs zu sein).* One may resist, as Nietzsche seems to do, but at the same time, "one has to go forward, which is to say step by step further into decadence" *(man muss vorwärts, will sagen Schritt für Schritt weiter in der décadence).*[16] This statement, which recalls the words of Baudelaire on this subject, is a definitive legitimation of the decadent's claim to the right to their particular position in time and space. Nietzsche's realization of decadence's necessity within the historical development is also tied to his recognition of and a personal taste for the new and strange beauties it engenders. His critique of Wagner when put in the context of Baudelaire and Flaubert, gains the dimension and scope it was lacking when it centered around his own relationship to Wagner alone. In company of the artists of late French romanticism, Wagner and Nietzsche become part of what Nietzsche sees as a select group of individuals who transpose their will and energy into art:

> This secret self-ravishment, this artist's cruelty, this delight in imposing a form upon one-self as a hard, recalcitrant, suffering material and in burning a will, a critique, a contradiction, a contempt, a No into it, this uncanny, dreadfully joyous labor of a soul voluntarily at odds with itself that makes itself suffer out of joy in making suffer—eventually this entire active 'bad conscience' . . . as the womb of all ideal and imaginative phenomena, also brought to light an abundance of strange new beauty and affirmation, and perhaps beauty itself. . .
> *(Diese heimliche Selbst-Vergewaltigung, diese Künstler Grausamkeit, diese Lust sich selbst zu einem schweren widerstrebenden leidenden Stoffe eine Form zu geben, einen Willen, eine Kritik, einen Widerspruch, eine Verachtung, ein Loch einzubrennen, diese unheimliche und entsetzlich-lustvolle Arbeit einer mit sich selbst willig-zwiespältigen Seele, welche sich leiden macht, aus Lust am Leidenmachen, dieses ganz aktivische 'schlechte Gewissen' hat zuletzt . . . als der eigentliche Mutterschooss idealer und imaginativer Ereignisseauch eine Fülle*

von neuer befremdlicher Schönheit und Bejahung ans Licht gebracht und vielleicht erst die Schönheit . . . .) (GM 87, KSA V 326).

The will to nothingness, which Nietzsche sees as the profound reality of all decadent sensibility, is superseded by a will to aesthetic expression, and reveals itself after all as a stimulant to ever new and increasingly refined artistic inventions. To the impoverishment of life, as a result of this will to nothingness, against which Nietzsche pitches the Dionysian affirmation of life (in all its best and worst manifestations), corresponds at the same time an extraordinary enrichment of the arts. The decadent's heightened sensitivity, his nerves, his neurosis born out of his experience of life as dread rather than as joy make him less an idealist than a realist. The decadent's escapism into the realm of art represents itself as a strategy of resistance and self-preservation. As such, it is not an abdication of life but a form of affirmation of its darkest sides, which after all are the most interesting ones.

Notes

[1] See Jacques Le Rider, *Modernité viennoise et crises de l'identité* (Paris: Presses Universitaires,1990), and Antoine Compagnon, *The Five Paradoxes of Modernity* (New York: Columbia University Press, 1994).

[2] See Alan David Aberbach, *The Ideas of Richard Wagner* (New York: University Press of America, 1988), 121–22.

[3] Dieter Borchmeyer, "Richard Wagner und Nietzsche," *Wagner Handbuch,* eds. U. Müller and P. Wapnewski (Stuttgart: Alfred Kröner Verlag, 1986), 126.

[4] See Dietrich Fischer-Dieskau, *Wagner und Nietzsche* (Stuttgart: Deutsche Verlags-Anstalt, 1974), 190–205.

[5] Martin Gregor-Dellin, *Richard Wagner, sein Werk und Leben* (München: Piper and Co. Verlag, 1980), 748–59.

[6] Curt Paul Janz, "Die 'tödtliche Beleidigung': Ein Beitrag zur Wagner-Entfremdung Nietzsches," *Nietzsche-Studien* 4 (Berlin: De Gruyter, 1975), 262–78.

[7] In Mazzino Montinari, "Nietzsche-Wagner im Sommer 1878," *Nietzsche Studien* 14 (Berlin: De Gruyter, 1985), 20–21.

[8] See René Girard, "Nietzsche and Contradiction," *Stanford Italian Review* 6.1–2 (Stanford: 1986).

[9] Friedrich Nietzsche, "The Case of Wagner," in *Basic Writings of Nietzsche,* trans. W. Kaufmann (New York: The Modern Library, 1968) 641. (*KSA* VI 43).

[10] Wagner's quote in Kurt Hildebrandt, *Wagner und Nietzsche* (Breslau, 1924), 291.

[11] Massimo Ferrari Zumbini, "Nietzsche in Bayreuth: Nietzsches Herausforderung, die Wagnerianer und die Gegenoffensive," *Nietzsche-Studien* 19 (Berlin: de Gruyter, 1990), 248.

[12] Sarah Kofman, "Wagner's Ascetic Ideal According to Nietzsche," *Nietzsche, Genealogy, Morality: Essays on Nietzsche's Genealogy of Morals* (Berkeley: University of California Press, 1994), 196. A French version of this essay appeared under the title "Nietzsche

et Wagner: comment la musique devient bonne pour les cochons," *Furor* 23 (Lausanne, May 1992).

[13] Friedrich Nietzsche, *The Genealogy of Morals*, trans. W. Kaufmann (New York: Vintage Books, 1969), 95. Reference to this text is designated GM.

[14] Friedrich Nietzsche, "Nietzsche Contra Wagner," *The Portable Nietzsche,* trans. W. Kaufmann (New York: The Viking Press, 1968), 663.

[15] This is one of the points where Adorno meets Nietzsche. See Karin Bauer-Milliken, *Critiques of Culture in the Context of (Post) Modernity: Adorno Rethinks Nietzsche,* diss., University of Washington, 1992, 109–32.

[16] Friedrich Nietzsche, *The Twilight of the Idols*, trans. R. J. Hollingdale (Baltimore: Penguin Classics, 1968), 96. (*KSA* VI 44).

Bibliography

Aberbach, Alan David. *The Ideas of Richard Wagner*. New York: University Press of America, 1988.

Austin, Lloyd James. *L'Univers poétique de Baudelaire*. Paris: Mercure de France, 1956.

Bataille, Georges. *Literature and Evil*. Translated by Alaistair Hamilton. London: Calder and Boyars, 1973.

Baudelaire, Charles. *Oeuvres Complètes*. Edited by Claude Pichois. 2 vols. Paris: Gallimard. La Pléiade, 1976.

———. *Correspondances*. Edited by Claude Pichois. 2 vols. Paris: Gallimard. La Pléiade, 1966.

———. *Selected Letters of Charles Baudelaire*. Translated by Rosemary Lloyd. Chicago: The University of Chicago Press, 1986.

———. *Intimate Journals*. Translated by Charles Isherwood. Westport: Hyperion Press, 1930.

———. *The Mirror of Art*. Translated by J. Mayne. New York: Phaidon Publishers, 1955.

———. *The Parisian Prowler*. Translated by Edward K. Kaplan. Athens: The University of Georgia Press, 1989.

———. *The Prose Poems and La Fanfarlo*. Translated by Rosemary Lloyd. Oxford: Oxford University Press, 1991.

———. *Selected Writings on Art and Literature*. Translated by P. E. Charvet. London: Penguin Books, 1992.

———. *Artificial Paradise*. Translated by Ellen Fox. New York: Herder and Herder, 1971.

———. *Baudelaire on Poe*. Translated by Lois and Francis E. Hyslop. State College, PA: Bald Eagle Press, 1952.

———.*Les Fleurs du Mal*. Translated by R. Howard. Boston: D. Godine, 1983.

Bauer-Milliken, Karin. 1992. "Critiques of Culture in the Context of (Post) Modernity: Adorno Rethinks Nietzsche." Ph.D. diss., University of Washington, 1992.

Behler, Ernst. *Irony and the Discourse of Modernity*. Seattle: University of Washington Press, 1990.

———. "Eine Kunst für Künstler, nur für Künstler: Poe, Baudelaire, Nietzsche." *Athenäum*. Paderborn: Ferdinand Schöningh, 1994.

———. Nietzsche und die Frühromantische Schule. *Nietzsche-Studien* 7 (1978).

———. *Derrida-Nietzsche Nietzsche-Derrida*. Paderborn: F.Schoeningh, 1988.

Benjamin, Walter. *Illuminationen*. Frankfurt a. M.: Suhrkamp, 1977.

Berkowitz, Peter. *Nietzsche, the Ethics of an Immoralist*. Cambridge: Harvard University Press, 1995.

Blin, Georges. *Baudelaire*. Paris: Gallimard, 1939.

Bohrer, Karl Heinz. *Die Kritik der Romantik*. Frankfurt a. M.: Suhrkamp, 1989.

Bollon, Patrice. "La figure du Dandy." *Magazine littéraire* 273 (1990): 42–44.

Borchmeyer, Dieter. "Richard Wagner und Nietzsche." *Wagner Handbuch*. Edited by U. Müller and P. Wapnewski. Stuttgart: Alfred Kröner Verlag, 1986.

Bourget, Paul. *Essais de psychologie contemporaine*. 2 vols. Paris: Plon, 1931.

Burton, Richard D. E. *Baudelaire in 1859*. New York: Cambridge University Press, 1988.

———. *Baudelaire and the Second Republic*. Oxford: Clarendon Press, 1991.

Calinescu, Matei. *Five Faces of Modernity*. Durham, NC: Duke University Press, 1987.

Camus, Albert. *The Rebel*. Translated by Anthony Bower. New York: Vintage, 1960.

Carter, A. E. *The Idea of Decadence in French Literature*. Toronto: University of Toronto Press, 1958.

Cassagne, Albert. *La théorie de l'art pour l'art en France*. Paris: Lucien Dorbon, 1959.

Cauchi, Francesca. "Nietzsche and Pessimism: The Metaphysics Hypostatized." *The History of European Ideas* 13 no. 3. New York: Tarrytown, 1991.

Caws, Mary Ann, ed. *City Images: Perspectives from Literature, Philosophy, and Film*. New York: Gordon and Breach, 1991.

Champromis, Pierre. "Nietzsche devant la culture française." *Romanische Forschungen* 68 (1956): 74–115.

Compagnon, Antoine. *The Five Paradoxes of Modernity*. New York: Columbia University Press, 1994.

Culler, Jonathan. "Baudelaire and Poe." *Zeitschrift für französische Sprache* 100 (1989): 61–73.

de Man, Paul. *Blindness and Insight.* Minneapolis: University of Minnesota Press, 1971.

del Caro, Adrian. *Nietzsche contra Nietzsche.* Baton Rouge: Louisiana State University Press, 1989.

Ferran, André. *L'Esthétique de Baudelaire.* Paris: Hachette, 1933.

Ferrari Zumbini, Massimo. "Nietzsche in Bayreuth: Nietzsches Herausforderung, die Wagnerianer und die Gegenoffensive." *Nietzsche-Studien* 19 (1990).

Fewster, J. C. 1992. "Au service de l'ordre: Paul Bourget and the Critical Response to Decadence in Austria and Germany." *Comparative Literature Studies* 29 no. 3 (summer).

Fischer-Dieskau, Dietrich. *Wagner und Nietzsche.* Stuttgart: Deutsche Verlags-Anstalt, 1974.

Foucault, Michel. "What is Enlightenment?" *The Foucault Reader.* New York: Random House, 1984.

Froidevaux, Gérald. *Baudelaire. Représentation et Modernité.* Paris: José Corti, 1989.

Gautier, Théophile. *Mademoiselle de Maupin.* Translated by Joanna Richardson. Harmondsworth: Penguin, 1981.

Gilman, Margaret. *Baudelaire The Critic.* New York: Columbia University Press, 1943.

Girard, René. "Nietzsche and Contradiction." *Stanford Italian Review* 6 no. 1–2 (1986).

Gregor-Dellin, Martin. *Richard Wagner, sein Werk und Leben.* München:

Piper and Co. Verlag, 1980.

Heller, Peter. "Nietzsche in his Relation to Voltaire and Rousseau." *Studies in Nietzsche and the Classical Tradition.* Edited by James C. O'Flaherty. Chapel Hill, NC: University of North Carolina Press, 1976.

Janz, Curt Paul. "Die 'tödliche Beleidigung': Ein Beitrag zur Wagner-Entfremdung Nietzsches." *Nietzsche-Studien* 4 (1975).

Jauss, Hans Robert. *Toward an Aesthetic of Reception.* Minneapolis: University of Minnesota Press, 1982.

———. *Literaturgeschichte als Provokation.* Frankfurt a. M.: Suhrkamp, 1970.

Kaufmann, Walter. *Nietzsche: Philosopher, Psychologist, Antichrist.* Princeton: Princeton Univerity Press, 1974.

Knapp, Bettina. "Baudelaire's and Wagner's Archetypal Operas." *Nineteenth Century French Studies* 17 (Fall-Winter 1988–89): 56–69.

Kofman, Sarah. *Nietzsche and Metaphor.* Translated by D. Large. Stanford: Stanford University Press, 1993.

———. "Wagner's Ascetic Ideal according to Nietzsche." *Nietzsche, Genealogy, Morality: Essays on Nietzsche's Genealogy of Morals.* Berkeley: University of California Press, 1994.

Kopp, Robert. "Nietzsche, Baudelaire, Wagner. A propos d'une définition de la décadence." *Travaux de littérature* 1 (1988): 203–216.

Koppen, Erwin. *Dekadenter Wagnerismus.* Berlin: de Gruyter. 1973.

Kuhn, Elisabeth. "Nietzsches Quelle des Nihilismus-Begriffs." *Nietzsche-Studien* 13 (1984): 253–78.

Lacoue-Labarthe, Philippe. 1991. "Baudelaire contra Wagner." *Etudes Françaises* 17 (3–4):23–51.

Leakey, F. W. "A philosophy of opportunism." *Baudelaire. Collected Essays. 1953–1988*. Cambridge: Cambridge University Press, 1990.

———. *Baudelaire and Nature*. Manchester: University of Manchester Press, 1969.

Lemaire, Michel. *Le Dandysme. De Baudelaire à Mallarmé*. Paris: Klincksieck, 1978.

Le Rider, Jacques. *Modernité viennoise et crises de l'identité*. Paris: Presses Universitaires, 1990.

———. "Nietzsche et Baudelaire." *Littérature* 86 (1992): 85–101.

Loncke, Joyceline. *Baudelaire et la musique*. Paris: Nizet, 1975.

Mann, Thomas. *Pro and contra Wagner*. Translated by Allan Blunden. Boston: Faber and Faber, 1985.

Mansuy, Michel. *Un Moderne. Paul Bourget*. Annales Littéraire de L'Université de Besançon 38. Paris: Les Belles Lettres, 1960.

Matucci, Mario. "Les Essais de Paul Bourget, entre pessimisme et décadence." *Lettres et réalités*. Aix en Provence: Université de Provence, 1988.

Michaud, Stéphane. "Nietzsche et Baudelaire." *Le Surnaturalisme Français*. Actes du Colloque organisé à l'Université de Vanderbilt. W. T. Bandy Center for Baudelaire Studies: A La Baconnière (1979).

Milner, Margaret. "Putting the Emphasis on Music: Baudelaire and the Lohengrin Prelude." *Nineteenth Century French Studies* 21 no. 3–4 (1993): 385–401.

Montinari, Mazzino. "Aufgaben der Nietzsche-Forschung heute: Nietzsches Auseinandersetzung mit der französischen Literatur des 19. Jahrhunderts." *Nietzsche Heute*. Edited by S. Bauschinger, S. I. Cocalis and S. Lennox. Bern: Francke Verlag, 1988.

———. "Nietzsche-Wagner im Sommer 1878." *Nietzsche-Studien* 14 (1985).

Moss, Armand. *Baudelaire et Delacroix*. Paris: Nizet, 1973.

Nietzsche, Friedrich. *Sämtliche Werke. Kritische Studienausgabe*. 15 vols. Edited by Giorgio Colli and Mazzino Montinari. Berlin: dtv/de Gruyter, 1988.

———. *Sämtliche Briefe. Kritische Studienausgabe*. 8 vols. Edited by Giorgio Colli and Mazzino Montinari. Berlin: dtv/de Gruyter, 1986.

———. *Human, All Too Human*. Translated by R. J. Hollingdale. Cambridge: Cambridge University Press, 1986.

———. *Daybreak*. Translated by R. J. Hollingdale. Cambridge: Cambridge University Press, 1982.

———. *Beyond Good and Evil*. Translated by W. Kaufmann. New York: Vintage, 1966.

———. *Basic Writings of Nietzsche*. Translated by W. Kaufmann. New York: Modern Library, 1968.

———. *The Portable Nietzsche*. Translated by W. Kaufmann. New York: The Viking Press, 1954.

———. *The Twilight of the Idols*. Translated by R. J. Hollingdale. London: Penguin Classics, 1968.

———. *Ecce Homo*. Translated by W. Kaufmann. New York: Vintage, 1969.

———. *On the Genealogy of Morals*. Translated by W. Kaufmann. New York: Vintage, 1969.

———. *The Gay Science*. Translated by W. Kaufmann. New York: Vintage, 1974.

———. *Untimely Meditations*. Translated by R. J. Hollingdale. Cambridge: Cambridge University Press, 1983.

Norris, Christopher. "'What is Enlightenment?': Kant according to Foucault." *The Cambridge Companion to Foucault*. Cambridge: Cambridge University Press, 1994.

Paglia, Camille. *Sexual Personae*. New York: Vintage, 1991.

Pestalozzi, Karl. "Nietzsches Baudelaire-Rezeption." *Nietzsche-Studien* 7 (1978).

Pichois, Claude and Ziegler, Jean. *Baudelaire*. Paris: Juliard, 1987.

Pierrot, Jean. *The Decadent Imagination*. Translated by D. Coltman. Chicago: The University of Chicago Press, 1981.

Poe, Edgar Allen. *Essays and Reviews*. New York: Library of America, 1984.

Prendergast, Christopher. *Paris and the Nineteenth Century*. Cambridge: Blackwell, 1992.

Prévost, Jean. *Baudelaire. Essai sur l'inspiration et la création*. Paris: Mercure de France, 1953.

Pütz, Peter. "Nietzsche im Lichte der kritischen Theorie." *Nietzsche-Studien* 3 (1974).

Raser, Timothy. *A Poetics of Art Criticism. The Case of Baudelaire*. Chapel Hill, NC: University of North Carolina Press, 1988.

Rasch, Wolfdietrich. "Die Darstellung des Untergangs." *Jahrbuch der deutschen Schillergesellschaft* XXV (1991): 414–34.

Raymond, Marcel. *From Baudelaire to Surrealism*. London: Methuen, 1970.

Reuber, Rudolf. *Aesthetische Lebensformen bei Nietzsche*. München: Wilhelm Fink, 1989.

Rippel, Philipp. "Die Geburt des Uebermenschen aus dem Geiste der Décadence." *Der Sturz der Idole*. Edited by Philipp Rippel. Tübingen: Konkursbuchverlag, 1985.

Ruff, Marcel. *Baudelaire*. Translated by Agnes Kertesz. New York: New York University Press, 1966.

Singer, Armand E. *Paul Bourget*. Boston: Twayne, 1976.

Spackman, Barbara. *Decadent Genealogies. The Rhetoric of Sickness from Baudelaire to d'Annunzio*. Ithaca: Cornell University Press, 1989.

Starkie, Enid. *Baudelaire*. Norfolk: New Directions, 1958.

Stendhal. *Racine and Shakespeare*. Translated by Guy Daniels. New York: The Crowell-Collier Press, 1962.

Valéry, Paul. *Variety: Second Series*. New York: Harcourt, Brace and Company, 1938.

White, Geoff. "Nietzsche's Baudelaire, or the Sublime Proleptic Spin of his Politico-Economic Thought." *Representations* 50. (1995): 14–52.

Williams, W. D. *Nietzsche and the French. A Sudy of the Influence of Nietzsche's French Reading on his Thought and Writing*. Oxford: Clarendon Press, 1952.

Young, Julian. *Nietzsche's Philosophy of Art*. Cambridge: Cambridge University Press, 1992.

Index

STUDIES IN LITERARY CRITICISM & THEORY

Hans Rudnick, General Editor

The focus of this series is on studies of all literary genres that elucidate and interpret works of art in the context of criticism and theory. Theory and criticism are held to provide the hermeneutically most rewarding access to specific authors, works, and issues under consideration. Studies of a comparative nature with special reference to issues of literary history, criticism, and postmodern theory are the distinctive features of this monograph series. Emphasis is on subjects that may set trends, generate discussion, expand horizons beyond present perspectives, and/or redefine previously held notions about "major" and "minor" authors and their achievements within or outside the canon. Approaches may center on works, authors, or abstract notions of criticism and/or theory, including issues of a comparative nature concerning world literature.

For additional information about this series or for the submission of manuscripts, please contact:

Peter Lang Publishing
Acquisitions Department
516 N. Charles St., 2nd Floor
Baltimore, MD 21201